RUNNING

My Salvation from
Stage 4 Cancer

by

"Pacer Tom" Perri

ISBN: 979-8-8821-5199-6

Book design:
Y42K Publishing Services
https://www.y42k.com/publishing-services/

Table of Contents

Foreword

Are you a runner? If so, this story is meant for you and will likely leave you wanting to "go out on a run." If not, this story is intended for you and will have you wanting to "go out on a run."

You will be challenged to run more often, run farther, and run for a cause by the time you finish reading Tom's story. I have said before that the sport of running is a part of the entertainment industry. I can tell by someone's reaction whether they are a runner. Twenty-six miles entertaining? Don't forget the .2 miles. Race organizers go to great lengths to entertain athletes during the race. In some respects, the marathon has become a traveling circus, a whole of entertainment along the route to entertain its traveling performers.

We can likely agree with one another that the *sport* of running is much more than a sport. We are winning, finishing in the top three in an age group, qualifying for another race, setting a personal record, beating time, and crossing the finish line for the first time. The road race breeds competition and the opportunity to excel. It is the perfect participation sport.

And it is life-changing. It teaches us about ourselves. What we are capable of both physically and mentally. And how to overcome obstacles. During training, on race day, and all the days in between. You will learn about its impact on people's lives through Tom's stories, the people he has met on race day, and all the days in between.

As race director for the IMT Des Moines Marathon from 2006 through 2022, I have heard stories about the impact that running and the sport of the marathon has had from thousands of runners. It is a true community. Tom's story is one of them. And his story is worthy of sharing. For everyone to experience.

That has been my experience meeting and knowing him through my professional and personal running career. He has gotten thousands of athletes to the finish line. One day, one race, and one mile at a time. And on pace. He typically leads a group to the finish line and volunteers as a pace team leader. If you have ever completed a marathon in Tom's pace group, you have learned he ensures it is never about him. It is about you and your life experience.

In these pages, you will read that he has run a lot. It is pretty much every day and most likely somewhere right now. His running accomplishments total more than 650 marathons. Including 50 states, seven times over. And, as a sub 4 hour, 50 state finisher, to keep it challenging.

But it is not always about Tom's personal finish time. It is about others finishing times. Maybe yours if you have competed in one of the more than 1,000 races as a pacer, 17 just in Des Moines. His selfless approach to race day allows the first-time athlete to feel just as empowered to be on the course as the Sub-Four Fifty State chaser. I have had the opportunity to spend time with him at many race weekend expos and packet pick-ups. Chatting about the race ahead, how much sleep we will get, what we will eat in the next twelve hours, and how his running schedule and race goals combine with his treatment plan for cancer.

Tom shared with me how running has become therapy since his cancer diagnosis. And how it has changed his approach to one day, one race, and one mile at a time. He is eager to share his story with you. And what it has taught him so that we may be able to learn and apply it to our race in life.

I remember specifically a Grandma's Marathon weekend when Tom was pacing, and I was running in the half marathon. A first-timer to Duluth stopped by and asked how early to arrive at the busses, where the water stations were located, and so on. Without missing a moment, Tom switched gears from the "450 plus marathon's discussion to "we will finish this race together." For the first-timer that that he invited her to join him in his pace group and said he would get her to the finish line with a smile and a good story or two of encouragement along the route.

Tom runs so he can continue. One day, one race, and one mile at a time. While the sport of running remains the same, the game has changed. He continues to inspire by sharing his progress. Full of courage, triumph, and setbacks, his mental toughness has prepared him for the unknown and the challenges each day brings. On the race course and in life.

His story is about survival and winning *both* on the race course and in life.

Chris Burch

Des Moines Marathon Race Director 2006-2022

Acknowledgements

I could not have written this book without the support, inspiration, and love from all the people I have met along my journey. Whether they are runners I have paced, doctors and nurses who have kept me alive, race directors, family, friends, and a cast of hundreds of others, I owe them my deep gratitude and more.

You will notice as you read my book that I have used songs, quotes, and a word before I start talking about myself and my friends. You will come to know them as funny, inspiring, and filled with a passion for running, and I can modestly say, for me. I share each chapter with 27 of these people and of course I cannot forget to include my four-legged dog friends for a chapter. Remember we are all not runners, but we all had obstacles that we overcame to make us who we are today.

Any mistake within the book is likely my fault so forgive me for any mistakes I might have made. I wish I could have included every runner that has touched my life, so I apologize if left out mentioning you.

Thanks goes out to Steve DeBoer who helped make my starting and completing this book a reality. Special thanks to Gail Wausche Kislevitz who helped guide me along the way so I could get to the finish line so the book could be published. Thanks to Ray Charbonneau for putting all the final pieces into place.

Introduction to "Pacer Tom" Perri

Who exactly is "Pacer Tom" Perri?

Tom is one of the original pacers who has been running for over 47 years, and has paced over 1,000 running events covering a wide range of distances. He is acknowledged as the only runner in the world with the *combination* of 100K Lifetime Miles, over 2,000 career races, 50sub4 Marathon Club finisher, 7 time certified 50 State Marathon Club finisher, Six Star Major Marathon finisher, and a Titanium Marathon Maniac, as well as being in the Marathon Maniac Hall of Fame. Tom is one of thirty-seven runners profiled in the book "Running Past Fifty - Advice & Inspiration for Senior Runners" by Gail Waesche Kislevitz. He was inducted into the Minnesota Senior Sports Association Hall of Fame in 2022. Tom has a double Bachelor's degree in English and Psychology, as well as two Master's in Psychology/Suicidology and Human Development with a focus on HIV/AIDS. Pacer Tom has not let a Stage 4 cancer diagnosis stop his running and continues to pace and run races all over the world. Tom continues to inspire new pacers along his running journey.

How did you get the nickname "Pacer Tom?"

In 1995 I was pacing a group of friends for around a 1:30 half marathon. It was a fun half-marathon as I ran part of the course with the legendary Minnesota female runner, Gloria Jansen. I treasured that run as she was achieving many Minnesota female Age Group records at the time. When a friend saw me at the finish area, they yelled "Hey, Pacer Tom!" Just hard to believe that was nearly 30 years ago. So sorry, Steve Cirks, you do not get credit for my nickname "Pacer Tom."

Curious Question: Why and when did you start saying "It's my first marathon (race) today?"

I was in the starting corral at the Des Moines Marathon in 2007 and a lady asked, "How many marathons have you done?" I told her "This is my 123rd marathon." She asked me again and I had the same answer "this is my 123rd Marathon that I will be running today."

She stated, "I didn't ask you how many races you have done!" And she walked away, I guess being rather irritated at me.

It was right after that marathon when I started saying "this is my first marathon today." Still to this day that is my standard race day reply.

Hilarious is that my race total was well over 1,000 races in October of 2007, and I doubt she would have believed that number.

Poem

Holy One

Thank you for the sheer joy of being able to run today.

Help me focus on this run, today.

My talent to move how I do is a gift from you.

I need your courage, endurance, and drive to get through this.

Be my courage at the start.

My endurance through the run.

And my drive to the finish.

And may I enjoy whatever awaits me at the end, a cold bottle of water, good swag, warm food, and maybe a great beer!

LET'S DO THIS!

AMEN

Chaplain Karen Sersen, Retired Pastor
Hospital and Fire Department Chaplain,
USATF of IL Master Sprinter,
Veteran Distance Runner

Chapter 1: My Daily Therapy Time

Song: "Weightless"

Artist: Marconi Union

Quote: "Running is my private time, my therapy, my religion." - Gail W. Kislevitz

Steve's DeBoer's word for me: Infectious

The decision to start something can be incredibly simple or potentially complex depending upon what we are trying to accomplish. For most people if it is something that you are doing for the first time you will remember it.

Regardless of how we come into this world, as a runner we all eventually take our initial first running step. Whether it is playing tag as a kid or being chased by a sibling. Or maybe playing "Blindman's Bluff" as portrayed by JD Salinger in the book The Catcher in the Rye.

When we enter our first running event regardless of the distance of say a forty-yard dash or a half mile run or any race distance we are then forever linked as a runner.

Once we acknowledge ourselves as a runner then we can decide for ourselves what that means to us individually. For some individuals that might mean running occasionally. Then for others, it might become a few times a week or monthly occurrence.

Only a couple of select runners in the world will ever be able to challenge the likes of Usain Bolt or Kelvin Kiptum. If you are that fortunate and lucky to be that fast and talented, I wish you all the best. However, for us occasional or everyday runners we will never obtain or reach that level of performance. That is okay as we are still runners.

Running means so many different things to so many people. For some it really becomes their therapy to help get through a bad day or help clear one's head so they can solve a problem better or to relieve some stress.

Running is a very cheap and simple activity. A pair of decent running shoes, socks, shirts, top, hat, and sunglasses is your basic outfit. Note that I am not talking initially about an expensive pair of running shoes to begin our running, as I am referring to the basics of what we need to begin our running journey.

A few runners prefer to run barefoot. You are even allowed to run barefoot at the Olympics. Abebe Bikila entered the 1960 Olympics and ran the marathon, barefoot, on the cobblestones of the Appian Way. Tied for the lead for much of the race, he broke ahead in the last mile and won in 2:15:16.

The barefoot runner Eddie Vilbar Vega ran 101 marathons in 2014 obtaining at that time a Guinness World record for most barefoot marathons in one year. Eddie was also the first known runner to have completed a marathon in all 50 states while running barefoot.

Tim Brennan is usually mentioned regarding inventing the barefoot shoe about 20 years ago. He helped create Vivobarefoot, which is probably the best-known barefoot shoe company in the world.

If you wear shoes, the weather will determine the other items of clothes you might wear. If you are running indoors on a track or treadmill, it might be just a singlet on top.

Once you decide to start running you will figure out what works best for you and your desire and personality. After finishing your first running event, you are entering a completely new adventure mode in running.

For most runners their first running event will be a 5k. For some it might be a 10k or 1/2 marathon. Then for a select few it will be a marathon. I am not sure how many runners' sign up for an Ultra as their first race, but I am sure it happens.

Most runners will not start running every day. Most will be 3 or 4 days a week runner. However, if a runner progresses from a 5k to marathon distance or an ultra - a running event further than a marathon - then more frequent daily running occurs.

Not all of us are daily runners. However, for some people the allure of running daily becomes such s big part of their daily lives that they cannot go a day without it.

Like the runner that runs an inaugural event and keeps going back year after year, the streak runners run daily to keep their streak alive. They become adept at avoiding excuses for not running. No little twinge or weather issue within reason will hinder their attempt at keeping their streak alive.

Like the Legacy runner of an event who keeps coming back each year, nothing within reason will hinder attempting to keep their streak alive. Maybe they do not complete the marathon, but they do one of the race weekend events like the 5K, 10K, or 1/2 marathon. The race just keeps bringing them back yearly. Nothing seems to get in the way of these individuals from accomplishing their goals.

Steve DeBoer
Rochester, Minnesota
Steve's word for himself: Determined (or **Deter-minded**)

Despite what Bruce Springsteen sang about me, I was not born to run. Though I was a breech birth, the rumor that I hit the ground running is stretching the truth a bit. It took me 15 months to learn how to walk! In grade school, I ran as part of sports but cannot say I enjoyed it or was very good at it, finishing 2nd to last when we ran the 50-yard dash in 6th grade.

The only reason I started running regularly was to get in shape for basketball, and that was all Roy Magnuson's fault. He convinced me to go out for 8th grade football since they did not have enough guys for a team. I injured my left knee at our last practice and was not allowed to exercise for a month. I was so out of shape when 8th grade basketball began, I realized I needed to do something to be more fit to try out for B-squad basketball the following November. So, on March 29, 1968, I ran about 1/3rd of a mile, doing those 7 days in a row, my first run streak!

By November I was up to running 3 miles most days but still did not make the cut for B-squad basketball. Along the way, I decided running was OK. I started running again the next spring. Starting April 9, 1969, I ran every day for 10 1/2 months (including my first cross-country season) until a bad ankle sprain in basketball practice (I did make the team in 10th grade) . After a family vacation, brother Dave and I ran 2 miles on July 20, 1970, and I have not missed a day since. In 1998, I found out George Hancock was keeping track of people who ran every day, so I sent my data to him.

I finished dead last in my only two varsity races, spending the rest of my high school career on the junior varsity. Despite that, I was named co-captain my senior year. The other co-captain, Tim Broderick, also ran junior varsity but we got our team to their first state meet with brother Dave one of the varsity runners. Sometime in the next year I decided I was comfortable running down to 32 degrees without a shirt on. As a result, I have been called many things, including "loco" by the Ecuadorians when I served there in the Peace Corps for two years.

Maybe my warm-bloodedness comes from my extensive warmup routine, which includes 100 pushups. I started doing them the year before regular running, since I was only able to do 5 in our Phy Ed fitness class. By April 1999 I had completed over 1,000,000 pushups, about the same time I surpassed 100,000 running miles. Since 1975, I have run more than 3000 miles each year, the longest string among "streak" runners.

At the end of 2000, the US Running Streak Association was formed. I was the second person to join, after Robert "Raven" Kraft, who has run every day on Miami Beach since Jan 1, 1975. Their first newsletter came out in April 2001, and my 30-year streak put my #5 of the 113 individuals listed. In 2002, a survey of the membership resulted in a decision that running a minimum of one mile was required to have one's daily runs certified. I have met that minimum of one mile since June 7, 1971. Though I lost 10 1/2 months of my "official" streak, I remained in 5th place longevity-wise.

There have been a few challenges along the way, including a kidney stone (2000) , broken ankle (avulsion fracture in 2007) , and double pneumonia (2020) , which included a one-week hospital stay, since I also had influenza b and was too contagious to leave my room. So, I ran around the bed in my room, even during my consult with the head influenza doc. It was during those times I only ran one mile - 7 days total over the last 52 years) . The pneumonia happened, ironically, when I went to Washington to help Jim Pearson celebrate his 50th anniversary of daily runs. His run streak since Feb 16, 1970, is the second longest in the world. I am now at #3. Jon Sutherland, who recently moved from CA to UT, has been #1 (started May 26, 1969) since Ron Hill retired in January 2017.

Until April 2000, I had not missed a day of school or work due to illness since my streak began. However, on April 11th, I woke up at 11 PM with terrible back pain, which my wife, Gail, diagnosed as a kidney stone. I had a fitful sleep and went out to run a mile about 5 AM, which did not make the pain better or worse. I then headed to the ER and had surgery to remove the stone. The avulsion fracture occurred at the 8-mile mark of a trail race, when I stepped in an unseen gopher hole and heard a pop. I stopped and fortunately, after the ER x-ray, was told I did not need a cast - just weight bearing as tolerated. So, I "tolerated" a 15-minute mile the next morning without the boot, with my ankle heavily taped. It did not hurt any more than walking in the boot, and I was back to 15 miles three weeks later.

Over the years, I have enjoyed the competition in my age group, even winning a few races. Of the 804 events I had finished through 2022 (4 drop outs - the avulsion fracture, the 2006 hot Med City Marathon, and two other marathons in 2021 when I had a stress fracture in my right heel) , I won 32 of them, and finished 2nd another 51 times. Since reaching age 40, I have won my age group 98 times (sometimes being the only person in my category) and was second to cross the line at 73 races. I won an open 5k in NC (1985) , and my interview ended up being the lead sports story that evening, before the Kentucky Derby. Unfortunately, I did not own a TV until I got married, so I never saw it.

Among streak runners, MN has always had the highest rate of all states based on population, and Rochester (now with 25 over the years) has the highest percentage for a city over 25,000 residents. When comparing metropolitan areas, the Twin Cities ranks 2nd with 201 (NYC has the most at 294) , but, again, has the most percentage-wise. It must be the balmy weather, or maybe the fact that we are used to dressing for anything and running keeps us a little warmer in the winter.

I would remiss not to say a little more about my family. Brother Dave was the 3rd person in MN to run daily (1972-1978) before being sidelined by injury. He moved to WI and then MO, where he had another running streak. I was second to run daily in our state, so Dave and I were the first related streakers in the world. Bruce Mortenson was the first MN streak runner from 1970-1972 while living in Rochester. He has since had four more strings of daily runs over one year, the last was his longest (2011-2022) . My dad, Wendell, started exercise and then running in his late 40s, after his dad died of heart disease at age 66. His first running streak began in 1978, making him the first person over age 50 to run daily at age 54. He was also first over age 60 and age 80. He had bypass surgery at age 68 but returned to running within a couple of months. In his 70s he ran 360–364 days per year but did not do it daily again till age 84. He lived over 20 years longer than his father, dying just before turning 90. As you might have guessed, Dave, Dad & I were the first family to have three members streaking.

There are many challenges to running every day. For me, it helps that I like to go out first thing in the morning, so I do not have to worry about it when things get busy later in the day. I can probably list over 20 illnesses/injuries that made it difficult to continue. The most recent was the development of a stress fracture in my heel the summer of 2021, when I was 66. I was having some heel pain for a few months, but it always went away later in the run. Then on my last 20-mile run before the MedCity Marathon (held in the fall that year), the heel pain came back the last three miles.

I wisely scheduled a visit to see my doctor, who had an x-ray taken. I was told I could see a sports med MD the following week, so I was surprised to get a call later that afternoon, asking if I could come in the next day. I could and I did. I had a stress fracture and was told to stop running and wear a walking boot while not in bed for six weeks. I agreed to the walking boot, but we did some negotiation about the running. I cut my distance from 10 to 3 miles per day and wore a heel cushion in my right shoe. I also bought a pair of Nike Invincibles because of their extra cushioning, using them for half my runs (I always rotate shoes). After three months, I quit wearing the walking boot and started gradually increasing my mileage. I continue to wear a heel cushion and enjoy the pain-free running.

When I wrote about my kidney stone experience in 2000, I ended the article mentioning a couple of long-term running goals, one of which was to run the distance to the moon. In the last 23 years, I have gone from 100,000 to over 180,000 miles on my legs. That means I have less than 36,000 to reach the surface of the moon when it is closest to Earth (the perigee, which happens 12–13 times each year). If I can maintain my current mileage, I should arrive in 2035 or 2036. Of course, there will probably be shuttle service by then. I also would like to complete a marathon at age 90 (most recently finished the MedCity in May 2023 at age 68), which would be in 2044 or 2045.

I would be untruthful if I said I have enjoyed every mile I have ever run. There are aches and pains, inclement weather, fatigue, and times when my mental attitude is not the best. However, as I was quoted on Amby Burfoot's website, *Lifetime Running*, Life is not always fun or easy, but it seems easier after a run and gives me a greater sense of well-being." During this 50+ year odyssey, I cannot say I ever set a goal how long I would run, but the answer now is as long as I am able. It has always been one day at a time, doing what I can. And sometimes, even we ordinary people, can accomplish some amazing and extraordinary things.

God has allowed me to do this running thing, and I look forward to what tomorrow will bring. But there is much more to life than lacing up and traversing the tundra one more time. My advice to others is to follow your passion (something positive, not necessarily running) and see how far it will take you, but do not let it take over your life. For me, as a Christian, serving God is the priority, and that includes relationships, doing for others as the Golden Rule states.

Chapter 2: My First Race

Song: "Today my Life Begins"

Artist: Bruno Mars

Quote: "Look at the stars look how they shine for you and everything you do." - Cold Play, "Yellow"

Kim Zabel's word for me: Supporter

As Maverick, Tom Cruise, so famously quoted in the movie "Top Gun" that "I feel the need, the need for speed," some of us though simply feel a deep desire to register for our first race. Okay, maybe not all of us will feel a deep desire, but it is something that we somehow feel a desire to do. We register for our first race regardless of whether we feel the need for speed.

For myself my first race was in 1975 when I ran a one-mile race that was simply 4 loops around a track. I thought I would be the brilliant runner that would stop at DQ - Dairy Queen for those that are not from the Midwest - and if I remember correctly, I had a large shake about an hour or so before my mile attempt.

Well, my mile race did not go as planned, which frequently happens with one's first actual race attempt. I threw up on the side of the track on my third lap. Yet I still finished the mile run and I was still proud of myself because I was not the last runner despite my projectile vomiting.

A little bump along the way of my mile run did not stop me from finishing. This was the start of my running career and this was just the beginning of my ignoring the bumps along the way in my life and running journey.

I then ran two years of track in high school finishing the hundred in 11.3 my freshman year. It was listed as "one of freshman's best" at that time in 1976 at my high school Cretin. At that time Cretin was a Catholic, all male school, and with JROTC. Now I doubt it would even be in the top 100 of freshman bests as runners are now running on the modern rubberized tracks that are significantly faster. They have shoes that far surpass my old Adidas spiked shoes that I wore that was bought at Steichen's sporting goods store in 1976.

One can only remember the sting or burn when you fell on those cinder tracks. Hurdlers in those days would have raspberries from their falls, so no thank you to doing the hurdles. Besides I was never adept at jumping and running so I knew I was never going to be the next Edwin Corley Moses. Between 1977 and 1987, Moses won 107 consecutive finals and set the world record in the event four times. Edwin, your records were safe with me, but thank you for some incredible memories.

Funny part of the 100-event time was that I did not even remember about this event until my parents had passed away and my sisters found it in the collection of stuff that my mom had kept on me over the years. As we get older, we tend to forget about events that happen in our lives. I guess that day I felt "the need for speed."

Once my brother graduated from high school, I stopped running track as I never truly cared back then about earning a varsity letter. That was not important to me as I was more focused on getting into National Honor Society, being in the various bands from marching band to jazz band, etc., Only a few times have I maybe had a little regret for not trying to obtain a varsity letter but that regret quickly fades.

However, I never stopped running as I was still running with some of my friends. I never had any desire to run in college, as competing and running seven days a week just was not for me. I honestly did not know anyone that had ran every day. So, Steve DeBoer's streak has and never was in jeopardy with me running every day.

If I remember correctly back to 1976, small races were from .50 cents to two dollars - possibly three dollars if you wanted a t-shirt at some races. There were rarely any medals unless you won the race, or rarely given an Age Group award. Most races wanted you to be at least 16 or 18 years old and so on maybe a few forms I had lied about my age when I was younger. I guess my good old fashioned Catholic guilt is making me confess my sins now. So, my running career had officially started with that one-mile race and some nearly 50 years later I am still running and doing races.

When I started running, I did not have all the fancy running gear such as blister free socks or a Gortex jacket. I had a basic nylon windbreaker jacket from Montgomery Ward that was worn to simply keep "the chill away." It would be a far stretch to say that that the windbreaker nylon jacket kept me warm.

It was probably the mid 1990's when I personally started to notice technological advances in running gear.

For example, the brand Under Armour was founded on September 25, 1996, by Kevin Plank, a then-24-year-old former special team's captain of the University of Maryland football team that is headquartered in Baltimore, Maryland.

With the advancements of running gear, an individual could tolerate running in most weather conditions. A run that you might not go outside to complete in the past, might now feel doable.

When you live in Minnesota you see every year at least a 100 degree's temperature difference from the lowest to highest temperature for the year. So, the advancement in outdoor running gear probably was getting a significantly higher proportion of runners outside to run.

This was a good side of the advancements in technology to make us survive the elements of the weather. This was especially true for us runners trying to brave the Minnesota cold and sometimes brutal winters.

When you sign up for a race in advance you never know what the weather will be, so prepare to be prepared.

Kim Zabel
Rochester, MN
Kim Zabel's word: Connected

My dad and I were always close. He was a brilliant engineer, loved to discuss science and numbers, tutored calculus students at our kitchen table, and he also loved to run.

When I was in high school, Dad would get up around 5:00 am before work to run. I would often join him before I got ready for school. These were not chatty runs, though. Both of us are thinkers, our time spent together was often spent in silence, just enjoying a sunrise, the pavement under our feet, and each other's company. He did like to push me further than I thought I could go, though. He'd pick up the pace, so I would be inspired to keep up with him. He always supported me and had such confidence in me. He always expected the best from me, and he knew I had those same high expectations of myself. Besides running, my dad and I shared a favorite color: yellow. As a kid my room was decorated with yellow curtains and bedspreads. Dad built yellow radio-controlled model airplanes and named them after me.

Yellow and running tied us together and connected us to one another, even when we no longer lived in the same house, the same town, the same state - it connected us even after he died.

In 2016, my dad's prostate cancer came out of remission with a vengeance. He had come through the radiation treatments just fine, but two years later, his prognosis was grim. In January, he called me to tell me that the cancer was back and that it had metastasized. It was in his spine. Nothing was sure or clear except for the aggressiveness of the cancer. By March, it had spread to his brain. Experimental treatments were not working. By April, he was put in hospice. Three weeks later, my dad was dead.

Very little would comfort me during that time except for physical activity. Walking, running, my Zumba classes - I had the energy to do these things but little else. It was those things that kept me going because while I was active, I did not feel as bad. There were moments where I felt a slight lift, a little more relief from the grief, a reprieve from the heaviness in my heart. So, I kept going. I kept moving my way through the sadness. Even though I was running, I was not running very far. My longest distance before I started training for my half marathon was a 10K (6.2 miles) . But I usually just ran 5Ks, and three miles or so was my limit. And I really loved the 5K distance. Short and reasonable. It did not take me any heavy training to accomplish it, and it felt so good to just get out there and run.

And although I was content with my 5K distance, I had always had the half marathon on my bucket list as a distance race that I wanted to accomplish. Being the manager at our local running store, TerraLoco, gave me plenty of opportunity to meet runners who had run half-marathons, marathons, and ultras. In fact, this is where I first met Tom Perri. Talking to all these runners intrigued me further about the 13.1 miles, and when my assistant manager, Haley, signed up for the Hot Cider Half Marathon in Rochester, I thought it would be a great way to cross that half marathon off my bucket list. Plus, I would have a training partner if we ran it together. I would not have to run it all by myself.

But that did not happen. Haley and I never could find the time to train together. I planned on getting a run coach but could not fit it into my schedule, so I downloaded Hal Higdon's half marathon training app and started to train. Alone. This is not what I wanted. When my training app told me it was time to run 10 miles for my long run, I started having some major doubts about whether I should continue. I had never run that far before and doing all that training by myself was difficult for me. Now I would have to do a new and difficult run all by myself.

I consoled myself by finding a route that took me through neighborhoods and main streets of a rural nearby town. This kept me in touch with people who might be outside in their yards or on the street. It helped me not feel so alone.

And then right at 10 miles, I stopped my watch and looked up. Parked in front of me was a large yellow tractor outside one of the implement dealers in town. I saw the yellow and thought of my dad. It was like he was making an appearance just then to cheer me on.

Then yellow started popping up everywhere. During my next long run, I spotted a bouquet of yellow flowers sitting in the middle of the road. After that, more yellow appeared on every run. I was beginning to understand that I was not so alone after all. On race day, I planned to wear a little yellow in honor of my dad. I brought a lightweight yellow moisture-wicking jacket along that could be easily tied around my waist, if needed. I had been training with a hydration vest since all my long runs took place without any aid stations, so I did not want to change anything up that I was used to on race day. I wore the same running gear I trained in. I kept everything the same, for fear that any change in nutrition or gear would result in a major mishap or gastrointestinal distress.

Other than being a bundle of nerves, my half marathon started off just fine. I had a secret race goal of 2:30 that I told no one about for fear I would not make my goal, but I did notice the 11:26 pacer nearby in the pile of runners at the start line. Maybe I should stick close to that guy, I thought. But then he did not cross my mind or my path again until much later.

The race began a bit unexpectedly for me with the 5K runners and the 10K runners all starting at the same time as the half marathon runners. It felt like mass chaos. I lost my assistant manager, Haley, near the beginning. I was not sure if she was in front of me or behind me. Finally, though, I passed the 5K and 10K turnarounds, and the chaos subsided. There were less runners on the course. At one point, there was this stretch where there were not any people around me at all. I thought I was going to have to do this race all by myself, and even though I had trained alone, I started to doubt my ability to finish alone.

While contemplating how I was going to complete the half by myself, the 11:26 pacer that I noticed at the beginning of the race ran up beside me and started up a conversation. I recognized him as Tom Perri because he would often come into TerraLoco where I worked, and I had chatted with him before. I knew that he was a big deal. A marathoner who paced a ton of races. A man battling prostate cancer just like my dad. He loves numbers and statistics and could rattle off a kazillion stats about running, racing, and cancer. Just like my dad. He obviously loved to run. Just like my dad.

Tom asked me what my race goal was. I told him 2:30, but I did not think I was going to make it. He was pacing at 11:26, which was a little faster than my average 11:30, but it did not stop him from pacing with me. We ran together and talked about his prostate cancer, how he has survived it so far, how he has kept running through it.

I kept thinking about my dad. I had not seen very much yellow on the race course yet, but here was a real person who was very much like my dad, who had the same cancer as my dad, who was still doing what my dad loved: running. And he was running with me. It began to dawn on me that I would not be running this race alone after all.

Tom was such an excellent pacer for me. He told me to run in front of him, to get ahead of him. He changed the way in which I was running the race by changing the duration of my walk breaks. Instead of 30 second walk breaks, he was giving me 10 second walk breaks. He pushed me through my hardest training miles, and our conversation kept me running faster and harder than I thought I could ever do.

Tom told me that I would make my goal. He had that same confidence in me that my dad had.

Tom not only taught me and ran with me, he would run beside other runners that he could see were struggling and talk with them as well, ask them how they were doing, what they needed. I wasn't the only one he supported as a pacer that day.

When I finally reached mile 12, Tom told me he had to push ahead to make his pacing time. He told me that he knew I would make it. And as he took off ahead of me, I watched him run down the course and got this overwhelming realization that in a weird sense, I once again had the opportunity to run with my dad, or at the very least, someone very much like my dad.

I started to cry.

Crying at mile 12 just made things worse. My heart was already working overtime, my legs were on autopilot, I had never run this far in my life, and I started to dry heave some tears. It took my remaining energy to focus my eyes on what was in front of me: a very teary, watery-looking Tom Perri getting further and further ahead of me.

I kept running through the tears until I could see the finish line. I saw Tom crossing it in the distance. He made his pace. I knew it.

What I did not know was whether I would make my goal. As I neared the final stretch of my first half marathon and was finally able to step across the finish, I saw two things: First, I saw Tom on the side cheering for me. Second, I saw my time: 2:29:54. Tom was right. I made my goal.

But I would not have done it without him.

And I did not have to do it alone.

Chapter 3: Accidental Marathoner

Song: "Unstoppable"

Artist: Sia

Quote: "Fear doesn't exist anywhere except in the mind." - Dale Carnegie

Linda Juretschke's word for me: Unstoppable

As John Bingham clearly states one needs courage to start, then really the rest is a miracle until you get across that race finish line.

The mystique of running a marathon is usually what entices a person or runner to complete their first marathon. However, for a few marathon runners it is the gigantic marathon medal or all the race swag one gets when registering and completing a marathon.

Did you notice I said person running a marathon? On an extremely rare occasion I have been pacing a marathon when I am talking to someone that signed up for the marathon because they lost a bet or their friend is doing it so they wanted to do it. They had the courage to start the marathon, and now they are seeing if they have the strength to simply finish the marathon.

Deciding to run your first marathon is a major decision. For some it is a bucket list item that they will do only once. If it is a bucket list item, I strongly encourage you to do when younger, rather than waiting a decade or two before attempting your first marathon. Also, if by chance you like the marathon experience, then you have decades more to run another marathon.

Sometimes you need a little help to keep you going and to get you across that finish line especially during a marathon. You still must take every step, but during the marathon someone can help you along the way. Most commonly that person is a pacer. The designated pacer is a person running a set pace per mile, so runners finish at a designated time.

In races without designated pacers, you may to try to follow or run close by or with someone that is running close to your running pace. Or maybe you have a running buddy that you trained with that you are running with.

For some marathon runners they will complete their first marathon and when they finish, they will swear they will never run another marathon. Then a few weeks or months later the mystique of the marathon brings them to register for another marathon. Maybe the person wants to better their marathon finish time, or to run a marathon with a spouse or significant other, or to raise money for a charity, or even earn that humongous finisher medal. There are plenty of reasons of why to run a marathon.

But to get to your second marathon finish, you first must finish your first marathon. Once you finish your second marathon, then third marathon, etc., you might become fascinated with the marathon experience and become a Marathon Maniac.

Just be careful with the allure of the marathon as before you know it you might be joining the 100 Marathon Club North America. A club made for people that have completed at least 100 marathons.

So, you hopefully started the marathon with a pair of running shoes that work for you. This is a very important part of the running and especially the marathon experience to run in shoes that are best for your running form and needs.

Then the next step is literally taking one step at a time until you cross the finish line. Again, if you don't cross the start line you can't cross the finish line.

When running your first marathon and you are not a barefoot runner, it is important to have the right running shoe. Running 26.2 miles is a long distance and the amount of time to be in a pair of shoes that doesn't fit properly isn't a brilliant idea.

It is generally believed that humans started wearing shoes about 40,000 years ago which was long before I was born.

The first running shoemaker was believed to be an English company called J. W. Foster and Sons, now better known as Reebok. In the 1890's it was started by Joseph William Foster, a keen runner who wanted to design shoes that could help him run faster. J.W. Foster made leather spikes worn by British athletes Harold Abrahams and Eric Liddell who won medals in the Paris Olympics in 1924. Their story was told in the Academy Award-winning film Chariots of Fire in 1981.

Bill Bowerman, a field-and-track coach, and Phil Knight who was

Bowerman's former student at the University of Oregon, founded Nike which would become a leader in the running shoe industry.

It was Nike that made around 12 pairs of running shoes for competitors at the Olympic Trials in 1972. The style earned the unofficial name "Moon Shoe" because the grip pattern looked like the footprints left on the Moon by American astronauts.

Bill Bowerman apparently developed the Moon Shoes waffle-like grip pattern after examining his wife's waffle maker. He used that same waffle maker to mold rubber for the design's first prototype. I am thinking that I would not have wanted to have the next waffle on that waffle maker.

It is interesting to note the shoes Roger Bannister wore when he ran a mile in 3:59.4 seconds were very light and weighed approximately four and a half ounces. Roger clocked 3:59.4 seconds in the historic race at Iffley Road Track in Oxford on May 6th, 1954. He became the first known person to break the four-minute mile when he was a 25-year-old medical student.

Most beginner runners start with just one pair of running shoes. If you begin slowly increasing your running mileage it is best to have at least two pair of running shoes and wear them on alternate days. Then if you begin running off the road and onto more of a dirt and grass or trail then it might be time specifically for trail shoes.

When I started running my running shoes were purchased at discount stores. Now nearly all of my running shoes that I wear I get at marathons that I pace. The occasional free pair of running shoes is a nice perk of being a pacer. However, occasionally the running shoes I receive do not feel or fit properly, but at least I can donate those running shoes to a charity.

It was not until the COVID pandemic that I had to buy a pair of running shoes for the first time in years in 2020. My usual pacing assignments were not happening, thus, no free shoes. So, off to purchase shoes I went. I wear what is comfortable for me and that fits properly. I do not wear the same shoe my friends wear or what some elite runner wears.

Linda Juretschke
AKA The Accidental Marathoner
Bolingbrook, Illinois
Linda's word for herself: Fearless

1) The main obstacle you faced when training for your first marathon?

I had never run in my life, and I really had no idea what I was doing. I kept procrastinating starting a training program, and about 12 weeks before the race, my husband was severely injured in a bicycle accident, which really threw a wrench into things. Just two months before the marathon, I hadn't even run a block.

2) How did you overcome that obstacle?

I essentially did not train, though I did do some distance walking in the final weeks before the race. Determination played a big role. I convinced myself that if I could power walk at a 15-minute per mile pace, I could get it done. I would set small goals to 'run to that fire hydrant' or 'run past that mailbox.' I could eventually run two city blocks without stopping, which seemed like an amazing feat at the time!

3) What about your running shoes and how you picked them for the marathon?

A good year or more before I even entertained the idea of running a marathon, I was on a plane reading a fitness magazine. It happened to be a 'best-of' issue, with a section on running shoes. One brand and model were listed as the 'best shoe for first-time marathoners.' I tore the page out and saved it, eventually buying that pair for my first marathon. I ran in those shoes (updated models along the way) for a full ten years before officially being fitted at a local running store and completely switching brands.

4) Why did you decide to visit the pacer booth at the Chicago Marathon where you going to run your first marathon?

I almost did not! I really felt that I could do it on my own, but then decided at the last minute to see what they had to say. I was in line waiting to talk with the 5:25 run/walk interval pacer (having pulled that time out of the air) , when

I started chatting with you, who would be pacing the 5:25 running group. I said I did not think I could keep up with running the entire time, since I still had not run more than a quarter mile by that point. You explained that both groups would be finishing at the same time, and to think about it; I would have to be running faster in those 4 minutes to slow down to a walk during the 1-minute walking intervals. You explained it so clearly (and confidently) , and it made perfect sense. You simply said that "just stick with me, I'll get you through," and I believed you! I never did talk with that run/walk pacer.

5) *What was the marathon experience like for you?*

I met up with you before the race and decided I was going to stick to you like glue. You told it me it was your 259th marathon, and I was blown away. We hit Mile 1 and I could not believe I had just run an entire mile! Then two, then five, then ten, and so on, all the way to 26.2. You were pacing 5:25 and brought me in at 5:24:58, which still amazes me to this day. It also remains my fastest marathon finishing time, and I owe that all to you! That first marathon experience was nothing short of amazing. I could have cared less about the actual running part, but the experience of the crowds, the camaraderie with other runners, the volunteers, and all the excitement was like nothing I had ever experienced. I grew up on the west side of Chicago, and running through the many different neighborhoods brought back so many great memories of growing up in this great city. I am so glad my first marathon experience was in my own home town.

6) *What did it feel like to finish that day after the medal was placed around your neck:*

"I JUST FREAKING FINISHED A MARATHON!!!' I felt so incredible and had the biggest smile on my face when I got to the finish line. I was so grateful to the volunteers all along the course, but that person who physically put the medal around my neck was the most special of all! She seemed just excited as I was to have finished the race. As much as I felt I could not believe I finished...I honestly always knew I would.

7) *Anything else that is important and would like to share:*

Almost NO ONE knew I was doing the race, not even my best friend (of course my lack of training made it easy to hide) . The only people who knew in advance were my three boys, because two were away at college and I wanted everyone in town for the race. I did not even tell my husband until two weeks before the race, and only then, so he could plan to have the weekend free. Race weekend coincided with our 25th wedding anniversary, so it was perfect. We spent the entire weekend in the city and had a fantastic time, with the race being the icing on the cake. Having my entire family there to support me was so incredibly special. I literally called my best friend after I crossed the finish line and said, "guess what I just did?" She did not believe me until I sent her a photo wearing my medal!

Chapter 4: Keeping Me Waiting - Three Attempts to Finally Finish My First Marathon

Song: "Stronger"

Artist: Kelly Clarkson

Quote: "If we can accept whatever hand we've been dealt - no matter how unwelcome - the way to proceed eventually becomes clear." – Phil Jackson

Joyel Barnard's word for me: Caring

So, on Saturday, May 20th, 2012, I was running Fargo marathon for the 7th time and pacing the 4:30 group. I finished in 4:29:37 so another marathon successfully paced. I had no clue at that time how important the Fargo marathon would be in my running career. So, one marathon completed that weekend and off to another marathon.

No after party celebration after completing the Fargo marathon, as immediately after the marathon I was showered and then driving to Green Bay. The Green Bay Marathon was on Sunday, May 21st, 2012, and I would be pacing the 4:45 group.

Getting in the car for a long 7 and a 1/2-hour drive immediately following the Fargo marathon - or any marathon - is not recommended. After any marathon a long car drive is never really a great idea. A few breaks to use the bathroom and stretch happened but even these were kept to a minimum as the goal was to get to Green Bay by 8pm if possible. Graciously Rat - AKA as Kathy Waldron a running Legend in Wisconsin - was letting me stay with her. I just remember it was very warm out still when I finally arrived at her house.

Looking back, I do not clearly recall all that happened that day for the Green Bay marathon. I just remember the race announcements at the start telling all the runners "it will be a hot one today!" or "runners please slow down today!"

The marathon started right on time as I was pacing the 4:45 group. I just remember by the first mile seeing runners already laying down on the side of the road. Some needing medical attention before even the completing the first mile. More runners were receiving medical treatment before we even completed 3 miles on the marathon course. In my opinion it was very warm, but not incredibly hot.

I am pacing the 4:45 marathon group and right on schedule at all the mile markers. I was keeping equal effort versus equal pace, a pacing strategy that I had been using for nearly 30 years. The marathon course is relatively easy and fast with no challenging hills or miles that one must worry about. The half-marathon came up and we hit it right on schedule, but rumors were spreading that the marathon was going to be stopped due to race conditions. Way too many runners were receiving medical treatment out on the course. The temperature was slowly getting warmer as the marathon went on.

We had reached just about mile 15.5 and I was told that the marathon had been canceled. My pacing duties were done for the day. The marathon was canceled/stopped because of the heat and overall weather conditions. This would become my second marathon that was affected by heat and weather conditions. The other marathon I successfully finished, this marathon I had no such luck. So sadly, my marathon that day was over.

This was by far the most confusing marathon and/or race cancellation that I have ever experienced. My pacing day was over so time to head to the finish line.

One of the runners in my pace group was Joyel. She was running her first marathon. Joyel was staying close to me and looked like a possible 4:45 finisher until the marathon was stopped.

Imagine you are running your first ever marathon and it is canceled less than 11 miles from the finish. What are you feeling and thinking? Why me? Are you feeling intense anger and frustration? A few marathoners regardless of whether a first-time marathoner or an experienced marathoner might be secretly saying thank you as I was having a bad day. I guarantee you that every runner on that course had a very strong opinion as to what was happening to them during the marathon.

Your dream of having that marathon medal around your neck is gone. No photos sent to friends about your first-time marathoner finish. No Facebook post about your accomplishment.

Again, this quote comes to mind:

"There is only one certainty in life and that is that nothing is certain."

G.K. Chesterton (June 1926)

Joyel did not actually fail her first marathon attempt. The marathon failed Joyel. I had total confidence Joyel would have finished the marathon had the marathon not been canceled. Would Joyel have stayed with my 4:45 pace group? That was not the main goal as my goal was simply to see her finish her first marathon. I truly believe she would have finished that day, but she did not get the chance that day.

So, what does one do when you go out and try to run your first marathon and all does not go as planned? Well, you sign up for a marathon three weeks later and you try again. You do not let a marathon race's failure keep you from succeeding and getting that marathon medal around your neck.

As the saying goes if you try and fail then you try again. You keep trying until you succeed.

On Sunday, June 3rd, I paced the Minneapolis Marathon 5-hour group. This was my fourth time pacing this marathon and being a Minnesota native I had probably run hundreds of miles on most of this course. The 5-hour pace group was small as this was a smaller marathon with approximately 900 runners.

Joyel joined my 5-hour pace that morning. Joyel had just some 21 days ago has been told "your marathon has been canceled." She had made it 15.5 miles with me, so now we were trying to finish this marathon together.

"If you fall off a horse, you get back up and on it," is a known saying. Basically, it means you are not a quitter. Joyel was not a quitter as it takes a good deal of emotional and especially physical courage to try another marathon just 21 days later.

The Green Bay marathon was in the past and the Minneapolis marathon was current and the focus of today. I finished the marathon in 4:59:37, so for me a successful pacing day and another marathon completed.

This would be a major accomplishment for Joyel to finally finish a marathon. She certainly got to the start line and this time she got herself to the finish line and completed her first marathon.

They say that less than 1% of the population will run a marathon in their life time. I cannot even imagine how incredibly small the percentage must be of people that for whatever reason that is outside the runner's control had their first marathon canceled while they were running the marathon. For some people the one and done philosophy takes hold regardless of whether you accomplished your goal or not. I hope all those first timers that day on Sunday, May 21st, 2012, in Green Bay, Wisconsin, eventually were able to successfully have a marathon medal placed around their neck.

Per the great Muhammad Ali:

"You don't lose if you get knocked down; you lose if you stay down."

If you feel defeated by a race, just try again, and sign up for another race and just keep trying. There are plenty of races to help you achieve your goal and succeed.

Joyel Kautza -Barnard
Wautoma, WI
Joyel's word for herself: Resilient

I have always loved running since I was a kid, but it took me some time to realize it. Running became my therapy: How I overcame depression and anxiety.

I had just recently been divorced and the age of 40 was creeping up on me and so was my weight. 5 feet and one inch tall and two-hundred and thirty–five pounds to be exact. I did the gamut of methods to try to get rid of the weight. Different diets, I joined "Curves," but nothing seemed to work. I felt hopeless, worthless. I was not motivated, no energy. I tried all different types of work outs and diets, but nothing seemed to work for me. I was stuck in a dark hole, and I did not know how to get out.

Then, one day, I decided to try something new. I put on my sneakers and went for a run. It was hard at first, but I pushed myself to keep going, from one telephone pole to another. In my head I would say, Hey Joyel, you used to run in college, you can do it again. As my 40th birthday was coming up, I booked a trip to AZ to visit my folks. Something occurred to me. Have Dad map out 10 miles in the desert for me to run on my birthday. For me it always has been go big or go home. No hesitation from my dad, as he was always the one to push me past my limits. He went ahead and mapped a 10-mile loop for me in the desert. I remember him telling me, you better get going, the Packer Bear game starts in 5 hours. Funny, right? As I ran, as slow as a turtle it felt like, I felt something else. Yes, my lungs burned, my muscles ached and excited while my friends riding an ATV with a Bloody Mary for me to chase. But I also felt something else: a sense of accomplishment, a release of tension, a boost of mood. The first time in a long time!!

It was not pretty, but I never walked and got the whole 10 miles in. That was 2005. I never stopped after that. I was finding out it was not so much weight loss or getting in shape as it was the mental therapy running did for me. That was the beginning of my journey. Running became my way of coping with stress and negative emotions. Running gave me a purpose, a goal, a challenge. Running made me happy.

I am not saying that running was my cure all. I still have bad days. Running taught me that I am strong, resilient, and capable of overcoming obstacles. Running showed me that there is a lot of good in this world. And it also brought me closer to God.

If you are suffering from depression or anxiety, or any other mental health issue, I encourage you to give running a try. It does not have to be fast or long or intense. Just start with what you can do, and gradually increase your distance and speed. You will be amazed by the benefits that running can bring to your physical and mental health.

Running became my therapy, and it can become yours too.

So, as the years went on from December of 2005, I decided to push it a bit further. Because of course I am always up for a challenge. And running a marathon is a huge challenge. As I kept running, I thought, could I run a half or a full marathon? So why not go BIG right away and signed up for a full marathon as my first race in Wautoma in 2010. I know it would require a lot of preparation and dedication. But I was not ready for everything I was about to learn about myself.

I started my training about six months before the race date. I followed a plan that gradually increased my weekly mileage and included long runs, speed work, recovery runs, and cross-training. I also paid attention to my nutrition, hydration, and sleep habits. I wanted to be as fit and healthy as possible for the big day.

What I was not ready for was setbacks, as on my 18-mile-long run, I suddenly had a shooting pain in my Achilles tendon. I thought to myself, "well just slow down and it will be fine." As I always told my kids, I do not see blood or bones so keep going. Not the best advice for this situation I found out the hard way. So close to race day in Wautoma for my first full marathon and I am running hours in our local hotel pool just to keep up with the training. It was not getting better. I went to doctor, and he told me, "Go ahead and run this race but you won't run another again." So, with a heavy heart and big disappointment, I did not run the race.

One of the most important aspects of marathon training is mental toughness. With this big disappointment I decided not to give up. I reminded myself of my goal and how far I had come. I also connected with and found support from other runners who shared my passion. They motivated me, cheered me on, and gave me valuable advice.

Next up Green Bay Cell Com Marathon, 2012. The day of the race was an unforgettable experience. I had so many friends and family who stayed with me the night before and were there to cheer me on the whole way. I woke up early, ate a light breakfast, and jumped on a bus to take me to the start line. Once I got there, I heard they had pacers that I could run with. So, I sought out the 4:45 group as that is what I had been training at. There was Tom! I felt a mix of nervousness and excitement as I waited for the gun to go off. When it did, I started running at a comfortable pace, trying not to get carried away by the crowd. Listening to all Tom was telling our group to do. God put the right person with me that day. I really enjoyed seeing all the spectators, the signs people were holding up to cheer us on and with the heat the homes that had their sprinklers going for us. It was an AWE type of experience for me as I have never even spectated at a race much less ran one. I saw people going down with the heat but thought I have run in hotter weather than this training. I listened to Tom and was on track to finish. Then WHAM 15.5 miles they kicked us off the course. I thought to myself not again!! Am I not to finish a race? The feeling of 2010 all over again. When you are halfway through your 2nd attempt at a full marathon and the race is canceled because of the heat, I felt a mix of emotions. Extremely disappointed that I could not finish what I started, and frustrated thinking that my training was wasted. I remember my brother coming to pick up some of us in my pacing group along with Tom. My brother said out of all the family and friends that came to cheer me on none of them wanted to pick me up knowing my "mood." Too funny. While in the car driving to the finish line that I was not able to cross, and to meet everyone that cheered me on, Tom said, "Come run the Minneapolis marathon in 3 weeks and use this as a training run. You can use this experience as a learning opportunity and a motivation for your next challenge." Well of course I said YES!

Tom was so good and set us all up for that race the Minneapolis Marathon. Registration, hotel rooms, and pre-race dinner. Words cannot thank Tom enough for all he did to get me finally to that finish line! That is the cool thing about running, you meet so many amazing people in the process and make lifelong friends along the way. Tom is one of them.

The race started out amazingly and I was on track for 5-hour pace. That rush of Green Bay all over again. My parents and my brother Bart were with me this time. They were so amazing about being at different mile markers and my brother with his Red Shirt making sure I had my "jellybeans" along the way. Tom was pacing and one woman (I wish I knew her name) stayed with me to the end! My last 3 miles I hit that brick wall they talk about and WOW what a wall that was for me. I thought to myself I cannot even turn my head from side to side, But the women that stayed with me kept me going. All I could think of was one foot in front of the other you got this Joyel.

My legs were super heavy, my lungs burned, and my mind was telling me to stop. But I pushed through the pain and challenge. I thought of all the people who believed in me and supported me. I thought of how proud I would feel when I crossed the finish line. And then I saw it. The finish line was in sight. I heard my name and I sprinted with all my strength and raised my arms in triumph. I had done it. I ran a full marathon! I still tear up when I think about it.

It was one of the top moments of my life. I received a medal, a blanket, and a hug from a volunteer and sheer happiness when I saw my family. I felt a surge of emotion as I realized what I had accomplished. I DID IT! I ran 26.2 miles. I had fulfilled my dream. Having the post celebratory beers was not bad either,

Since then, I have run one additional full marathon in Las Vegas and multiple half marathons.

My race days are fewer now and I do get my runs in not just as far, as having ACL replacements are not fun. But I am still running and trying.

Running a marathon or even that first mile is an amazing journey that taught me a lot about myself and what I am capable of. It is never easy, but it is so worth it mentally and physically. It is an adventure that I will never forget and continues to push me harder in anything in life.

My advice for anyone that thinks they cannot do it, and that does go for anything in life..........UMMMMMMM YES YOU CAN!! You can do anything you put your mind to!! I did and so can you!

Trivia

Note one trivial part of the Minneapolis Marathon in 2012 was that Tom Tisell finished second overall in the marathon. Tom had won the first three Minneapolis Marathons, and barely missed his fourth win. But that is not what the legendary Tom Tisell is best known for and I bet you don't have a clue why Tom Tisell is a famous trivia answer? Remember some professional athlete known as "Prime Time" or otherwise known as Deion Sanders? Tom was chosen the "Most Athletic" over Deion Sanders in high school in his Senior year.

Chapter 5: Ups and Downs - It is all about the Attitude at Altitude

Song: "Altitude"

Artist: Dave Drinker

Quote: "It's your attitude, not your aptitude that will determine your altitude." - Zig Ziglar

Angel Brock's word for me: Altruistic

I had been to Colorado numerous times before for sightseeing, visiting friends, and attending a few workshops and conferences before I headed to Colorado to run the American Discovery Trail Marathon on Monday, September 5th, 2005. At just over 6,000 feet the city stands just over 1 mile above sea level. Colorado Springs is near the base of Pikes Peak, which rises 14,115 feet above sea level on the eastern edge of the Southern Rocky Mountains.

The simple reason I did this marathon was I needed the state of Colorado for my first time of doing a marathon in all 50 states. It was Labor Day weekend and the marathon was being run on Monday which was Labor Day so it fit my schedule perfectly.

I had knee surgery in March of 2005, so this marathon was just about six months after the surgery. My original thought when I signed up for the marathon was that I would run under 5 hours which would be a slight challenge.

One of the challenges was I was just slowing getting back into a normal running schedule so my running pace was still not anywhere near what it had been at the start of 2005.

My second challenge was that I would be running at an elevation of over 6,000 feet for most of the marathon. I was traveling from Maple Grove, MN, where the elevation was at an estimated 935 feet. That is at least 5,065 feet of elevation change which would present a small challenge.

I had won a 5k race in the 1990's in Colorado and breaking 19 minutes in the 5k in Colorado at elevation was almost an identical effort as compared to my 18:55 5k at the Victory 5k race years later that was in Minnesota. The Victory 5k race was a race that used to be held on Labor Day, which I completed several times usually doing both the 5k and 10k race.

The one thing I knew from all the articles I had read in Runner's World about running at elevation was that basically for every 1,000 feet of elevation change you would potentially be running an average of 2% to 4% slower for an average runner. The higher the altitude the slightly higher the percentage your actual running will slow.

Note that when running a 5k a loss of 10 seconds per mile does not sound like a lot when only running 3.1 miles, as that is around 31 seconds' slower overall time. Please remember I am specifically referring to running at that altitude versus doing a downhill run of 10,000 feet to 6,000 feet.

However, if using a slightly higher percentage of decreased running speed for the marathon due to the marathon distant and potentially slower running pace during the marathon, that might mean potentially a twelve to fifteen second per mile slower pace. That could mean nearly a 7-minute slower overall finish time.

Remember that this is just highlighting the possible seconds per mile slower one might need to run. Some people may tolerate the elevation change better than others so they will be in the less than 1% range and others not tolerate it all and be safer at a 2% slower running pace.

So, I finished the American Discovery Trail Marathon in 5:17:49. I knew I would be needing to take the marathon course slower than what I would have liked as I would have loved running a sub-5-hour marathon, but with the challenge of still recovering from knee surgery and the elevation challenge I was very happy with my marathon time. Also, I know I lost a few minutes of time as I was busy taking photos during the marathon as I was just having fun and enjoying the run.

The next time I would do the American Discovery Trail Marathon would be on Monday, September 6th, 2009, pacing the 5-hour group to a 4:58:34 finish. Then I came back in 2010 pacing the 5-hour pace group in 4:58:20. I continued to come back for two more years pacing the 5-hour group in 2011 in 4:59:00, and then my last time pacing the 5-hour group for this marathon was in 2012 finishing in 4:58:18. To my knowledge this marathon no longer exists if you were looking to pace or run it.

As a runner just do not be afraid to run slower when above 5,000 feet elevation change. As mentioned in a 5k event you might feel the difference immediately due to the immediate harder effort, but with the marathon distance or longer you possibly may not feel the difference when you first start your run, but it will probably make for an unpleasant second half of the run. So, if you were running 8:57 pace at 1,000 feet elevation comfortably, you might very well want to slow potentially to a 9:07 pace or even a 9:09 pace or slower above 4,000 feet.

I would also advocate to run 10% slower than your normal pace at altitude to have an overall more enjoyable experience running if your goal is simply to complete the race.

One other important consideration is that with running a race at significant altitude change, it is potentially best to arrive at least ten days before which helps allow the body to somewhat adapt to the demands of altitude.

Altitude can be basically looked at as three levels with high altitude being 4,900 to 11,500 feet (think Leadville Marathon and this marathon does go slightly higher than 11,500) , very high altitude at 11,500 to 18,000 feet (think Pikes Peak Marathon) , and extreme altitude at above 18,000 feet (think Everest Marathon) .

However, for a weekend runner that is coming to do a race at altitude and has minimal time to arrive early to adapt to the altitude, it is usually best to arrive as close to race start time as possible, preferably within 18 hours to two days.

It is generally believed that the most prominent performance inhibitors of altitude typically are experienced within the first 48 hours up to 7 days from arrival date, but again that varies with everyone.

So, if you do show up for a race at altitude it is better to show up less than two days early, or at least be in your race area at a minimum of ten days early. Again, this is just in case you are seeking potentially your best racing experience at altitude as everyone handles altitude differently.

One other thing to make sure you have a basic understanding of is "altitude sickness" or "mountain sickness." Symptoms tend to occur within hours after arrival at high altitude and include headache, nausea, and shortness of breath.

Note that if you arrive to an area at higher elevation and are not feeling well, you may want to contact your primary physician to discuss your symptoms. If serious symptoms you may want to seek medical attention immediately.

Just always enjoy the running experience as it really becomes about your attitude especially when at altitude. There is no reason to fear a race due to altitude, but you do have to readily accept the challenge. Just be okay and prepared to run at a slightly slower pace.

Angel Brock
Fountain, Colorado
Angel's word for herself: Living

I was diagnosed with ovarian dysgerminoma September 30, 1996. I was 27 years old. By the time they did surgery the tumor was 4lbs 9.5oz and 22cm. I ended up with 2 surgeries and chemotherapy. So, I lost my hair but not my will. I was not into running at that time as I was more into the stair climber, aerobics, and bench pressing. A few months after my 2nd surgery they had a bench press competition and I heard this bodybuilder girl was worried that I would enter and so I did. And I won. I won because I did not have all those muscles like she did and bench pressing is based on your weight to bench ratio. But most importantly I was lucky because they left part of my left ovary that would allow me to give birth to my son 4 years later!

I ran my first 5K in September of 2008 as my introduction to running races. I had just turned 39, and my initial goal was to run a half marathon before turning 40 in June of 2009. I met my goal early in December of 2008 at the Zappos Las Vegas half marathon. Then I figured I would train for the marathon. You know the old saying be one and done. I ran my first marathon in April 2009 at the Salt Lake City Marathon in Salt Lake City, Utah, in just under 5 hours. I then just kept going and doing more races, especially marathons.

I live in Colorado near Colorado Springs. I signed up for the American Discovery Trail (ADT) marathon on Labor Day in 2009. It would be my 2nd marathon and just like a teenager I thought I had it all figured out. I did not know what a pacer was until the ADT marathon. Tom Perri was pacing the 5-hour group. That was about the time I expected so I thought I would join his group. Tom was very engaging with the group, and told us the first mile he would go a little easy. Entertained us with jokes and trivia. He was nice and all, but by mile 2 I lost faith that he would get us there in 5 hours. It just really seemed too slow and I mean this was my 2nd marathon so I know what I am doing. I was pretty sure I knew more than this guy! This other woman runner and I decided to go ahead.

By mile 9 I am struggling. I had all this energy and unearned confidence at mile 1 and now I had none. My pace dramatically slowed and I had to start walking/jogging. I was devastated as I did not walk in my first and only marathon or any of my training runs. I was proud of the fact I could run for 5 hours, just not pretty, but I could do it. It was very warm too which with all my marathon wisdom I did not know about the effect on my running. Most of my training had been in the fall/winter months. Well Pacer Tom and his posse passed my walking sticks about mile 10 and it was to say a little bit embarrassing.

Well after 5 hours I am still out rethinking my life choices and trying to keep putting one foot in front of the other hoping to make the finish line before Thanksgiving. I think it was about mile 24.5ish I see this guy running the opposite direction and it is the Pacer guy! Oh my gosh ..... pleeaaasssseee help me! Tom stopped and sure enough he paced me to the finish line. Not thinking anything of it, except that I was beyond grateful I asked Tom if he would hold my hand as we crossed the finish line! He obliged but told me not through the finish line, probably because of the timing mat. I think I finished in the 5:40s.

I found out later that Tom had gone back to help another runner but I had pleaded with him first. And I think he had just about 198 or more marathons than me. I have had the pleasure of seeing Tom at other races ... ¦super knowledgeable, of course experienced, caring, and most of all humble. I am grateful to have him as my friend!

Yes, Tom did go back after we finished to get that runner that he originally had planned to bring to the finish.

Trivia:

The Pikes Peak Marathon, founded in 1956, takes runners from Manitou Springs, Colorado, with a starting elevation of 6,412 feet, to the summit of Pikes Peak at 14,115 feet. It is approximately 7,815 of elevation ascent and descent, for a total of 26.2 grueling mountain miles to complete this marathon.

The sister race, the Pikes Peak Ascent, climbs 7,815 vertical feet up the historic Barr Trail on the east face of the mountain. The Ascent, which climbs 13.3 miles to finish at the summit, used to be held on the same day as the Marathon but became its own event in the 1980s due to its popularity. In case you are thinking of registering for the Double, both the Ascent which is on Saturday and the Marathon which is on Sunday, you must have previously completed the Ascent or Marathon prior to registering for both races. Also, you must be at least 16 years old on race day to register.

Chapter 6: It is All in the Planning with Some Surprises

Song: "Don't Stop Believin'"

Artist: Journey

Quote: "You can be a victim of cancer or a survivor of cancer. It's a mindset." - Dave Pelzer

Emily Enyeart's word for me: Toughie

You can plan your life all you want. You can plan your hourly, daily, and weekly routine. But guess what? Cancer simply does not care what you plan or when you plan it. Cancer has a mind of its own. Cancer will dictate your life if you let it. Cancer can and will consume your entire life if you simply let it. Welcome to my new world that was put into place on December 26th, 2018.

But guess what cancer? You decided a Stage 3 cancer diagnosis was not stopping me, right? So, you upped the ante to giving me a Stage 4 diagnosis, right? Do you think I care what frigging Stage of cancer you give me?

Cancer, you just gave me an upgraded Stage. Big deal as you gave me basically a higher number. As the saying goes "sticks and stones will break my bones but words (or numbers) will never hurt me."

Sure, I had to take into consideration that I had cancer. Yes, I understand how cancer was changing my life and affecting me. Yes, I clearly understand how serious Stage 4 cancer can be. But let me make this clear. Do you have a clue cancer how tough I am?

I guess cancer you were trying to give me a knockout punch to keep me from my running goals. Guess what cancer I am tougher than you are. I *have* been continually planning my marathon and running goals since December 26th, 2018 when I was told that I probably had cancer.

So, you decided to play tough guy with me? Let's show the reading audience just how tough you are. Since 12/26/2018 when told I had cancer, I have completed 191 marathons. Since 7/30/201 when I was diagnosed with Stage 4 cancer, I have completed 170 marathons. Did you know that I completed five ultras within those 170 marathons?

I am still pacing and running marathons. I am still winning my Age Group and overall races since my Stage 4 cancer diagnosis.

I have multiple dreams and goals to accomplish and plan. Cancer is just a little distraction trying to impede my progress and I am currently not letting cancer derail me from the goals I want to accomplish.

Cancer I am like the bullet train in Japan going up to 199 mph and nothing is going to stop me from getting my goals accomplished. Sure, cancer you are fast as well trying to multiple and get through to my bones, and various organs and my brain. Just remember I am visualizing leaving you behind and enjoying my next destination that I hope is as beautiful as Mt Fuji. I hope all you people with cancer plan on getting on the bullet train with me and leaving cancer behind so we can enjoy our next journey. As Dolly Parton said, "If you don't like the road you're walking, start paving another one."

Sure, some days I spend doing a radiation treatment. Some days I spend getting another blood draw for a PSA. On other days I am getting a hormone injection shot. Some days I am just driving to Mayo Clinic to get another scan done. Not even to mention how many times I had to take a COVID test so I could simply have a procedure done.

Most of my appointments I had to plan, while others I was given a date/time/place to show up. I spent hours on hold while I was simply trying to make an appointment. During the pandemic simply trying to call to simply get a call back was exacerbating at times. On many days it was not easy. But it is what I had to do and I got through it all.

But between all my appointments, phone calls, and treatments I still had my life to live. I was still running and lifting weights and going to the gym. Sometimes I did not even have the physical energy to do a simple workout, so I went to the gym to just sit in the whirlpool for five minutes. Note that I simply did *something* and on some days that was a struggle to do but I did it.

I simply wanted my day and my life to feel somewhat normal.

Being active is normal to me. Just like my planning marathons and races to pace and run is normal too me. Normal felt good for my body and brain, so I have not ever stopped planning or running races. In fact, I found pushing myself to do marathons and races I had never done before, to be invigorating and extremely motivating.

What have I accomplished since my Stage 4 diagnosis? Well let me tell you just a few of the goals I have accomplished with my running in the order they were completed below.

- My 500th marathon completed.
- My 5th time 50 States Marathon certified finish completed.
- My 6th time 50 States Marathon certified finish completed.
- My 100th Marathon with Stage 4 cancer completed.
- My 600th Marathon/ultra completed.
- My Six Star World Major Marathons completed.
- My 7th time 50 States Marathon certified finish completed.
- My 150th Marathon completed with Stage 4 cancer.
- My 650th marathon/ultra completed.
- I reached 2,350 career races.
- I reached 120,000 lifetime miles.

Okay, so those goals were accomplished, so now you want to see what else I am planning to accomplish and what is on my near future bucket list that I am currently working on?

- Approaching my 300th career race since my initial cancer diagnosis.
- Still need the states of Louisiana and New Jersey (for New Jersey I completed an ultra but just not the marathon distance) to run a marathon in, so I can complete my goal of a certified marathon finish in all 50 states with Stage 4 cancer.
- I still need the state of Hawaii to accomplish an overall win or an Age Group award so I can have one for all 50 states.
- Still need to pace a marathon in all 50 States with Stage 4 cancer and just 13 states left.
- My 200th Marathon/ultra completed with Stage 4 cancer.
- My 700th marathon/ultra completed.
- My 8th time 50 State Marathon certified finish with only 10 states

to go currently.

- Still seeking my second Six Star World Major Marathon finish with only Boston and Tokyo left to do.
- Run a marathon and complete a marathon when I am 70 years old.
- Still seeking my 100th Sub 4-hour marathon, as I am currently at 99.

Okay, so you want to see what else I am planning to accomplish and what is on my distant bucket list?

- Still seeking my 9th time 50 State Marathon Club certified finish with only 23 states to go.
- Still seeking a marathon on all continents with three continents down, and five to go!
- Still need to run an ultra in all 50 states.
- Still seeking my 14th time 50 state certified marathon finish.
- Still seeking my 1,000th career marathon/ultra.

Okay, so you want to see what else I am planning to accomplish and what is on my dream distant bucket list now that I have Stage 4 cancer?

- A BQ time so I can officially qualify for the Boston marathon.
- A BQ in all 50 states.
- A 50sub4 Marathon certified finish for my second time, as I only have 32 states to go.
- Run a marathon when I am 80 years old.

So, what is on *your* bucket list?

When you have a goal to accomplish just go for it. You might even have family members, friends, and siblings that can help you along. As T.S. Eliot said, "Only those who risk going too far can possibly find out how far one can go."

So how far can you go? And maybe, where in the world might you want to go?

Enough said.

There was a *rare* day when I got home from my third cancer related surgery in 2021 that involved taking out a growth on my neck and I was depressed. I was basically sitting home and anxiously awaiting the results. Was the growth on my neck going to be a cancerous growth or not? The actual results of the biopsy were something that was totally out of my control. That thought pattern was actually depressing me.

Then I changed my thought pattern from negative and worry thoughts, to a positive memory of thinking of my helping Heather at the Honolulu Marathon in 2015, and a big smile appeared on my face. Sure, it was winter in Minnesota so thinking of palm trees and relaxing on Waikiki Beach was a powerful image. It was an incredibly good feeling inside my heart that helped me the most that day. I had an incredible memory remembering helping a friend achieve a goal. I helped her that day and she paid me back by *giving* me that positive memory to think about.

Consider your mind like a light switch, and turn off the negative thoughts and switch on the positive thoughts.

Regardless of what that biopsy found I told myself that I would pace another marathon. I promised myself that I would pace another marathon and I did.

So, I can always thank Heather for that few hours that we ran together that we never planned as it was just meant to be. I helped her that day in Honolulu, Hawaii, in 2015, and she helped me in Maple Grove, MN, that day in 2021. I have that incredible memory forever.

Sometimes things you do not plan on turn out to be simply the best. Just like meeting Emily at the Burlington, Vermont airport, and finding a running connection. As the saying goes "the rest is just history."

Oh, that biopsy from the growth on my neck was benign.

Time to start planning some more marathons and races is what that was telling me. Just don't stop believing.

Emily Enyeart
Anchorage, Alaska
Emily's word for herself: Unbeaten

In 2014 my husband had a 24-hour running event that was a fundraiser for

POW/MIA that we went to participate in. I thought I could never run because I had never learned how and was not an athlete of any sort. My husband and a coworker of his had me tag along for a few laps around the track. They talked me through the beginnings of a run with little mind tricks and how to hold your hands and breathe. We ended up running 4 miles. A complete miracle for this girl! Then I wondered what else I could do.

My local running store had a 10k program that led into a race. They also had their half and full marathon programs that went through the winter to prepare for the spring races. Being from Oklahoma City we have a big hometown race that is the Oklahoma City Memorial Marathon which is a Boston Qualifier and benefits the OKC National Memorial and Museum. It is also well known for being one of the country's most meaningful races. I figured I could at least learn how to run a 10k and if that was all I wanted to do I could stop after that. It was not easy but having the structure of the training program got me in shape and in a good habit and I got 3rd place in my age group for my first race ever. Well, that was it for me. I enjoyed the use of my physical body to meet challenges and have time set aside to see new friends and have time outdoors with my own thoughts. It felt good to know I was doing beneficial things for myself several times a week and I was building a baseline of making running a steady part of my life.

My first half marathon felt like a massive accomplishment and so I turned around and ran two more which qualified me for the running group Half Fanatics. It was surprising to me that something which takes so much effort to be able to do the first time could be repeated relatively easily if you keep after yourself and have the mental strength. I started seeing folks traveling to run races and going to all kinds of wonderful and beautiful places, so why not me too?

I had not seen much of our country and so I started researching. I made my mom go with me to Santa Fe, New Mexico, for the Santa Fe Thunder International Half Marathon. This is an event that is high on culture and is one of the more scenic races I have seen. It is a point to point that starts in the cold and dark with a mile uphill and then you get to the Old Pecos Trail. You make a turn and start down the outdated two lane and there is this sunrise that just takes over your whole attention. The valley lights up and the smell of sage washes over you. It was one of the most amazing scenes I have ever experienced.

America is so diverse and so vast that now, how could I not see it all? Running the country has been more of a gift that I ever considered possible. I have walked the Freedom Trail in Boston, ran with thoroughbreds in Kentucky, snorkeled the Florida Keys, surfed off the coast of Southern California and kayaked the rapids of Missoula, Montana. Coffee in Seattle, hiking the Pacific Crest Trail in Oregon, and catching the view from the crown of The Statue of Liberty have all been gifts I would never have known without running and a little bit of nerve.

Running can give you so much and I try to gracefully accept what it offers. Five years ago, my husband was transferred to Anchorage, Alaska and I've tried to take advantage by expanding my running and hitting the further spots and the more costly which also allowed the best opportunity to treat my parents to Maui. Seeing my dad playing in the warm waves of the perfect beaches on Hawaii just beats all. Running gave that to me, and so much more.

I have run a half marathon in 33 states and figured this last summer might be a good opportunity to train for my first, and maybe only, full marathon. An imposing feat to most as I was intimidated by the 26.2 miles. I was training to do a trifecta in June with 3 half marathons in 3 states in three days. I figured that would put me in prime shape to go further.

In July, I ran the Mad half marathon in Waitsfield, Vermont. When at the airport, I started visiting with a couple in the airport on my way out of town. They turned out to be Tom and Amie. I have seen God do many moves in my life and when Tom told me they were pacing the marathon I was training for and that I should just train, take it easy and run the race with him and that he would get me to the finish line, I just knew then for sure that was my plan. Race day came and I found Tom a few minutes before start time, gave him a high five and we were off. I have no idea how he paces these things but that is a whole level of racing that I may never get to. Fine by me, I will leave that to Tom. We had almost 6 hours of "getting to know you" and now I have a friend for life. Tom paced the 6-hour group and I finished just ahead of him at 5:58:33. My first and *probably* my only marathon completed.

I think if I were to describe Tom in a word it would be â "toughie." He is just a toughie. By the time I met him in August 2023 he had been undergoing cancer treatment for the Stage 4 prostate cancer for a while and he is just going to keep going till he cannot anymore. That is just like a runner. You just keep going. You do not stop until you are done. There are not really a lot of secrets, you just do not stop. That is Tom. I am so glad God put him in my path.

Note that I am a Registered Nurse and my current position is at an Imaging Center where we run the breast cancer and lung cancer screening programs. We speak to all the ladies after having a breast biopsy. There really are not many nursing jobs that are easy and this one certainly is not, but the opportunity to guide someone through the beginning of a terrifying experience that no one is signing up for is very rewarding. We can give information that the patient does not have as well as perspective on what they really are dealing with and if nothing else, where is the hope in all this. Finding the hope is one of the most important things a person can do no matter what they are facing, especially if it is cancer. Breast cancer is not preventable but detectable. Mammogram is the number one way to screen for breast cancer and the American College of Radiologists recommendation is to screen annually with mammography beginning at age 40 if of average risk. Risk for lifetime development of breast cancer should be figured for every woman by their primary care provider beginning in their 20s as women at high risk could be recommended to begin screening earlier than 40 and may be recommended additional screening modalities such as annual Breast MRI along with the annual mammogram. Breast cancer in its earliest stage would not be detectable without imaging. It cannot be felt and gives the woman no clue as to its presence. Diagnosing breast cancer in its earlier stages leads to the highest survivability chances as well as the lesser of the treatment needed to tend to it. My hope is that all people find a way to care for themselves by getting all their cancer screenings as recommended to allow for the best opportunities for quality life after diagnosis.

It is important to note that men can also have breast cancer and if they have a family member with genetic related cancers, they should consider genetic testing and/or counseling to see if screening would be recommended.

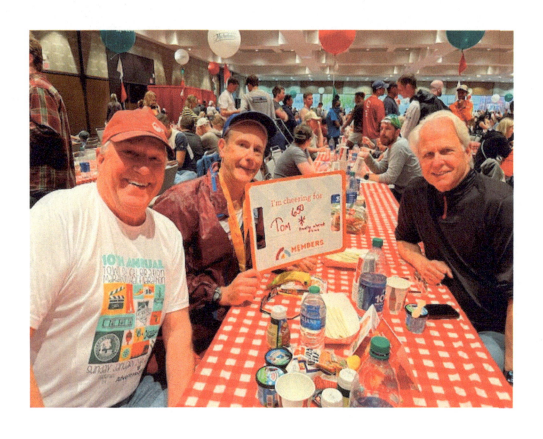

Chapter 7: I Wish I Could Have Met My Grandmother's

Song: "I'm Gonna Win"

Artist: Rob Cantor

Quote: "A grandma is warm hugs and sweet memories. She remembers all your accomplishments and forgets all of your mistakes." - Barbara Cage

Mike Swanson's word for me: Pacer

(This should be noted this was a difficult choice for Mike between the word Malone's)

It was about time that I finally ventured up to Duluth, Minnesota, in 1994 to be a real participant in Grandma's Marathon weekend festivities. For the first time I would not be just a "bandit" running a few miles on the course or pacing a friend unofficially during the marathon. That basically translates to I paid to be a participant in 1994. I had actually sent in my race registration form to compete in a Grandma's event. Let me take that last sentence back and change the word from compete to the more proper word complete. I do not think the marathon winner was too concerned about me that day, but I did not ask him so I will never know the truth.

I remember driving that 2 1/2 hours to Duluth that weekend as I was staying in the Duluth dorms that weekend. If my memory serves me correctly it was $99 back then for two nights stay at the dorms.

The dorms in the lower level had a "welcome reception" that included beverages, fruits, and snacks. So, after that quick visit to the reception, I was off to the shuttle bus to take me to the expo. It is a nice feature of the dorms as parking is included and once you park your car on Friday you do not have to move your car until you leave as shuttle buses basically take you around. Meaning that the shuttle buses will take you to the expo on Friday, the 5k on Friday evening if you are running it, the race start on Saturday, and then back after the marathon or half/marathon on Saturday.

When I was finally done walking around the expo and done eating at the "all you can eat pasta feed," I ventured out to see them completing the setup for the Irvin 5k. While watching them setup I watched a guy doing long strides who looked incredibly fast, so I immediately picked him to be the overall winner of the 5k.

While patiently waiting for the 5K to start someone asked me if I would be willing to hold the banner for the winner of men's and women's division of the 5K which I agreed to do. The race started and the guy I had picked to win the race overall finished in 14:40 which is still the men's course record for that event.

It was only when he had crossed the finish line that I realized he was the legendary Jon Sinclair. No wonder he looked so frigging fast from a long distance away from me. Jon was the USA National 10,000 meters track champion and a finalist for the 5,000 meters in the 1984 Olympics along with being a finalist in the marathon in the 1988 and 1992 Olympics.

I have two regrets that evening. One is that I did not have Jon Sinclair sign my marathon race bib after he had won the 5k. My second regret is that in hindsight had I signed up for that 5k then I would have very likely completed all the Irvin 5k's to date. I would have been a rare runner to have completed all the 5k's as well as Grandma's Marathons since the inception of the 5k.

Note if you do want to do Grandma's Marathon it is called the Grandma's Challenge and you sign up together for both races - which can be either Grandma's marathon or half-marathon with including the 5k.

It was on Saturday, June 18, 1994, that I ran my first official Grandma's Marathon as a registered marathon participant finishing in a very comfortable 4:01:27 as I was pacing friends to a sub-4-hour finish. I did not finish in under 4 hours as I was too busy visiting with friends the last 1.2 miles of the course. The free beer on the course derailed any concern of me running a sub-4-hour marathon as my friends all easily had a sub-4-hour marathon that day.

That was one of many marathons that could have easily been under a sub-4-hour marathon time. Note that when I completed this marathon there was no 50sub4 Marathon Club or sub 4 Marathon Club in existence, so that was not a particular goal I was focused on. I was focused entirely on helping my friends meet their goal pace time and having lots of fun and some beer. If you know me at all, I do tend to get extra beer/drink tickets.

Just like after my first marathon finish, I never honestly thought that I would be running Grandma's marathon again the following year. Several friends talked me into coming back in 1995, which I finished in 3:50:34. I was helping pace some friends to a sub 3:50, with again slowing down and visiting with friends during the last 1.2 miles. I guess I finally did get my sub-4-hour marathon at Grandma's Marathon, but back then I honestly really did not care.

I continued to question coming back to Grandma's Marathon year after year but I did come back again in 1996 and have I been back every year since 1994. This is obviously minus the Pandemic year of 2020 when I ran a virtual Grandma's marathon.

Note we should all be incredibly grateful to Grandma's marathon because in June of 2021 they were one of the first larger scale marathons that started happening after the Pandemic. Grandma's marathon showed that having a marathon could again happen and that somehow life would slowly be getting back to pre-pandemic living. Remember I said the word slowly here."

So, on June 17th, 2023, I completed my 29th Grandma's marathon in 5:59:15 while pacing the 6-hour pace group. This was a monumental marathon and race weekend day for me as I had just completed my 650th marathon or ultra. Completing #700 in 2024 is now one of my main goals.

It was my 154th marathon since my Stage 4 cancer diagnosis on 7/30/2019. So, let us say that the world population is approximately 8 billion, and it is estimated that less than 1% of the population has run a marathon. Then take my at least 100 marathons completed without Stage 4 cancer and then at least 100 marathons completed since my initial Stage 4 cancer diagnosis and I am a rarity.

This was a goal I never planned on back when I ran my first official marathon in 1993 was running some 600 plus marathons. It just happened that if I wanted to keep pacing and running marathons then it would be an inevitable goal I would have to achieve.

And I did just that when I ran Grandma's Marathon on June 17th, 2023.

If you are thinking that was my highlight of Grandma's Marathon weekend in 2023 then I have you completely fooled. Could I by chance ask you about buying an Aerial Lift Bridge that I might be willing to sell to you for significantly less cost than the London Bridge? My ultimate highlight for the weekend was holding a sign at the Michelina's All You Can Eat Pasta Feed with the sign clearly stating 650th marathon. You see I had finally passed the legendary Swanson brothers - Craig and Mike Swanson - that are from Minnesota in *total* number of marathons completed. Their combined marathon numbers were 642 - Craig had 336 and Mike had 306 marathons.

As Julius Caesar stated so succinctly – "I came, I saw, I conquered."

I started that goal when I did not have any notion that cancer would try to stop me from accomplishing my goal. I was not about to let the word "cancer" stop me. In fact, all the motivation I needed was "two against one" and then I knew they did not stand a chance - with or without me having cancer.

One final note to all Grandma's out there is "thank you" for all you do. I was not lucky enough in my life to have met any set of my grandparents. However, when I finish Grandma's Marathon, I always hug a grandmother I know, so maybe by chance that was you who is reading this book at this time.

Thank you!

Mike Swanson
Plymouth, Minnesota
Mike's word for himself: Friendly

I was 45 in the fall of 1996 and, during a physical my doctor said I need to lose weight or quit drinking beer. It was an easy decision. I decided I would start running. I had never run in my life. At that time, I belonged to the Northwest Health Club so I ran around its track which was about half a block long, so lots of circles.

This was in the fall so I got my brother, Craig, and best friend from High School to run the Turkey Trot in downtown Minneapolis with me. This was my first race a 5K. Well, it was kind of a run until the hill, then it was a walk. I should say I was wearing cotton sweatpants and a sweat shirt and baseball hat all cotton.

After that was done, I ran every 5k that the Twin cities had to offer.

By February I was pumped. I ran an entire Valentine's Day run around Lake Harriet without stopping.

Feeling like a runner while a champ, while drinking a couple of beers with

Craig and friend I said I might do a marathon, and they agreed to run a marathon with me of course. Back then everything was by mail, so I registered all of us for the 1997 Twin Cities Marathon. In early June they were surprised to receive the green postcard saying they were signed up for the marathon. You should have heard the complaints. But we read Hal Higdon's Red book and in that book was a program for 13 weeks of training for those that want to finish a marathon. Ironically it was developed by Bill Wenmark from the Cities who started ALARC and his wife Monica owned the STARTLINE, a running store. Eventually that is where we bought all our Mizuno shoes.

So, for 13 weeks we trained religiously doing a long run on the weekend. It was a struggle with lots of knee complaints. In the old pictures we all wore some kind of knee brace.

Race day was approaching so we all went down to the Cafe Napoli in Minneapolis for Pasta. Even had a friend (Don) from out east and his sister run. Don was inspiring. I watched him run Twin Cities the year before and stop and have a cigarette during the race.

1997 was the hottest Twin Cites Marathon up to that time. But we ran the whole way finishing together with a time of 4:36. I did not know if the group would do another but we saw a new race called the Suzuki Rock n Roll Marathon that was going to happen in San Diego the next summer. We decided it would be our next one. And we recruited a real runner my brother-in-law to join us.

It was a nice vacation. The morning of the San Diego marathon we had to catch a bus to get to the start. By the time we got to the stat we had been on our feet for 3 hours. This was the largest first-time marathon ever with over 20,000 people. We lined up but were way back. We could hear announcements but could not make out what was being said. The race was delayed for 45 minutes.

With not enough toilets everyone had to use the Banyan trees in Balboa Park, and the park quickly became men and women trees. You get the picture.

The race started. It was hot and no shade but we ran better than the last one. There were no bands, and water was limited. They dumped water from the freeway overpasses into garbage cans at the water stops. We did receive a nice apology letter from Rock n Roll. But we did another 7 of the Rock n Roll races.

Then it was on to Twin Cites again and had done 21 marathons of those to date. The next year I did 3 marathons, then 5 the year after.

My brother said "How about we do the 50 states?" So that was the beginning of our running quest and by 2007 I had run all 50 states. I finished at Whidbey Island marathon with 50 running friends and family from all over the country.

3 years ago, I ran with my sister and brother. I was 69, my sister was 68, and my brother was 67. My mom and other sister came to watch it was truly a family affair. This last Saturday I ran my 310th marathon and the 5th time I have run on my actual birthday, which is October 7th.

I am hooked on Marathons doing all the states and running the majors: Boston, New York, Chicago, London, Berlin, and Tokyo.

Along the way you meet people who become lifelong friends. One of those is Tom Perri, who also happens to live a couple miles from my brother and me. The long-time standing joke is that Tom is trying to catch up to the Swanson brother's number of marathons. Well, he has finally done that and we will never be ahead of him again. I guess it is my turn to buy him a beer at our local watering hole Malone's.

Chapter 8: Two is Better Than One - Just Simply Believe Me

Song: "(I've Had the) Time of My Life"

Artist: Bill Medley & Jennifer Warnes

Quote: "Where is love there is life." - Mahatma Gandhi

Georges Gonzalez's word for me: Driven

Jonathan Rushnak's word for me: Motivating

One common statement that people make after finishing their first marathon is what a life changing event running and completing a marathon is. It is entirely irrelevant whether the marathon has fifteen finishers or 50,000 finishers. Or if the course is lined or not lined with thousands of spectators. It does not matter If you won the marathon or simply finished last. The result will be the same - finishing the marathon will change you *forever.*

The training can be challenging for a marathon. Simply blocking out the time to run can seem impossible some days. What happens if you miss your weekly group run? Or your Saturday long run? Of your Wednesday speed workout? If you are missing an occasional run or training day do not stress out on what you missed. Just think of it as an extra rest day for your body and mind. Life will get in the way of training for a marathon. Just do not let the stress of training for the marathon affect you.

My suggestion is that you have a wall calendar and then start making notations to note the date of your marathon and plan out a possible training schedule. If your marathon is in 2025 that you are training for use the 2024 calendar to get you started, and once you find a 2025 calendar you can hang that up as well. You usually can order in July of the calendar year, an 18-month calendar which should nicely fit your needs into the following year.

I know we can all do schedules on our cell phone, but seeing the calendar on the wall shows the very *visual* side of what you are doing. I suggest a week before the next month comes start filling in dates of your running and training plan. Every time you complete the run just write the time and miles from your run on the calendar. Maybe even get some gold stars to place on the calendar after each successful completed run.

Remember when training three basic things: 1) be kind to yourself, as not all runs go as planned; 2) when you complete a run that is longer than your last training run treat yourself; 3) remember to get extra rest if possible as your body will thank you while you are training for a marathon.

Just getting to the marathon starting line is a huge accomplishment in and of itself. So, you have started the mental preparation to get to the start of the marathon. Every week spend time on working on your mental toughness. It will not be until you finish your first marathon, when you will be amazed at how big of an accomplishment you just completed.

No one said running a marathon is easy! Otherwise more than 1% of the population I am sure would be completing a marathon if it indeed was easy. You may have used up all your mental and physical power within you that day to simply accomplish this goal. The more you train your body and brain the better you will be prepared.

These are my suggestions to make your first marathon (or mostly any race) more enjoyable by following Baker's Dozen tips below:

1) The #1 thing you need to do, or be thinking about, is *have fun with the experience.* You may only do one marathon (race) in your lifetime so make it the best marathon experience that you can.

2) Soak in the experience. If you have your cell phone take pictures of what is happening around you so you can readily recall the experience.

3) Do not be surprised if you experience a "nervous bladder syndrome" where you feel the need to constantly pee. Just make sure you allowed plenty of time to use the bathroom before race start. Just try not to over hydrate the night before, or the morning of the marathon, to help avoid any extra bathroom issues. If you are a coffee drinker, I would strongly suggest limiting your coffee intake. Note that you may want to do a single shot or two shots of expresso for your caffeine kick, versus say at 12-, 16-, or 24-ounce container of coffee to hopefully help reduce bathroom breaks.

4) Hopefully you reviewed where the bathrooms are along the course, so you know which mile or aid station you need to reach if by chance a bathroom is needed.

5) Drop off your gear drop off bag, if there is one, before the gear bag check closes. Don't be that runner carrying your gear check bag to the finish. Tip: I suggest either place inside, outside, or attached to the gear check bag, your name/email/cell phone number. Those paper airlines tags work as well as address mailing labels that you can add your phone number on. It is rare actually that gear bags get lost but your bib number has been known to fall off, or if by chance someone accidentally gets your gear check bag, they have a way to contact you.

6) When you get into the starting corral have someone take your picture if you have your cell phone. Just make sure your bib number is showing!

7) Strongly encourage you to have your ears open - no ear buds in, etc., - so that you can hear any announcements such as delayed start or any updates about the race that might be relevant to you. Also, then you can hear the National Anthem if played, as well as the start of the marathon.

8) If there are pacers at your race, I suggest introducing yourself to the pacer and tell them "This is my first marathon (race) " so the pacer is aware of you. Just "checking in" with the pacer does not obligate you to run with the pace group. The pacer is there to help you throughout the race so take advantage of using the pacer at the start or anytime along the race course.

9) Be careful running that first mile. A marathon is more than 26 miles, so today is not the day to run your best mile ever. In fact, you should *slowly* build up to your marathon pace by the 3 mile, or 5k spot.

10) Do not run by your GPS. By that I mean, it is highly unlikely your GPS watch will match *exactly* what the mile markers are on course and the overall mileage when you cross the finish line. Use your GPS as an approximation or guide to the course, and trust that the course is accurate. I suggest wearing a "pace band" to help guide you along the course. If they are not available at the expo you can print one to wear to use as a guide. A pace band shows you overall time as well as the time for each mile. Note that if the race is in KM (Kilometers) , then I suggest having your pace band show the race in KM's to clearly and easily show your time.

11) Check in with yourself at the 3-mile mark, or 5k mark, to see how you are feeling. If you feel you are going to fast and your heart rate is higher than you would like, then slow down as you still have a long way to go. Think

negative split, where your second half of the race is faster than the first half. Checking in at every 5k, or three miles, is a good way to know how you are doing overall. So basically, eight check-ins during the marathon, and then you just simply finish.

12) When you get ready to cross that finish line DO NOT look down and be looking at your watch. Pump your arms in the air! Wave your arms! Scream and yell "I just finished my first marathon (race) !" You will see official results to grab your race time, so forget about your GPS device or watch! Please enjoy that finishing moment. What you just did is an amazing accomplishment, so let the photographer capture your look of utter amazement and joy.

13) When you get that medal around your neck your feeling of accomplishment will be amazing. It will be life changing. Soak it all in. Make sure to get a finisher picture with that medal that you earned that you are proudly wearing around your neck.

If you are to train and run and then finish a marathon, what other accomplishments are you capable of achieving? What did you learn about yourself within this journey?

When you started the marathon, you may have had doubts running through your head. How can I possibly do this? Is it possible to run 26.2 miles when my longest run is 16, 18, 20, or even 22 miles? How can I run possibly run some 6 to 10 miles further?

If you never run a marathon again, if does not matter as you are *forever* labeled a marathon finisher. You earned the label *marathoner.*

But hopefully a few weeks after you are done with your marathon, you may be thinking another marathon (race) might be in your future.

In my opinion, *two is better than one.* Maybe you will find out for yourself that two is better than one. If you see me, please let me know if you agree.

Warning: this can become addictive.

Georges Gonzalez & Jonathan Rushnak
Tampa, Florida
Georges word for himself: Competitive
Jonathan's word of himself: Haphazard
For both of us we are: Driven

Why you both started running?

Georges: I started running to get my cholesterol and weight under control. I did not want to take medications at 41 years of age. At 41 years old, I had never been a runner or considered myself an athletic person at all. But as one would have it, a friend of mine from work had several mini strokes at the office and that really bothered and scared me. I came home and told Jonathan I wanted to go running with him. I guess a life scare change how one looks like one's life and health. I was scared enough to attempt and make a lifestyle change.

Jonathan: For me, my first journey into running was signing up for the Miami Corporate Run 5K when I was 22 years old. The thought of running 5K was completely foreign to me. Once I finished the race, I was hooked. I was never a runner in my youth, unless you count the horrible experiences in high school PE class being made to run laps around a brutally hot football field. The thrill of finishing a race and the sound of the crowd was exciting and made me feel like a true athlete.

Any obstacles you had to overcome in your 50-state marathon competition goal?

For Georges, I had many obstacles. I had to get a training schedule put together so I can stay focused. Balancing work schedule, business travel schedule, school schedule (I was attending college during the evenings) , managing my weight and training schedule. Not to mention my eating habits, which I had to get under control.

I did not start by thinking I was going to complete a marathon in every state. In fact, that was not even a goal of mine at all. Not a dream, not a desire, it was not even in my vocabulary. I simply wanted to get my weight under control and not take cholesterol medicine.

I joined Jonathan on Thursday evenings for a running group at a local running club in Tampa. There I met other runners and people Jonathan knew. There was one lady I met in the group, named Lynn, who is still encouraging and an inspiration to me.

A major obstacle for me was being able to practice my long-distance training runs. I really dislike training runs, especially once I achieved and conquered the 18-mile plus training runs. Another obstacle for me was managing the travel schedule to the different states and races. Scheduling flights, vehicles, hotels, restaurants, and vacation time was challenging, but after the first 10 marathons, and some extra unnecessary expenditure, double bookings, etc., I got pretty good at keeping track of our races and schedule. I created a schedule board in our home office, I kept it simple, so we would not be overwhelmed with non-value information, but rather a quick glance would allow us to be prepared. With this information we knew what was scheduled, booked, and/or paid for (see table below) , the table kept us organized and on track.

Marathon Schedule Board table.

Race Name	Date	Race Paid?	Hotel?	Flight?	Vehicle?
Marines Corps Marathon	Oct 28	Y	Embassy Suites	Not Yet	Yes

Jonathan: For me, the biggest obstacle for completing the 50-state journey was the COVID-19 pandemic. At the onset of the pandemic, we literally had 3 states to complete. One by one, they were cancelled. Each race director handled the situation differently. While some offered postponement to the next race or even a refund, others offered no alternative and simply turned the race into a virtual event. Eventually, we were able to complete the three and only had to change one race we originally planned.

What did you learn about yourselves in this journey?

Georges: As someone that was not considered an athlete by myself or anyone else in life, I began my running career as one would imagine. However, having a partner that was a runner, it helped me a lot. Personally, at the beginning, I started by joining an online local running group called Run Tampa on Facebook. Through the group, I learned everyone in the running community was welcomed. No matter how slow, fast or anything in between, everyone was welcomed.

The right equipment: the biggest lesson was to ensure to purchase the correct running shoes so as not to get hurt. The right shoes help to avoid foot injuries and help with the running form. A great lesson I learned was to trust myself. Trust the training. To achieve the marathon distance, one must put in the training time, which to me is not easy due to the amount of time necessary to ensure one stays healthy and injury free. I learn the different equipment offered at local running stores, large department stores and online. Everyone in the running community will have an opinion, thoughts, feedback, and recommendations. Putting in the time is the key. I spent many hundreds of dollars on unnecessary equipment, almost every time it was a lesson for me on what not to do.

The year I ran 14 marathons, my left foot began to hurt. I was asking around, and once again, different thoughts and ideas of what the pain could be. After several visits to doctors and running stores, I learned I had plantar fasciitis. The diagnosis sent me on a path to spend hundreds of dollars on special socks, massages, and doctor appointments. One day after several months of painful running I was on Facebook checking the Runner's World magazine site, I came across a short video from a trainer providing feedback and guidance for runners experiencing plantar fasciitis. The video is approximately 2 minutes long, recommended runners should purchase a hard ball (a lacrosse ball or similar) , please it on the floor, after every run (short or long) , take off the shoes, leave socks on, roll each foot 5 times over the lacrosse ball from the ball of the foot to the heel of the foot, back and forth. To my surprise, that fixed it after a short couple of weeks, and I still practice it to this day. I have not experienced foot pain since.

A funny lesson I learned along the way was to carry toilet paper in a little plastic bag. Sounds silly, but one never knows, especially on long runs when one may have to go.

Jonathan: What I learned most about myself in the journey, is not to judge before I get to know. I always considered myself somewhat of a big city, cosmopolitan, person. Some of the biggest marathons have been met with the biggest disappointments. For example, when we ran the Chicago Marathon (I know, I know...) , I found myself disappointed at the anti-climactic finish. This was completely surprising to me as I really enjoy the city and went the highest expectations after watching my favorite documentary, "Spirit of the Marathon." I do not want to bash The Chicago Marathon, because I do think it's a great race. To my surprise, I found that I really enjoyed some smaller races in states that I may have pre-judged based on old stereotypes. The Hogeye Marathon in Northwest Arkansas certainly comes to mind. Running this race in a small Arkansas town, I was amazed how beautiful and progressive the area is. The parks and trail system rival many big cities. And being a vegetarian, I expected no dining options. I was completely wrong as there were some wonderful vegetarian friendly restaurants.

Something else I learned along the way is not to take myself so seriously and not compare myself to others. A few marathons in, I learned that everyone, including myself, has a personal story and goals that keeps them motivated. I realized that I will never achieve the "elite runner" status, and I am good with that. Looking back at the kid that was hospitalized multiple times for severe asthma and I am so proud of what I accomplished. Mine is just one of hundreds of personal stories and that is what makes running marathons so special.

What did you learn about yourself as a couple in this journey?

Jonathan: I can safely say, we learned each other's quirks when it comes to travel. While we were already together for 18 years at the beginning of this journey, there were still new things to discover. For me, Georges quickly learned my distaste for free hotel breakfasts. I am trying hard to overcome that! I learned that Georges can be a silent complainer. If we check into a hotel and the air conditioner is not quite right, I always know just by looking at him and he never has to say a word!

But in all seriousness, the travel journey taught us how to live life to the fullest in what short time we have. Having been to each state, we learned from each other to enjoy what may be just a weekend and that each one of us really enjoys nature and being part of it. In the beginning, we always enjoyed big cities and the amenities they offer. Throughout the journey, we discovered we both have a passion for the National Parks. Any time the geographic location of a marathon allowed; we planned a visit to a National Park as well. After running the Missoula Marathon in Montana, for instance, we ventured up to Glacier National Park for a few days. We are hooked.

We are also each other's biggest cheerleaders. When either of has a bad day and does not feel like getting up for our daily run, we find it in ourselves to motivate the other. This is true for running marathons as well. When we ran the Wyoming Marathon in 2019, Georges had one of his worst experiences. The last mile or so consists of a 1000 feet ascent to the finish. He was seriously spent and not sure he could finish. I had to coach him with a lot of positive affirmation.

Additional things we learned along our journey, is that on race day we found that wearing a hat or visor is a must for race day. I am personally not a hat person, but I did find it helpful on either sunny or rainy races. A hat for me and a visor for Jonathan was a must on race day. I carry a string backpack on race day. For several reasons, I keep my phone in the bag, I keep snacks, credit cards, ID, toilet paper and cash. The bag is very helpful at the end when races provide drinks and snacks. I just place them in the bag and do not have to carry them in my hands.

During the race we found that we liked syrup and salty snacks. We did not like the Gu or many of the other energy items available. So, we found that Vermont syrup really helped us. We also prepared small plastic bags with salty snacks. We found that salty kettle chips kept the best. We tried many different salty chips and cracker snacks during our seven-year journey, most did not survey the shaking of running and did not do well during the race.

For the after the race item, we found that the backpack I carried was the best idea and worked at almost every race since races usually pass some sort of food or drink at the end. I do not like carrying things in my hands after running 26.2 miles, so the bag was helpful, and it came handy at many races.

Chapter 9: Mission Accomplished: 50sub4 State Marathon Goal

Song: "With a Little Help from My Friends"

Artist: The Beatles, from their 1967 album Sgt. Pepper's Lonely Hearts Club Band

Quote: "Life is 10% what happens to you and 90% how you react to it." - Charles R Swindoll

Cade Remsburg's word for me: Goals

When running in Minnesota in the 1970's the primary running club was MDRA, which was an acronym for Minnesota Distance Running Association. It should be noted that this club was originally called the Minnesota Road Runners Club which was apparently the eighth regional club in the country of the Road Runners Club of America that had originally formed in 1958. I believe I joined this group in 1993 the year of my first marathon at Twin Cities Marathon. It has since changed its name to Run Minnesota which basically is now saying that we are "here for the long run."

Then in the late 1990's when I started running a few more marathons each year I was seeing a wide variety of marathon clubs forming. There were multiple running clubs in each of the 50 states, just not running clubs that were based on statistics or total number of marathons.

The 100 Marathon Club North America, founded and directed by Bob and Lenore Dolphin was started in 2001. It has since changed its name to the 100 Marathon Club of the Americas. My 100th marathon would be at the Billings Marathon, in Billings, Montana, on Sunday, September 17th, 2006, finishing in 4:13:25. I will always remember this marathon for four things: 1) it was my first news interview outside of Minnesota about my running, 2) I stopped to take pictures along the way and wasn't concerned about running a sub 4 hour marathon as I had no race goal and I wasn't pacing it, 3) a runner that I had passed very early during the marathon who was walking magically appeared before me in the last 5k - having never passed me running on the course and never could have passed me, and 4) I was able to share the news video with my parents which made my mom and dad especially happy. This would sadly be the only news segment that my parents and I ever shared and watched together in my running career.

Then there was the 50 State Marathon Club started by the legendary Steve & Paula Boone in March of 2001. As Paula Boone told me that this club was created "so people could have a fun running goal but also to create a community of runners." I would eventually become the 314th finisher on Saturday, September 29th, 2007, at the New Hampshire Bristol Marathon in 4:24:46. Also, it should be noted that I was a "certified" finisher.

I was basically joining multiple running clubs and groups so I would have the opportunity to pace races in all states. At the time there was no one pacing group that had marathons that they were pacing in all 50 states. There is still no known pace group that paces marathons in all fifty states. So, to pace at some marathons and races I joined the local running club so I would be on the pacing roster to pace particular races specifically in that state. This led to me becoming the first pacer to have ever paced a marathon in all 50 States. The story about my pacing career is a topic for another book, so if you like this book please look for that one soon.

Then Marathon Maniacs started on May 25, 2003, by Steve Yee, Chris Warren, and Tony Phillippi, in the state of Washington. I would become the 181st Marathon Maniac to reach the Titanium level by running marathons in 30 different states in 365 days. There are various ways to achieve the Titanium level and that was the route I took. Then in 2018 I was fortunate enough to be entered into the Marathon Maniacs Hall of Fame. This was my first of three Hall of Fames that I am now currently inducted into.

Then along came another club the 50sub4 Marathon club that was founded on January 1st, 2009, by Jeff Hill. I did not initially show any interest in joining the club, as I thought I would not be doing the 50 states again.

At the time I was approaching belonging to over 150 different clubs as some did not have club fees as you simply had to be on the roster so I could be eligible to pace races, but many did have fees. I have since significantly cut down to belonging to just about a dozen different running clubs to keep my email box from overflowing. With the growth of a variety of pace teams throughout the

United States belonging to all the running groups no longer made sense.

Note this was fairly similar situation with half marathons. The 50 States half marathon club started in 2008, and so I decided not to join this club immediately as I had just completed my 50 State Marathon goal. I had well over 200 half marathons by then but I did not really care about my half marathon statistics.

Then Marathon Maniacs started the Half Fanatics Club which was born on July 4, 2009. At this time, I am not a double agent even though I am running and pacing anywhere from one to twelve half marathons every year. I would eventually like to get to at least 500 half marathons but that is not a priority. If I can no longer run marathons, then I might switch my focus to half marathons. One group that surprisingly is not yet out there is the 50subHalf Marathon group, for those that have completed a sub two-hour half marathon in all 50 states. I think that would be an interesting group to be associated with, but that is just my own opinion.

Once I started on my second time of completing a marathon in all 50 states, I was beginning to become closer to completing a goal of a Sub 4 marathon in all 50 States. I was pacing 4-hour marathons so it was helping with my goal of a sub-4-hour marathon in all 50 states. I even was thinking of pacing specifically a 4-hour marathon in all 50 states.

The issue was I was pacing the same marathon at 4 hours each year which was limiting my chances to do other marathons at Sub 4 on that weekend or in that month. For example, I had paced the Myrtle Beach Marathon 4 hour pace group in 2014 at 3:59:26, then 2015 at 3:59:36, then in 2016 at 3:59:18. But see what I am trying to convince you is that I am not totally insane as the *next day* I would pace the Little Rock Marathon 4:45 pace group in 2014 in 4:39:54 (the weather year) , then in 2015 in 4:44:38, and then in 2016 in 4:43:59. I stopped doing the double marathon weekend when hurricane weather related issues made it impossible to get to the Little Rock Marathon in 2018.

I was just a few marathons away from getting my 50sub4 State marathon finish in 2016. I needed just the states of Oklahoma and Montana as my final sub 4 marathon states.

The Runners World Tulsa Half & Half Marathon was on Sunday, December 11th, 2016, which was my chosen marathon for Oklahoma. I guess maybe with the windy conditions and less than ideal marathon conditions the weather kept the faster runners away. I seriously doubt that anyone saw my name on the Half & Half Marathon registration list and decided not to run. So, I finished in 3:57:16, so Oklahoma was finally checked off for a Sub 4-hour 50 State Marathon certified marathon finish. The one thing I had not known while running this marathon was that when I finished that I was indeed the "overall winner."

Along this journey I was able to join another group called the 100K Lifetime Miles group, which is a web site about runners that have logged at least 100,000 total lifetime miles. I reached that milestone on Thursday, December 15th, 2016. The legendary Amby Burfoot, who won the Boston Marathon in 1968, created this website. It is interesting to note that even with the brutal Minnesota weather and winters, that Minnesota is a state that has as many 100k runners as almost any other state. We are tough runners in Minnesota.

It is interesting to note that on December 15th, 2016, I had 100,000 miles. As of October 31st, 2023, my lifetime miles are currently at 120,715. So, if my math is correct that means 20,175 miles logged since joining the 100k group. So regardless of my cancer diagnosis or the COVID Pandemic or whatever obstacle I was given I was still getting in my minimum of 2,000 miles a year. My goal is to eventually hit 150,000 lifetime miles, which should be around the fall of 2034.

The Billings Montana marathon on Saturday, September 17th, 2017, was to be my sub-4-hour marathon attempt for my final state needed which was Montana. My marathon bib was to be #50 to reflect my final 50th State for my Sub 4-hour marathon goal but somehow my bib #50 went to someone else. I thought that was a bad omen, but I did indeed finish in 3:56:45 for a first place in the 55 to 59 Age Group for the marathon.

"Believe you can and you're halfway there" is a quote by Theodore Roosevelt. I believed in myself to accomplish this goal and I did. The power of positive thinking has always been a significant part of my life and it was shown on September 17th, 2017, when I ran that sub-4-hour marathon.

However, to accomplish this goal I did need a "little prodding" to get this goal accomplished. I was not in any sense of rush to accomplish this goal as when I turned 60, I was going to BQ in all 50 states so that would accomplish that goal at the same time. I would just need a sub 3:50 marathon in all 50 states to get that goal as that was my current BQ time for a 60–64-year-old male.

This might make me *possibly* train to run a sub 3:50 marathon consistently in all 50 states. At the time however, I had no idea that a cancer diagnosis would derail this goal. Correct I am saying "derail" as I have not 100% eliminated this from ever happening. Miracles can happen and when I turn 65 currently my BQ time would change to 4:05.

I remember Cade continually gently prodding me to get my 50sub4 Marathon states goal completed. Okay, maybe a few times being a little more *direct* and less prodding until I eventually clearly got the message and accomplished my goal.

Just like most 100-mile runners need a little encouragement and prodding to potentially help them finish the 100-mile race in the last few miles, I needed someone to encourage me to make my 50sub4 Marathon state goal a reality as I only had a few states remaining. Mission accomplished.

Thank you, Cade.

Cade Remsburg
Philadelphia, PA
Cade's word for himself: Goals

I had known Tom a few years before this story occurs. I was newer to the nationwide marathon circuit than he. I was a couple years younger and not as financially successful so he was able to start the hopeful plan to run the states 14 times much earlier than myself. I was trying to just run the states 5 times and the one thing I did have on him was speed. I was not incredibly quick but if you wanted to see someone run a 3:30 marathon there are very few who can do so as consistently as myself. We had talked a few times about his goal to 14 and I am sure I seemed exasperated with him. That is fine and all but you have to quit a couple of these legacy streaks and all this pacing!

I do not think it was a rebellion against his pacing but I have more of a rebellious attitude. He was telling me about his Fall running schedule and all the pacing he was doing and I must have just blurted out, "but when are you going to finish 50 Sub 4?"

Fifty sub 4 is a small unique group of runners whose goal it is to run under

4 hours in every state. Tom was pacing around 4-hour marathon time and only had 3 or 4 states left. To know someone this close to the goal and not completing it so he could pace again and have a streak of 8 years in another town seemed ludicrous to me! Tom is on top of his stats so I am sure he brought up that part and how close he was. He has given me credit for then pushing him to do so. I am sure I did on a couple occasions and I do know that I was a nag about it when I would see him. To me, sometimes the best time to do things is now.

When I first started running my marathons, I would wait your typical 6 months to run another only to cut it down to a couple months about 6 marathons in. I had my own training plan and would give up alcohol and soda for a couple weeks and then run the best race I could. I met the right (or wrong) people and they got me to run more and more closer and soon enough I would have to give up everything if I wanted to keep running marathons so they just became my life. I knew Tom was the same way with not as bad of habits and he was in the shape at the time to get it done.

I had a girlfriend at the time who had a medical issue a couple years before. She ran as many marathons as she could under the coveted 4-hour mark but the issue became larger and after a while there were some days where under 5 hours was very difficult. I had seen this firsthand and though there was nothing she really could have changed, it changed me. I realized the time to hit these things is now. Why wait? Anything can happen tomorrow. I had moved up my schedule to run the states 5 times and until COVID I was looking to get it done very quickly. As a person always concerned about keeping my speed, it meant everything to me to make my goals complete while I was in the best health possible. Not to mention, that if you don't know this or not, but runners usually do get eventually injured.

But project these thoughts on to Tom I did! I told him he had to get it done and he did! And actually, pretty quick at that. I guess he felt my sense of urgency and to finish that goal he accomplished. I cannot say I was proud of him because he always had it in him. I don't feel like I put him into another gear or anything like that. I just feel he had a race to run. I just pointed out that it can be limited.

What he has been through since then has been awful but he always kept that goal - and I assume he just made it to the next race. I can do this treatment so I can be at Fargo on Friday. Then there he is running and smiling though I am sure part of him is almost dying inside with the pain. The goals keep him going. The goals keep him alive most likely.

To quote a not-so-great song, I didn't start the fire but I am glad that I helped keep it going. I am thrilled that I woke up that part of him to get that goal. For it was not long after that he was diagnosed with cancer. He got it done not just in time but when he needed too. And he used that fire to keep burning through and running through every obstacle he could possibly face. But it never beat him - he had another goal to go get.

Chapter 10: One of Only Two People

Song: "In My Life"

Artist: The Beatles

Quote: "Experience is not what happens to you; it is what you do with what happens to you." - Aldous Huxley

Kathryn's White word for me: Engaging

The Oklahoma City bombing of the Alfred P Murdoch building occurred on Wednesday, April 19th, 1995. It still remains as one of the deadliest acts of terrorism in United States history. A total of 168 people died because of this attack, and some of them were even children. A truly sad part of the history of the United States. I wasn't there in Oklahoma that tragic day, and when I look back nearly thirty years ago, I can't even remember where or what I was doing that tragic day.

In 2001 the inaugural Oklahoma City Marathon was created and approximately 5,000 runners ran that weekend. Per the website 1,853 full marathoners received the Inaugural Oklahoma City Marathon medal. This race weekend has become a Runner's World top "must do race" that one needs to do regardless of which of the many events you participate in. Per the website the Marathon is now the Memorial and Museum's largest fundraiser and averages over 24,000 participants annually.

Taken directly from the Oklahoma City Marathon website the mission of this marathon is to celebrate life, reach for the future, honor the memories of those who were killed on April 19, 1995, and unite the world in hope. This is not just another marathon it is a: Run to Remember. People have been "Running to Remember" since 2001.

Sadly, I was not able to make it to the inaugural Oklahoma City Marathon in 2001. I knew I had to complete this marathon, so it was basically just figuring out the logistics of how and when.

In 2004 I was having issues with my right knee so of course the logical step was to have an MRI done. Knee surgery was recommended and Dr. Smith stated to me "it isn't if, it is simply when you are going to do it."

So out the door I went thinking I could wait a few years. Maybe knee surgery to celebrate turning 50 sounded like a good idea to me? I was just 43 years old and running consistently and still on occasion playing softball. However, my occasionally "falling down when I pivoted" started happening much more frequently, so I knew I needed the dreaded knee surgery.

So I had four major concerns with completing the surgery: 1) What happens if I have the surgery and I can't run again?, 2) I needed to make sure I could complete the Med City Marathon scheduled for 5/29/2005 as I didn't want to lose my Legacy status, 3) I needed to make sure I could complete a marathon in April of 2005 to keep my monthly marathon streak alive, 4) that I would not miss any marathons already scheduled for the year due to the knee surgery.

Once the surgery was completed, I *immediately* started on my physical therapy program of riding the bike and doing my weight exercises. Was there pain and discomfort when doing this? Definitely. Was I doing this so I could run again? Definitely. Did I take pain pills to manage the pain? I sure did as I took only *one* pill 12 hours after the surgery. That was all I needed or wanted.

I was more on the side of being told "you should probably not bike and do the weights and walking as much as you are" than being a sedentary person. If there is one thing you will learn about me from this book is that I am not a sedentary person as I and hopefully will never have the two words "couch potato" in the same sentence as my name.

Might I get sidetracked here and ask you when Mr. Potato Head first came out and by what company? It was first distributed by Hasbro in 1952. What is one surprising fact about this toy? It was apparently the first toy advertised on television and has been in production ever since. I am not done here yet, as Mr. Potato Head appeared in the Toy Story movies and was voiced by Don Rickles.

One note that I think is important to note that I do not like taking or being on any narcotic pain pill while I was experiencing pain and hoping to run. I knew very well what my running pain tolerance was from my nearly 35 years of running when I had the surgery. I embraced the running pain as I was not covering up my running pain with any pill or narcotics. I needed to know if I was simply having real pain when just simply running. I did not want any pain pill masking that actual discomfort or pain. Believe when I say the recovery from my knee surgery was not easy, but to me it wasn't ridiculously painful.

So, the four goals were all completed with me finishing the Oklahoma City Marathon on 4/24/2005 in 7:41:25. I signed up for the early start knowing I had 8 hours to finish this marathon. I simply would walk and rest and rarely ran any part of the marathon course. The pace I tried to maintain per mile was under 18 minutes per mile to give me enough cushion to finish under the 8-hour official cut off time. I was proud that I made a pace time of closer to 17:40 per mile. This remains my slowest marathon finish currently regardless of whether I am pacing or running any marathon on the road or trail.

It was an emotional walk - I would not call it a run as each step was a reminder of the pain that the people experienced in the attack that day on Wednesday, April 19th, 1995. I was completing this marathon to remember those 168 killed that day, not to mention all the family, friends, first responders, survivors, etc, being affected by this tragic event. My discomfort that day from my right knee was minuscule compared to what those people went through that day and possibly every day since that tragedy.

See what I tried to do here? I took an incredibly tragic situation to make my knee pain and surgery seem less significant. My pain was nowhere near what thousands of people experienced that day. Note I did not state my knee surgery was insignificant.

Some days in life we get to choose our battles and other day's life gives us battles and obstacles that we did not choose. That Sunday, April 24th, 2005, I went to a starting line hoping to conquer a marathon course at not 100%, and I am so happy that I accepted that challenge. Not simply because I accomplished my marathon completion goal, but because I had the initial courage to get at least across the start line when a successful marathon finish was not a given.

I also did complete the Med City Marathon on Sunday, May 29th, 2005, in 5:53:45 and therefore kept my Legacy status. I basically did a run and walk strategy as having done this marathon previously my #1 goal was to finish and #2 goal was to finish in under 6 hours and I indeed accomplished both goals.

The rest of 2005 found me finishing all my scheduled marathons and races that I had planned on for the year. Not one single race was missed due to my knee surgery and my monthly marathon and/or race steak was kept in place. My #1 goal of being able to successfully run again was accomplished as I was running everything from 5ks to marathons. I had not yet ventured into the world of ultras just yet, as that was still going to be awhile before my first ultra.

I most recently paced the Oklahoma City Marathon in 2022 pacing the 5:30 group and finishing in 5:29:16. I met multiple runners along the way especially a runner named "Jellybeans" - real first name is John - who we shared several miles running together. John was working with the Indian Education department for Norman Public Schools. It's s a federally funded program that provides supplemental academic, financial, & cultural support to Native students. It has a presence in 38 states and Oklahoma had 407 recipients of these federal funds.

There are several Indian Education programs throughout the state of Oklahoma & also throughout the United States.

Oklahoma though receives the bulk of the funding due to the massive presence of Native Americans in Oklahoma.

John worked as a tutor & secretary, so he was helping tutor middle school students with their homework, often one-on-one or in small groups. John also took students on field trips, hosted events, & collaborated with different organizations (like local universities) so that they could learn more about their culture & learn about opportunities at college. They have over thirty school sites in Norman Public Schools, so John & a small team of tutors covered all the school sites. John had a unique challenge and he made the best of it and basically became a "Pacer" to help the students move towards their goals.

John did not reach the 5:30 marathon pace goal that day as he finished in just over six hours.

I want to highlight that he clearly did not stop when he was not going to finish with me being the 5:30 pacer. He simply continued and finished the marathon in just over 6 hours. Congratulations to all who finished the marathon that day and to all who overcame whatever obstacle they needed to cross the finish line and earn that Oklahoma City Marathon medal.

Kathryn "Captain Insane-O" White
Tulsa, Oklahoma
Kathryn's word for herself: Provider

I have always been athletic, participating in multiple sports at any given time, but running was just different. I was drawn to it before the Jim Fixx era when recreational running was just not a thing. My parents were not particularly athletic and there were just not any local runners to serve as role models. At the age of 12, I would go to bed early donning the best clothes ever known to a runner; polyester and cotton. I have learned many valuable things about clothes and running in general since that time.

I awake at 0300 to run; sometimes enticing my sister to join me on her bike with promises of buying her pecan pinwheels for breakfast. Quite a sight to see two little kids out early in the morning; one running and the other trailing on a bike with a Pomeranian, Dixie Lou, in the handlebar basket. You know that kind of basket; white weaved plastic with a purple flower affixed to the front. Classic! It really was like a Forrest Gump moment; I was sitting or running in the waking hours. Nothing in between. I once asked my mom why she let me run so early. At the time, I thought it was such an odd thing to do. She said she admired me, plus we were in safe areas. Well not exactly in safe areas. The only store open at that time of the morning was a convenience store on the other side of the tracks. I suppose that will forever be my own little secret.

From there, I lettered in cross country and track each year in junior and high school. Although I was a staple in the local 5k and 10k race scene, I trained for a marathon in high school. Unfortunately, the race was cancelled due to an ice storm, and I moved on. I walked-on in college for about a half a second. I realized that I was never really going to be a good college runner and running just became too overwhelming tedious. A chore really. I began to focus on classes to obtain degrees that would generate a living for me and hit the gym. It was not until post-college that the passion for running incidentally came back.

My other passion is soccer. I was playing competitive soccer in Houston where I lived at the time. I wanted to get into peak shape. One morning on my way to a soccer game, I passed numerous cars parked on the shoulder of a major roadway. It was an abnormal occurrence for a Sunday morning. When I got to the game, I was told the Houston marathon was being held. I recall the look of admiration and awe on the faces of my teammates by the mere mention of the race. It was settled. I would be running the marathon next year. I was ready and willing when training started. Training often occurred by running the longest runs before and then playing a full soccer game afterwards. I still have no idea why I thought that was a good thing and cannot fathom doing that now. I miraculously made it through training injury free and completed my first marathon.

I honestly truly never planned to run another marathon. A few months after the first, I broke my tibia plateau and tore the meniscus playing soccer. I had surgery and was on crutches for over three months.

A coworker told me that I would never be the same again. You know he was right?

Some 216 marathons later, average of 7.2 marathons per year for 30 years, and one of only two people (Stephen Abernathy is the other person from Midwest City, Oklahoma) that have run all Oklahoma City Memorial Marathons and Route 66 Marathons (40 including virtual races) , Boston Marathon qualifier, 35 states, 2 European countries and streaking Houston Marathon (30 years in a row) .

The best outcome? Lifelong friends made along the way!

Chapter 11: Pump it Up and Make Some Changes

Song: "The Times They Are A-Changin"

Artist: Bob Dylan

Quote: Failure is not fatal, but failure to change might be. - *John Wooden*

Brock's word for me: Relentless

The Arnold 5K Pump & Run, which tests overall fitness by measuring both strength and endurance, is currently the largest race of its kind in the United States. In 2023 more than 30 states participated in the 2023 5K Pump & Run as nearly 800 runners competed in the competition which was held in the Columbus Convention Center in Columbus, Ohio.

In this type of competition, participants bench presses a percentage of their body weight. Each lift (up to a max of 30) reduces their 5-kilometer run time by 30 seconds. In this competition they limit the maximum number of repetitions.

It should be noted I have never done this competition - The Arnold 5K Pump & Run - so I can't comment on this particular event. However, I absolutely love competing in these types of running events so hopefully one day I can compete in this event.

It should be noted in some Pump & Run contests participants also do arm curl repetitions based again on a percentage of their body weight.

Note that the Quad Cities Marathon in Moline, IL, has a Pump-N-Run division offered in the 5K, Half, and Full Marathon as of 2023. All Pump-N-Run proceeds go directly to Quad Cities Marathon Charity Partners - Shoes for Kids & The Prostate Cancer Initiative. They have both the bench press repetition and arm curl repetition for their scoring. In this contest there is no limit of repetitions that you can complete per either bench press or arm curl.

I last competed in a Pump-N-Run at Quad Cities Pump-N-Run division for the marathon in 2014. That Sunday, September 28th, 2024, I ran a 3:55:29 in the marathon. In the Pump-N-Run competition I did 22 arm curl repetitions and 36 bench press repetitions. My adjusted marathon time became 3:26:29.

This to me was just a creative and fun way to see that my weekly weight training sessions were adding to my overall fitness and strength. With the strength training came the bonus on working on my endurance.

At one time I was looking to do a Pump-N-Run 5k in all 50 states, but when I researched it less than twenty states appeared to have such a competition. The one thing that makes running such a fun sport is all the creative run combinations that can be created like duathlons and Pump-N-Runs to name just a few.

Weight training is a great choice for an alternative form of exercise to lose weight. It is also a strong cross training alternative when starting running or to build your performance and speed as an experienced runner.

It is important to note that weight training can help you build strength and promote muscle growth. The result can then raise your resting metabolic rate (RMR) which is basically how many of calories your body burns at rest.

The combination of running and weight training will make you a better and stronger runner. With the added benefit of increasing your RMR to help you become a leaner runner.

When doing weight training you will be increasing your muscle mass, which can reduce your body fat percentage and improve your overall body composition.

One thing that is important to note that with strength training it may cause you to gain weight. However, if you increase the amount of your lean body mass, you will look leaner and toned.

When I was too tired to do my running from my cancer treatment's I could still do my basic weight training with significantly lighter weights. It at least made me go to the gym to get a workout in.

I never wanted to become the next Arnold Schwarzenegger, I just wanted to improve my overall health and wellness. I clearly accomplished that mission with my weight training. Even with my cancer diagnosis which forced me to no longer do heavier weight sessions, I can still do lighter weights and continue my weight sessions. With my continuing the weight sessions it helps add definition and toning to my overall body.

Some days it is simply just easier to do basic weight training than doing a run, due to my level of fatigue. This was especially true when in active treatment, especially when I was doing both the hormone treatment and the radiation treatment at the same time. With weight training I could rest between sets and it at least felt like I was doing something, and when I finished my workout, I was not completely exhausted. Just getting to the gym was a major accomplishment in and of itself, yet alone doing any type of workout.

Brock Jenkins
Newfolden, Minnesota
Brock's word for himself: Implacable

How I learned to stop worrying and love the run.

Where does one begin a story like this? Background? I was a 290-pound sedentary man with a job that involved a lot of heavy lifting but required little to no endurance. I was the guy that got winded going up a flight of stairs, no matter what the speed. I drank a lot of beer, I ate a lot of pizza, and life was basically just passing me by without anything other than momentary rewards to look forward to. I had no passions other than video games. In January of 2012 I stopped eating pizza as a staple and started to "clean up" my diet in general. I did not stop drinking beer, I didn't really lose any noticeable amount of weight, and I basically still physically felt like crap.

On June 2012 I found out a friend was on medication that would not allow her to drink wine, so I brought up the idea of me not drinking beer as a sign of solidarity. She was less than thrilled with the idea because she knew I could not, but I did it anyway.

Not drinking freed up a lot of time, so I knew I would need something else, and I wanted to try running again. I had a brief 6-month stint as a runner when I was in my early 20's, and I loved how it made me feel about myself, and life in general. I had pipe dreams of being that guy with a dresser drawer full of 5k shirts, because that is what I do for fun in those pipe dreams.

In June of 2012 my running slowly begins. My goal? To run a 5k without dying. My secondary goal was to not finish last. I dug out an old pair of Puma cross trainers that I had, and just started running. I knew shoes were important, but since I would be running mostly on gravel and grass right away, I was not too worried, and besides I did not know if I would stick with this crazy running thing. To start, I did not follow a plan, I always recommend to new runners to start with a couch to 5k, and I wish I would have, but I did not. I just ran until I got extremely winded, then walked until I could catch my breath.

I did not make it 100 yards the first time, and if I had to guess my pace, I would put it around a 15-minute mile for those 100 yards. I knew I should not run every day to start, so I did this every other day seeing small and gradual improvements. About 2 weeks after starting I got to a half a mile sustained.

I then started informing people that I was going to run a 5k later that summer, and that I would love if someone would run it with me. The reactions were not exactly what I had hoped for, as there was much laughter, which was basically the mean hearted, evil laughter. I would go so far as to call them hearty guffaws of evil laughter.

My sister did agree to run a 5k with me though! So, I trained on knowing that I had a buddy who would be there for my first "Race" and I would not have to go through such a scary experience alone. Now it is July, and I can go almost 2 miles and I have lost weight, still not sure how much because I do not own a scale. I have set my sights on a small local 5k midway through August. My schedule the first month and a half? Monday, Wednesday, Friday was run/walk intervals until exhaustion 1-2 miles. Saturday a long run. This was a very loose schedule, as I was not actually this regimented, but this was what I would try for.

Towards the end of July something magical comes together, and I learn to control my pace by constantly monitoring the two L's (legs and lungs) Suddenly, I break the 5k barrier. Every Saturday now the long run becomes longer than the previous, by a lot. Suddenly running becomes enjoyable.

Between the end of July, and the 2nd week of August I realize through constantly monitoring my muscle fatigue and cardio capacity and controlling the stresses put on them by slowing pace that I could rocket past my previous long run distance of 4 miles.

On August 10th, I plod myself an unbelievable "10" miles. The "10" is approximate, pedometers such as iPod nanos are NOT GPS devices and are prone to gross inaccuracies.

I cry, the feeling that accompanies this run is that I have finally done it. I no longer hope, I KNOW the change has come, something that has plagued me my entire life is on the way out, and this is a new Brock. Still drenched in sweat and reeling in the post run glow I sign up for a half marathon at the very end of September. Now this has gotten real, as I just signed up for a half marathon, having never completed a 5k. Now is the time for research, and Google starts becoming my best friend! I go to DSW Designer Shoe Warehouse and pick up a pair of Saucony Progrids 5's, so now I have actual, real running shoes.

During one of my Google searches, I find Marathon Rookies "beginner half marathon" 10-week schedule and start it at week 4. No pressure. Right?

So now it is August 18th, my first 5k, in Viking, Minnesota. I am the first person there and all alone.

My sister did not train and as such, she will not be running with me. I am ok with this; I realize that running is a selfish act. It is the most selfish thing I do. I enjoy it. If I must enjoy it alone, so be it. By now I have lost 40 pounds so I am a svelte 250 and I feel like I do not belong here, but I am going to do it. We find out where the starting line is and I line up, and I am literally scared to death. I have so much adrenaline coursing through my veins that I can stop anaphylactic shock from 5 feet away with the right breeze. I have read about this, I knew this was going to happen, that does not stop me from taking off with the leaders when the gun goes off. Within a quarter mile my adrenaline has dumped, I am now on rubbery legs with a LOT left to go. I push through. I do finish, despite battling with a girl who is roughly ten years old for placement for the majority of the 5k and I finish. Triumphantly I do not finish last.

More importantly at the finish line waiting are my mother, my sister, and my nephews! Motivation! They apologized for missing the start, but it is all good right? My time? 33:48. I am disappointed, yet overjoyed. I have met both of my goals, but I seem slower than I thought. I realize the pedometer that told me I was running a 9-minute mile, may have been inaccurate. I continue to train on the half program.

So, on September 29th, 2012 is my first half marathon - the Wild Hog Inaugural half marathon. Training for this has gone as well as can be expected. I missed one of the long runs on the schedule but I did fill that day with roughly 14 hours of canoe paddling so I know the cardio is there. I am the 1st person there again, and I am alone again. This time though, I KNOW I will have a lot of support in the crowd. The people who laughed meanly, and guffawed heartily are there, but they want me to succeed. Urge to cry rising again. I have dropped another 25 pounds, and I am now 225 pounds, I look fit but soft. I am nervous, but no longer with the crap scared out of me. This is something entirely different from the 5k, this is big and loud. There are pomp and circumstance here, this is a spectacle. This is simply awesome.

It is cold, and now I am wishing I had a throw away shirt like a lot of the websites talk about. I am in shorts and a wicking running shirt, and my nipples are dutifully taped. I am so ready for this. Within half an hour I had finished my sports drink, tucked my Gu into my pocket, and prepared for the start. 15 minutes prior to the start, we are herded to the line, despite just waiting in line for 20 minutes to go pee half an hour ago. I feel I need to pee again.

Now I line up towards the back of the pack, and the music starts playing. My adrenaline starts building but I do not let it take control. Going into this run, I am not viewing it is a race, as there is no time goal. There is no goal of not finishing last, as all I want to do is finish. I give zero crap about my final time if I cross that finish line 13.1 miles later under my own power. Most definitely somewhere before the course closing. We start, and I start out slow and continue slow, to me this is just another Saturday afternoon long run, but this time I have friends running with me. It is nice to have friends. I make conversation with complete strangers, as I am happy to be alive.

Around mile 8, the urge to pee has not left me and I realize I need to stop. I know I will regret this, as the pace I had maintained will be lost because of this bathroom break. Nine miles in I am worn down, but I am still happy, and I am still running. I had consumed my original Gu packet; plus, the Gu packet they handed me at mile 8. Checking the 2 L's constantly has me still moving under my own power, and my pace is good.

I have seen friends and family, and at mile ten I have more friends and family waiting. I cannot stress enough of how big of a boost ANY support is. This is where I meet crowd, and crowd loves spectacle, and the crowd wants you to succeed. Note that in addition to your friends and family, you will have people you have never met screaming their lungs out for you. Believe me it helps. Mile 11, I have developed bad cramping in my hamstrings and left calf but I know if I walk, I will not start running again, so I continue to plod along, but slower. At mile 13 I see my mom waiting for me close to the finish line. As she runs with me, she is crying. She sees in me that I have seen in myself. I finish. My lying pedometer tells me I have gone 17.4 miles. I hurt, my time 2:19. I am elated. I ice, I bathe, I eat, and I still hurt.

I then go to Schells and talk to an amazingly beautiful and lithe hurdles runner, she sets me up with what will become my longest shoe relationship to date, the Mizuno Wave Inspire.

Then in fall of 2012, I start looking online for more running events. I run across an ad in my very small home town for a local 5k fun run for Halloween. I shop online and get a Friday the 13th style hockey mask, as this is going to be fun. At the run I meet my local runner's group, as I want to become more involved and tentatively, I do. I start the run at the back of the pack wearing jeans and a flannel shirt and my mask. I scare the high school kids, as I am having fun. I make all the runs with them I can over the winter.

For Black Friday, I shop online and purchase a Garmin 405cx GPS watch. This is by far one of my best running purchases to date. I want to get faster, much faster. I decide on doing the Fargo half marathon in the spring, and pick out a new training program.

I decided on the Hal Higdon Intermediate half marathon training program. It has speedwork, so this is new for me. It is a 12-week program, which I can do twice before my next target half gets here. The first time through, I do not miss a single run, I rack up another 5k fun run, and two timed 10's over the winter/spring. My finish time was 28ish minutes for the 5k fun run in January, 2013. Then 55 minutes at the 10k Frozen Feat in February and 52 minutes at the 10k Shamrock Shuffle in March.

April comes, and having dutifully done 5 months of hard running training over the winter I sign up for the Autism Speaks 5k about an hour from where I live. My goal is to finish at under an 8-minute pace, and I do. My 5k time of 23:48 puts me just out of the top ten, I am elated. Two of my friends from NARC (The Newfolden Area Running Club and we do have shirts and hats if anyone is interested - Lol) show up and we have a great time afterwards laughing and joking. I have found a community. I continue to finish out the Hal Higdon intermediate half plan until Fargo.

So, in May of 2013 I am doing the "GoFar" challenge, which consists of a

5k the night before a longer distance race, and for me it's a half marathon. I am doing the 5k with my sister and her 3 boys, finally! Family to run with! My nephews were 16, 7, and 6 at the time. They wore the race shirt, along with 6000 of the other 7600 runners, this is not advised... this, is no longer fun.

We line up, assigning the 16-year-old to the 7-year-old, and my sister and I want to finish together so we try as best as we can to slow the 6-year-old down to her pace, this is not happening. Six-year-olds simply do not pace. I say good bye to my sister knowing we will likely see her shortly down the road as I chase off after my nephew doing sprint intervals in his bright blue shirt. He stops directly in front of a stranger who is jogging, and the stranger tumbles off onto the median, but my nephew is unscathed. Whose dang kid is this? I yell as I whisk him deep enough into the crowd to avoid the stranger's glare. My nephew is a trooper, so he does his sprints for 2 miles before he runs out of gas, and my sister catches up with us. Nephew, sister, brother finish in that order, this has been my most trying 5k to date... time? 47:40.

The next morning, I feel great, as I am wearing my "training for the zombie apocalypse shirt" I look dapper. I weigh ~175 pounds I feel fast. The run starts out cool and misting, at around 50 degrees. It is supposed to warm up, and I am leery of this, and, I must pee. I ignore this urge to pee. My friend Lori (from NARC) is here, and we both want to PR. We have not decided yet if we are going to PR together, or separate. So, we have decided to run the first mile together to warm up, and no faster than an 8:45 pace, which is what we do. After that first mile, I feel, AMAZING and I ask Lori if she feels up to a PR? She is a more experienced runner, as her half marathon Personal Record (PR) time is significantly faster than mine at this point, so I know that the call is hers to make because I will obtain a PR regardless. She nods and we take off, and immediately I lose her in the crowd within a half a mile. It is now starting to warm up. My Garmin tells me my pace is ranging between 8 minute and 8:15 minute pace. I stick with this pace most of the race and at mile 5 I see one of the band set ups that the race does and it is a high school classmate playing the Sweater song by Weezer. I cheer for him as I run by. It gets hot, so I slow down a bit but not noticeably. Some people do not slow down enough. It seems a lot of people do not finish due to overexertion and overheating, and I am luckily not one of those people.

I am constantly looking for Lori, and I cannot find her, but I do not let that slow me down. Around mile 8 a little girl in the crowd hands me a butterscotch disk. I love crowds. I love her. I continue to coast in on the simple carbs that disk provides. I have muscle fatigue but no cramps, and my breathing is fine. L and L working to perfection. With around a half a mile left to go I get a boost of energy, so I accelerate to the finish line. My watch tells me I am running approximately a 5:30 pace when I cross to the sounds of my sister yelling "WAY TO GO BROCK!" My time is 1:46:48, and I am very happy with this.

I stop abruptly, and nearly pass out while medical personal circling me like vultures. I recover and learn a valuable lesson. Do not sprint at the end of a race and then stop. Continue jogging a bit until your heart slows down if you must burn off the extra energy.

I still do not know what has happened to Lori, but now I realize I have no phone, and no way to contact my sister who has my stuff. I ask a burly young man who is talking to his mother if he can text my sister to tell her my location. So, he lets me do so, and I am so grateful.

I learned another thing and that is to always plan a post-race meeting point. We find our way to where Lori's husband is, and we find Lori, and she also has a PR with a 1:49, so it is a good day for NARC.

Now onto the Blue Ox Marathon which was their Inaugural on 10/12/2013. This is scaring the crap out of me. I am scared. I am the lightest I have been since I was in the 7th grade, 160 pounds of lean muscle and just a little bit of post weight loss flab. I have talked an old friend into doing the half so I would have someone to split the hotel room with. Lori will also do the half, and her husband will be there to help pick us both up after. You the man Mike!

The training program has gone decently, I did both of my 20 milers at around a 9:30 pace, but had a bad tendonitis flare up following the second. Between that and the half flare up I have now missed 2 weeks of an 18-week training program, so I am a bit concerned. My goal? To finish without dying. My secondary goal? To finish without dying, but under 4 hours. I took the entire week following the Wild Hog off, and then had a taper week after that. I had not put on any real mileage for a month or so before the full. The weather for this was awful, horrible, and rather typical fall Minnesota weather. At start it was 45 and overcast but not windy, so we were in high spirits. I was wearing a throw away sweatshirt, and a throwaway t-shirt on top of my wicking NARC shirt. We line up in the chutes, and I check my nutrition supplements, salt pills and 400 calories worth of Shot Blocks and whatever Gatorade I can consume should bring me home. I am shooting for around 750 calories to take in during the race.

We are asked to line up, and I am no longer feeling like the crap is scared out of me. I realize I can do this, but I am nervous. I just want it to start so I can do what it is that I have trained to do. Some guy in flannel with a musket says some words. Then we have a prayer, followed by the National Anthem. So, he fires the musket and away we go.

The first 15 miles go by so fast that I do not remember a lot of it. I know I was talking to a lady who was a Boston hopeful, and asked if I could pace her since I had a GPS watch. I agreed to do that to the halfway point because her BQ was in line with, or just slightly, faster than my race pace training. When we hit the half way point, she is right on target, I tell her to go on ahead, that I am going to slow down, and good luck! Unfortunately, I never did find out if she got her BQ time that day.

I dutifully consume my salt pills and Shot Blocks at the desired intervals, washing them down with water from volunteers. This is not as easy as it sounds, grabbing a cup of water while at a run with your left hand then drinking that water, while still at a run is not easy. It is the one thing that I have the most trouble with about long-distance running. The course so far is beautiful, the weather... is turning. I did not run the course beforehand, which is something you should do if it all possible. The course was basically 3 phases, a residential phase, a paved trail phase, and then an open road phase. We were told it was an open course, and it was. In the residential areas there were cars, and they would politely move over for the runners who would politely move over for them. The trail was by far the best feature of this race as it was beautiful. I saw an eagle, and it appeared to wink at me when I went by. I was amazed.

The open road portion, was just horrifying. After about 17 miles (which is where the hills started) the course dumps you out onto a county highway with about a 3-foot shoulder where you are running into oncoming traffic. Which, is bad enough in and of itself, but pair that with the temp change which is now in the high 30's. The wind which is now 20mph and gusting higher and the rain is now feeling like it is bouncing off my eyeballs and it was tough.

Shortly after the volunteers started asking me how I felt whenever I saw them, other than tired and in pain I felt fine so I told them that. I persevered, at some points on steep hills my ligaments and muscles had tightened to the point where it was not safe for me to continue to run up them, so I hobbled up them. I ran the flats as this could have been a byproduct of the cold. About a half a mile out my cousin was waiting for me to pace me in. Then within a quarter mile I saw Lori and Mike waiting, and cheering and my mom also cheering. I finished. Primary goal, finish without dying achieved. Also, I did not murder anyone. My secondary goal was to finish under 4 hours and that was not achieved.

My finish time was 4:09:00. I am and was faster than that time, but I did several things wrong during the race, and in prep for the race. During the race I had unfortunately ditched both my throw-away shirts, which was the reason the volunteers were so interested in how I felt. When I crossed the finish line, I was hypothermic, and my lips were blue. Had I stopped to rest at any point they probably would have made me go hold up for the sag wagon.

Race prep errors? I did not run enough hills, there are not hills by me so I did not run them. There were hills on the course, and lots of them. I also had nutrition issues, the Shot Blocks which had worked so well on my long runs made me sick after mile 18 so I could not eat them. I let myself go faster earlier which was a mistake. I still warmed up slow but I knew that going faster through the beginning part of the marathon would ultimately cost me speed in the end, and it probably did. This was a great learning experience, but one of the hardest things I have ever done, and there are portions of it that I do not remember.

Immediately following the race, I needed coffee to try to warm me up, water to try to rehydrate, and food to try to recover. This is where the cookies pic of me came from (thanks Lori!) , and yes, I would have stabbed the fool who tried to take them. I changed as quickly as possible out of my wet clothes and sat in my mom's car and violently shook for about ten minutes before finally warming up and heading off to post race nutrition.

In addition to the many different well-known running plans, I used during and following this period of my life I liked to do a bodyweight circuit that includes pull-ups, push-ups, squats, and sit-ups.

Pull-ups are a fantastic compound workout that uses many big and small muscles that makes my upper body feel less neglected. If my legs feel to beat up, I will also switch it up to cycling to keep my cardio fitness up to snuff.

That was the first 2.5 years of my running life. Since those first two and a half years I have had some stellar running years. In 2015 I ran four marathons and an ultra, three of the four marathons were in the 3:20's. That is also the year I started pacing with the Grand Forks Wild Hog (Half) Marathon. This is how I met Tom, I was named to be the pace team coordinator for the race and when the race transitioned to a full marathon Tom was a last-minute replacement to pace for me. He was recommended to me by Gwen Thomas who is the cofounder and head of Lost Dog Pacers. Pacing half marathons and staying fit enough to pace for the Lost Dog Pacers is what occupies most of my running life now a days.

Since my initial weight loss, I have managed to keep off most of the initial weight but have gained back some, as of this writing as currently I weigh 196 pounds. I continue to run knowing that the fight I have with my weight will be a lifelong fight. I continue to win my battle with alcohol. I have not had a drink since June of 2012, the week before I started running. When I started running, I was a morbidly obese alcoholic with little to no hope for my future. Since that start I have let my running life take me where-ever it may and it has let me experience so many things and meet so many people that have inspired me. One of those people I met on this running journey has a saying that I live my life by: "'never limit where running can take you" as stated by Bart Yasso

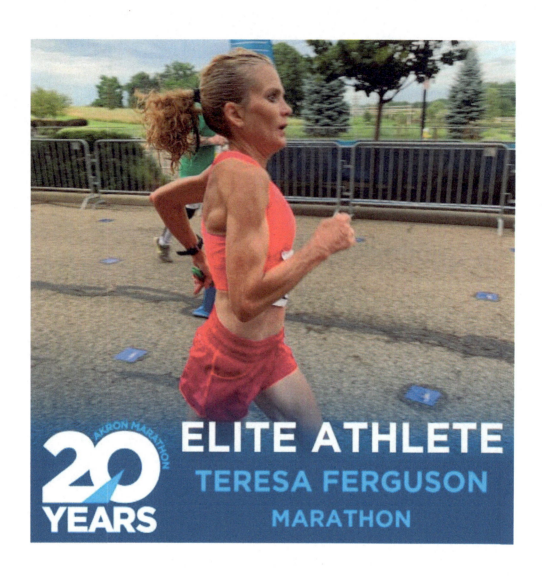

ELITE ATHLETE

TERESA FERGUSON

MARATHON

Chapter 12: Missed it by that Much

Song: "Carry On"

Artist: Fun

Quote: "In life, things can always go wrong, so always keep your heart strong, carry on, and never give up hope." - Mouloud Benzadi

Teresa's word for me: Motivator

On Wednesday, August 1st, 2007, at approximately 5:36 pm I had driven over the I-35W bridge that goes over the Mississippi River into Minneapolis, Minnesota. I had just completed a doctor's visits in Shoreview, Minnesota, and was heading to a Twins game at the Metrodome. I had Twins season tickets in 2007 so I was just going to a baseball game.

Why is that *time and day* important you might ask?

Shortly after 6pm and without warning, the I-35W bridge collapsed, taking with it 111 vehicles. Thirteen people died and 145 were injured per the local news reports.

My older sister Kathy called me that day as I was sitting in my seat watching the Twins warm up. An announcement went off about the bridge collapse. The announcer asked us to not leave the Metrodome. The game went on and the Twins eventually lost to the Kansas City Royals that evening by a score of 5 to 3. It was a chaotic scene when leaving the Metrodome that evening as the Twins announcer had advised us earlier in the evening.

When we go through life, we will be part of lots of near misses. Some misses could have been tragedies and some could have been successes.

Just like the odds of picking all the winning numbers for Powerball isn't the easiest goal to accomplish, we all can't pick and have success in everything we do.

Albert Einstein failed in the entrance exam of Swiss Federal Institute of Technology on his first attempt but succeeded in his second attempt.

In 1978, Michael Jordan was just another kid trying out for a basketball team and he did not get one of the fifteen roster spots out of several dozen's trying out. Michael used that motivation to become probably the GOAT (Greatest of All Time) in the NBA.

On Saturday, September 18, 2021, I was running a 5k in the small Wisconsin town of Antigo. The run was a benefit for childhood cancer. I won the 5k by *accident* as I meant for the younger runner by me to win. He did not know it but I was pacing him to win the 5k. Unfortunately, the race was chip timed so the runner must have started right behind me because I was declared the winner by 1 lousy second. Out of a small field of 41 runners I was the winner. I tried to intentionally finish in second place but I failed.

If you remember the TV show, Get Smart, played by Don Adams, he would have clearly stated that I "missed it by that much."

This was one of several races that I would win or get an Age Group award in since my Stage 4 cancer diagnosis. My Stage 4 cancer was not taking away my competitive side of me, it was simply a *motivating* factor to prove that I could still run.

In 2022 I still needed Alaska and Hawaii as the only two states I did not have an overall win or an Age Group award in. I was trying to have an overall win or Age Group award in all 50 states - meaning in at least a one mile run distance or longer - so I was going to attempt the Anchorage One Mile run on Saturday before the marathon. I finished the One Mile run in a solid 6:49 on Saturday, August 20th, 2022. I was ecstatic that I could still break a 7-minute mile over two years since given a Stage 4 cancer diagnosis. I thought I had certainly a chance at the Senior Grand Master One Mile award, but I crossed the finish line and no award. I was completely baffled as no one in front of me looked anywhere near as old as I was.

Oh, well I guess I gave it my best.

But wait. I had them check the results and I had won the Anchorage One Mile run for Senior Grand Master like I stated in 6:49. I finally completed my Age Group award in Alaska and my actual Age Group award was mailed and arrived less than three weeks later. It had inadvertently been given to the second-place person in the Senior Grand Master division.

A replacement I-35W bridge was designed and constructed on an accelerated schedule and opened on September 18, 2008, about 14 months after the anniversary of the collapse. The motivation was there to get the bridge replaced as soon as possible as that bridge is a crucial access road to enter downtown Minneapolis, Minnesota.

It was a feeling of mixed emotions when I drove over that new bridge for the first time. Survivor's guilt? Probably. I think how different my life could have been had I been on that very bridge when it collapsed.

Do you remember the date of the bridge collapse was August 1st, 2007? I was one marathon and state away from my first 50 State Marathon certified finish on that day. So had I been seriously injured or killed that day, I would have fallen short. I would have "missed it by that much."

I still need Hawaii so when will I get my overall win or Age Group Award? I guess I will just keep trying to go to Hawaii to get an overall win or an Age Group award. Being from Minnesota and going to Hawaii during the winter certainly does not seem like punishment to me. In fact, to me that seems to be an awesome *motivating* factor.

Teresa Ferguson
Akron, Ohio
Teresa's word for herself: Determined

I have run competitively for as long as I can remember. In grade school I was known as the fastest runner at Turkey Foot Elementary School. Fourth grade was the oldest grade in this elementary school and when a new student, Mike, arrived mid-year, I eagerly challenged him to the dual race on the playground during recess. With many of the students standing and watching, we lined up and prepared to defeat each other. Someone screamed "Go!" and we were off running. Poor Mike realized rather quickly that he was doomed. He lost to a girl no less!

I learned soon though to remain humble as there is always someone out there faster, or at least faster during a particular race. When I started a new school after my family moved, an opportunity arose at recess to run a race against Shelly, a fellow student. She put me in my place, and perhaps that was when I traded my desire to sprint for a living to something other than having dust kicked in my face. I never claimed to be a fast runner after that race with Shelly.

By the seventh grade, I was not only slower than just about everyone on the track team, but I was assigned to the distance group, as opposed to the sprinting group. The distance group was the collection of runners who were too slow to sprint, yet still had to have some purpose for the team since there were no "cuts" from the team. At that time, I had already proven that the hurdles, high jump, long jump and any other field event was even less achievable than my now poor sprinting ability.

During every track meet for that season, I came in last place in the 880-yard race. As a minor consolation, I came in second-to-last-place in that event at the last meet of the season. The second to last place finish was probably the motivator that made me begin running formally. In addition, my older sister began running daily and before long the entire family was running and racing the local road races.

Many who know me now are surprised at my description of my early years of running. I learned simply to enjoy the entire experience. I break the whole effort down to breathing, pushing off of my feet, the feeling of my feet in my shoes, and the warmth of my body repeating the push off of my feet becoming like a drumming effect from my legs as I take each step.

Do I think running impacts my mind to such a degree that it is addictive? Then I say "yes." I have accomplished faster times because I not only want to run, I need to run. Mental health is finally considered a part of the total person. We recognize that our belief impacts our ability.

Running has helped me battle my own mental health challenges and coping with a difficult marriage. I met Tom Perri at the Towpath Marathon on Sunday, October 10th, 2020, and shared the mental health challenges that impacted my family. After 17 years of marriage and my husband's attempts and ultimate successful commission of suicide, running was an avenue for coping with that burden.

During the summer of 2017, my closest friends would run with me and hear the darkest stories of what I was facing in my life. It was easy simply to share all the details on a long run-in part because running side by side I could never see the other's concerned facial expressions. Every mile with my friends was not only deeply therapeutic but also lifesaving. Caring for three children and holding down a full-time job while my husband made three attempts at taking his own life within that summer made running the only healthy and cathartic outlet available to me. I reflect now and remember the ongoing numbness and mental exhaustion.

The morning of his memorial service, which was five days following his death, I raced a 5K in downtown Canton, Ohio. Most people would not understand why I would do this. Run a race before one's husband's funeral? A runner would totally and wholly understand this. Throughout the entire race, I felt as if he was running right beside me. In my mind, I told him, "You were always annoyed by all of my running, and here you are running a race with me!" I won that race having posted a time sub 19 minutes while training for a marathon. So surprised with my time I had to verify the certified course was indeed certified. I was reassured by the race director that was indeed a certified 5k race course.

The Akron Marathon is always at the end of September. Even with his death, I was determined to remain mentally strong and avoid the rabbit holes of grief. I had every intention to remain focused and race hard and leave all the energy out on the course. Grieving is unique to everyone. When looking back I was grieving through my running. I raced well that day. Predicted to be in the top three masters, I raced next to one of my favorite competitors the entire race. She had no idea what burden I carried as we raced along as she and I knew each other annually only on this day at the Akron Marathon ever year.

Did I think about my husband's death while we went through each mile? Absolutely. In the last 400 yards turning onto Main Street, she took off. Now, did I respond? Did I think back to my early childhood days of being an amazing but short-lived sprinter? Did I muster it all up and chase her down to win? That would be an amazing ending to this little story, right? No, I looked at the beautiful blue sky and this overwhelming feeling of peace enveloped my body. I knew he finally was at peace and that through all the darkness he felt in his life that now he was safe. I crossed the finish line with a third Master's age group award that year. My mind was full of appreciation of all the kindness and love so many had given to me. I would go on and live my life knowing I was not alone.

Chapter 13: Running the Longer and Tougher Runs

Song: "Eye of the Tiger"

Artist: Survivor

Quote: "My strength is also my endurance. I can bear anything and everything." - Urfi Javed

Danny's word for me: Resilient

The Self-Transcendence 3,100 Mile Race is the world's longest certified footrace. Sri Chinmoy created this event in 1996 initially as a 2,700-mile race, and then in 1997 it was extended to 3,100 miles.

There is no shortage of endurance events. Each endurance event has its own challenges. One could easily debate about which endurance event is the ultimate toughest test. Is it the grueling Tour de France which is staged for three weeks each July - usually in some 21 daylong stages which covers some 2,235 miles?

Maybe the Ironman World Championships which is a grueling 2.4-mile swim, 112 bike, and 26.2 marathon?

Could it be the Badwater 135-mile foot race? The start line is at Badwater Basin, Death Valley, which marks the lowest elevation in North America at 280 feet below sea level. The race finishes at Whitney Portal at 8,300 feet, which is the trailhead to the Mt. Whitney summit, the highest point in the contiguous United States. If my math skills are correct that means at least 8,020 feet minimal elevation change.

One race that you could always argue is the Barkley 100-mile run. Only 15 runners out of about 1,000 have finished within the 60-hour cutoff. Imagine being the two participants who after several failed attempts completed the Barkley in 2001 together, only to be disqualified for inadvertently leaving the course to follow a parallel route for about 200 yards.

Is there anyone on the planet that has done all four of the above events and successfully finished all of them? With only 15 Barkley finishers I would say a high probability to that the answer is a definite no.

One component of the human mind that I have always been fascinated with is what is the breaking point of the human mind? I believe we all have a breaking point so what is our own breaking point?

The breaking point is a moment of stress in which a person breaks down. The intensity of how this happens and why varies from individual to individual. What is one's person's breaking point has no effect on another person. We all handle certain situations and stress individually.

If you feel you are "past your mental breaking point" that is not running related, it is never too late to get professional help. There are 24-hour help lines, EAP's (Employee Assistance Programs) , and free counseling centers that help. Any diagnosis like cancer is life changing, regardless of what grade or stage you have. Once the word cancer is associated you it will be with the rest of your life as either a survivor or a death statistic. Please do not go into the cancer battle alone. There are plenty of resources available for you, so please do not be afraid to ask for help.

The physical breaking point is when you are in say a 24-hour run and you have just reached a point of fatigue when you feel that you need to quit. Or you are running your first marathon and at mile 23 your body is telling you to quit.

It simply can become an issue of how tough your mind is. Can you overcome this temporary pain at mile 23 so you can finish your first marathon? Can you picture yourself at mile 87 of a 100-mile race finishing the race and getting the coveted belt buckle?

I ran my first Ultra event the Stuffed Turkey 30 miler on Saturday, November 30th, 2020 in Granger, Iowa, in less-than-ideal conditions and finished in 5:54:36. I finished 9th place out of 26 starters. I visualized myself crossing the finish line in under six hours and that is what I did. I really believe that made that race so much more enjoyable because I visualized my successful finish. I did not waste any energy during that race on negative thoughts.

This was also a race that helped me with managing my fatigue issues in later marathons and ultras due to my Stage 4 cancer. Yes, I *entered* the world of Ultra running after a Stage 4 cancer diagnosis, and so far, I have successfully completed 6 Ultra events. My goal before my cancer diagnosis was to complete an Ultra in all 50 states. Another new challenge I have is to eventually complete an ultra in all 50 states with a Stage 4 cancer diagnosis. So, my learning to run with an advanced cancer diagnosis is a steady continual learning curve where I learn from each race and run that I do.

So, can I still finish the Comrades Marathon? This was on my bucket list of running events when I did not have any cancer diagnosis, so what happens now that I have a Stage 4 cancer diagnosis? Then I must decide do I do the "up" or "down" course? Or do I hold out hope I can still run well enough in 2027 to run the 100th running of the Comrades Marathon? Or, do I just think crazy and think I could and might do both and then say I completed both the down and up version of the Comrades?

If you can find and work on your mental and physical breaking point you will be adequately prepared for what life throws at you. The more time spent working on building up and strengthening your breaking points the less likely that will occur in life or at a race.

My tip on this is to simply visualize positive outcomes. That is a key component when training for any athletic event or endurance event.

When you create a clear mental picture of your success it will give you the confidence and positive energy to work toward achieving your goal. The more you reduce your anxiety and fear the more likely you are removing negative energy and thoughts from your mind. You are not wasting any energy on negativity so you can conserve more energy that you can utilize on positive energy later on in the race when it is absolutely needed.

One successful technique for runners is goal pictures. If this is your first race, see if you can get a photo of the race finish line on the race website or taking a picture of the actual finish line if it is a local race. Then picture yourself crossing the finish line. Or maybe take last year's race results and picture your name being in those results. This is most helpful for longer races of say a half marathon or beyond where you are testing your mental and physical limits.

Index cards work as well to help build mental endurance and strength. You can write "quotes" that you like and write them on index cards, and then read one each day to motivate you. There is at least one quote in each chapter of this book that you could write on the cards if needed. Hint: that is why those different quotes are in this book as different quotes mean different things to different people. Pick the quotes that particularly stand out to you.

If you are not a visual person, then possibly writing in a journal may help.

Write about what goals you are working to accomplish and how you are going to accomplish them. Just like you are writing an outline for a story, simply create a plan and outline that you can use when the going gets tough. Keep that outline in a zip lock bag if needed and pin it your shorts to have when needed.

I personally spend time *every* day visualizing the cancer leaving my body. I truly believe I feel the cancer cells leaving my body. This incredibly positive way of thinking erases the doubts and fears I have about my body having cancer. The better I feel about myself the better I can live my life. The better I can feel about myself the more likely I will have a good race or run. The better I feel about myself the more likely I am to cross that start line and then cross that finish line.

Danny Ripka
Splits his time between Minneapolis, Minnesota, and Naples, Florida
Danny's word for himself: Unstoppable

1) When did you start running?

I was a runner in junior high and quit before senior high school as I wanted to be a cool hippie with the patched bell bottom pants and long hair. I was able to do anything I wanted as my parents were alcoholics, so with no supervision I ended up in drug rehab as a sophomore in high school and nobody wanted their kids hanging out with me after that. I was still a nice kid and would run after I got out of high school, but would still smoke weed before and during my runs.

2) How long have you now been sober?

Once my honey, and I agreed to quit using, I put myself into a 28-day program, and my honey went outpatient for six months. We have been clean ever since, and going on 33 years!

3) What was your first race you registered for and completed?

My first race was the 10K Wiener Run in Melrose, Minnesota, and I wanted to prove to Melrose that I was not the kid they thought I was. I also wanted to prove to my folks that I was worthwhile.

4) Please talk about your running with particular focus on your ultra running?

I started to really run ultras in the mid 1990s when they were not so popular. The Ultra Running magazine was black and white. The first 24 race I did was FANS around Lake Harriet. I won the race with 126.8 miles and I was hooked! I have won many 50 mile and 100k races and I did set a couple of North American records, running 216 miles in 48 hours and running 478 miles in the Sri Chinmoy 6-day race in Flushing Meadow Park in New York City on a 1-mile loop. I broke the old North American age group record by 90 miles. I would train 20 miles a day for three months straight to train for a six-day race. I would also run 846 miles in a month, 28 miles a day, to train for the 48-hour race in France on a 300-meter track.

I have also raced the Western States races and the Leadville trail races until my first knee problems in 2007. Then once they both went bad, I had them both replaced the same day in 2014.

5) Since you have had a double knee replacement how many marathons have you completed?

I have run about 25 marathons with total knee replacements. Then three years ago in 2020, I had to get one of my knee replacements replaced and that was brutal.

I have a great understanding with my doctor, and he knows better than to tell me to quit running. He just tries to get me to slow down.

6) What about your pacing?

I paced marathons for ClifBar Pace Team for 14 years and still pace the New York City Marathon.

7) What have you learned about yourself during your running journey?

For me, running is the best way to start the day as it gives me a boost and energy I need. I am very grateful to just run, but still have goals. I love sharing my knowledge and experience and enjoy, helping others by pacing races. I always want to be a runner and I am always willing to help others!

Trivia:

Do you know what Hall of Fame that both the legendary rock legend Alice Cooper & myself are both in? Note that there are multiple Hall of Fames in Ohio. The Pro Football Hall of Fame is in Canton, Ohio. The National

Aviation Hall of Fame is in Dayton, Ohio. The National Cleveland-Style Polka Museum is in Euclid, Ohio. The Rock & Roll Hall of Fame is in Cleveland, Ohio, and Alice Cooper was inducted in 2011, however I am currently not inducted and find it incredibly unlikely I will ever be inducted. However, we are both in a Hall of Fame in Columbus, Ohio, that Alice Cooper - the legendary "Architect of Shock Rock" - entered into this coveted Hall of Fame in 2014 and I entered in 2020. I am talking about the White Castle Hall of Fame, and you can find my Hall of Fame story only on the white slider box if you are so fortunate enough to get one. Please let me know if you find me on a yellow slider box as that would be a true collectible as my story was only told on the white box.

Chapter 14: Donating Will Make You Feel So Good

Song: "Ronan"

Artist: Taylor Swift

Quote: "The value of life is not in its duration, but in its donation. You are not important because of how long you live, you are important because of how effective you live." - Myles Munroe

Steve's word for me: Helpful

The song "Ronan" is a charity single by American singer-songwriter Taylor Swift that was created on September 8th, 2012. The three-year-old Ronan died from neuroblastoma in 2011. All proceeds from sales of the single were donated for charity causes to raise awareness of and for the fight against cancer.

September is Childhood Cancer Awareness month. Approximately 45 children a day are diagnosed with cancer in the United States. Which means around 17,000 children are diagnosed each year. Nearly 1 in 300 children will develop cancer before the age of 20.

Because of major treatment advances in recent decades, 85% of children with cancer now survive 5 years or more. There are an estimated 400,000 survivors of childhood cancer in the United States.

September is also Prostate Cancer awareness month. I felt incredibly honored that I was interviewed by Al Roker on The Today Show in September of 2022 to talk not only about my prostate cancer diagnosis, but also to talk about my staying positive and still actively pacing and running with my Stage 4 cancer. I will always have the memory of my original interview being "bumped by the Queen's death on September 8th, 2022."

What I loved about that interview is that more people have asked me about my beloved dog Otto, since that interview than about my Stage 4 cancer. It is imperative to note Otto is my "best buddy" and is a lovable goofball so he needs his own chapter in this book. I am not Otto's owner and his mom, Nora, will tell you Otto's story.

Per the American Cancer Society, for adult males other than skin cancer, prostate cancer is the most common cancer in American men. The American Cancer Society's estimates for prostate cancer in the United States for 2023 is that there will be around 288,000 new cases of prostate cancer, with approximately 34,000 deaths from prostate cancer. It is roughly estimated that about 1 man in 8 will be diagnosed with prostate cancer during his lifetime.

I was diagnosed with Stage 4 cancer on Tuesday, July 30th, 2019. At Stage 4, prostate cancer is unlikely to be cured. So, what is the bad news for me personally about that besides having a Stage 4 cancer diagnosis?

I will likely never be able to donate blood to the American Red Cross as I likely will never be cancer free. Sadly, I will miss not obtaining my ten-gallon blood donation, but I know in my heart I can give in other ways. Like my raising over $20,000 for the American Red Cross so I can run the Boston Marathon.

I truly believe that giving back will enrich your life. Helping someone else or your community is an opportunity for you to grow as a human being. It allows you the chance to better see how you fit into the world around you. I truly believe that giving is good for you.

The health benefits of giving when you help someone, is that your brain secretes "three feel good" chemicals such as: serotonin (which regulates your mood) , dopamine (which gives you a sense of pleasure) , and oxytocin (which creates a sense of connection with others) .

Also, I believe in Karma, meaning if you give to others, you are more likely to be rewarded, and receive something in return in the future.

I believe everyone has a skill or experience from which someone else can benefit, so it is important to share your knowledge on something you are good at.

If you are not putting your talents to their best use in your everyday life, volunteering can be a prime way to share.

In the 1980's I was a certified HIV/AIDS Instructor that did free presentations back when HIV/AIDS education was desperately needed. I also donated hundreds of hours over the years on suicide education and prevention. I believe knowledge is power, so I did my best to help those in needed some basic knowledge. Sadly, with my Stage 4 cancer diagnosis I had to basically sit back and watch the COVID Pandemic unfold as it was too risky me being out in public.

Maybe you have a natural gift like running which is easy for you. There are many way's runners can give back to the running community. You can volunteer at a local race on your "off day from running." Races this day desperately need race volunteers. Plus, as a bonus with some races is your volunteering can get you free or discounted future races, so a win-win for both you and the race. Another way to help runners is to volunteer as a pacer at a local run, as being a pacer is a great way to help and support other runners. Your knowledge and support can do wonders for that first time runner.

Or how about donating some of your race medals? I am sure Medals4Mettle would love to receive those race medals and put them to good use. That is a lot better than them being in a shoe box hidden away that no one sees. You can well imagine the smile on someone's face when they receive that medal after having a surgery or treatment.

https://medals4mettle.org/stories

How about those running shows that no longer properly fit or you just do not wear that still have some miles left on them that you can donate to those needing shoes. You can contact you locate running store to see if they are accepting shoe donations.

How about donating a pair of your season tickets that you cannot use to an organization like Ronald McDonalds House or to another charitable organization. Do not let those tickets go to waste and put a smile on someone's face. Or donate to an organization like Tickets for Kids:

https://ticketsforkids.org

Another obvious way to help others is by donating to charities either goods or money. There are multiple people collecting monetary donations for a variety of charities like when I am raising money for the American Red Cross to simply run the Boston Marathon being I am not able to run a BQ time.

Another type of donating is with on-line or live in person charity auctions where you bid on an item and the money goes to that charity. Over the years the American Association of Suicidology collected more than my fair share of donations due to the extraordinary auctioneer skills of one legendary Dr. Frank Campbell. I think Frank could easily convince me to give him a Grant ($50 dollar bill for those that are not familiar with the President's on which dollar bill) for a shiny new penny. Hopefully you know it was Honest Abe - Abraham

Lincoln - that was on the penny. So, the American Association of Suicidology benefits from my donation and I feel good about donating. I also help Frank feel great because I paid way over the value of the item so that again benefits the American Association of Suicidology. Simply a win for everyone.

Or how about donating a pint a blood? Just one donation can save up to three lives! Be like Mike who is working towards earning his ten-gallon pin. Or maybe organizing a local blood drive?

Or how about donating a body organ? I will let Steve share his story about unselfishly donating his kidney to his neighbor. That is an incredible donation and gift to your neighbor. Thank you, Steve.

Make sure in your life journey that you unselfishly give of yourself. The awards are many for yourself and others.

As the legendary singer James Brown sang "I Feel Good" and you will when you donate.

Steve Mura
South Orange, NJ
Steve's word for himself: inquisitive
Why did you start running?

I started running in high school. I ran all my freshman and part of my sophomore year. I always wanted to be in the top 5 on the cross-country team, but I could not quite make the cut. I felt that running more would make me faster, but unfortunately, the head coach of our team disagreed. So instead, I'd be told to hit the showers while the top 5 continue working out. After one workout, I was so mad that I quit the team.

Fast forward several years and I started dating an avid runner. I envied the glow that she, my now-wife, had when returning from her runs through Brooklyn. Nine years after I quit the team, she encouraged me to start running again. Her coaching tip was, "Put three songs on your iPod shuffle - any three motivational songs - and stop when those three songs end." The idea was to run to the beat of a good tune - to turn your brain off instead of trying to keep a pace or obtain a certain mileage.

The only problem was- I could not do it. I could not complete a run to three songs. I came back from that first run defeated. "Try again tomorrow," she said. After several more attempts at this, I completed the three-song run and was ecstatic. She then told me, "Add a fourth song." Over time, I kept adding other motivational songs, and then at some point, the number of songs went out the window, and I could master a 4-mile loop around Sunset Park.

Why do you still run?

The reason I run changes depending on where I'm at in life. When I first started running, it was for time. I wanted to get faster and go farther. I wanted my half-marathon time to be announced in minutes, not hours. I wanted my marathon time to qualify me for prestigious races.

After I achieved some of those time goals, I ran to coach others. I was fascinated with the new runner as it brought me back to the 2001 version of me on those cross-country courses. Training someone for their first marathon brought me back to the hundreds of miles I looped around Prospect Park training for my first marathon in 2010. I also started pacing runners during this time. Dedicating my race to those with goals of breaking 2 hours in the half marathon or 4 hours in the marathon. I felt pride at the finish line, being a small part of another runner's journey and helping them achieve their goal.

At this point in my life, while all those reasons still have a place in my running, I now run for community and connection. As a 39-year-old father of two living in the suburbs of New York City, the runs I do now are rarely a solo endeavor. They are with one or multiple other runners of various skill levels. The runs are not about running. They are about connecting with old and new friends. Sure, we sometime discuss running, but our conversations are loaded with much more. Without running, the chances of meeting the people I have met, from New York City to the other side of the world, would never have happened.

Why did you decide to donate your kidney?

My father-in-law had a liver transplant in 2019, so seeing the positive impact of organ donation rang true in our household. When my family learned that our neighbor Mike needed a kidney, my wife and I raised our hands. My wife underwent the testing process first but was ineligible for several reasons. I then proceeded through the process and passed each test. There is a lot of testing and waiting when donating an organ. From multiple blood tests, x-rays, 24-hour urine tests, and multiple interviews with doctors, nurses, and even psychologists; they ensure that what you are doing is safe for you and the recipient.

I questioned what life would be like after donating, as I have never met any donors. I looked online and found a community of athletes who have donated called Kidney Donor Athletes. Reading their post-donation stories opened my eyes; all were still running marathons, ultra-marathons, cycling, or hiking to a higher standard than pre-donation. I then realized I had nothing to worry about.

I am certain that after donating my kidney, I am a better athlete and person. Since donating, I have completed marathons, hiked Mount Kilimanjaro, and spent time advocating for living kidney donation. I have yet to be slowed down.

The roadblock that you overcame to accomplish your goal?

It was not so much a roadblock but overcoming the fear of slowing down. After donating my kidney, I started letting go of a time goal mindset. I took it easy as I picked up the miles and I soon realized it was okay to be a community runner. In fact, I found more happiness and peace with my running in this new mindset.

What did you ultimately learn from this experience?

Whatever mile I am in or the distance of the race I am pacing, I should walk away from a race having fun rather than a fast time. Those two can happen simultaneously, but the enjoyment of the process must come first.

Another example of donating and helping making you feel good.

Team: Determination - American Cancer Society and running the New York City Marathon

I raised over $3,600 with ACS (American Cancer Society) in honor of my grandmother, as I lost her to lung cancer. My sister is a breast cancer survivor and dear college friend is a Stage 4 colon cancer survivor.

Thank you again for getting me across the finishing line and for being such an amazing inspiration! I will cherish the memory of yesterday's run with you!

Anneliese Keil

San Diego, CA

Note that Anneliese was in the 5:45 pace group with me and ran the entire course with the 5:45 pace group at the New York City Marathon in 2023. She successfully finished in 5:43:24, running under her 5:45 goal.

Thank you, Anneliese for raising money for the American Cancer Society, and being an example of "donating will make you feel good."

Chapter 15: It Does not Matter How You Finish if You Finish

Song: "Winning Ugly"

Artist: The Rolling Stones

Quote: "If you enter a race and finish last, you are a winner. The loser never entered the race." - Roger Crawford

John's word for me: Ambassador

Sometimes the best laid plans do not go as planned. You make plans five years out and then plan every race and run but sometimes things definitely do not go as planned as they are out of our control. It is okay if we start something and somehow manage to finish what we started.

My first trip to Anchorage, Alaska, was to run Humpy's Classic Marathon on Sunday, August 15, 2004. I do not recall anything of the weather or how the race went, but I know I finished the marathon in 4:25:22 per the official results. I remember taking lots of pictures as we ran along the Tony Knowles Coastal Trail. I did not see any whales out playing, but I did see several eagles flying overhead, a moose along the course, and a few other animals.

One of the things I do remember is truly enjoying the Farmers Market. I remember trying several different jams and jellies that I had never tried before like salmonberry and fireweed. I remember going to Humpy's Great Alaskan Alehouse and buying Alaskan King Crab legs which were a delectable treat to eat. I remember having a meal of incredibly fresh salmon at the Glacier Brewhouse and Restaurant. I went to Alaska the first time for the marathon, but the food and scenery was what I remember the most.

I knew Alaska would be a state that I would visit again. I went back on Sunday, August 16th, 2015, to run what I believe at that time was called Big Life Wild Runs Marathon (which was formerly Humpy's Classic Marathon). I needed a sub-4-hour marathon this time for Alaska, so I wouldn't be carrying my 24 shot Kodak camera on me. Crazy to say that since the 11 years since I had been to Alaska the invention of a thing called the iPhone made carrying a disposable Kodak camera obsolete as the iPhone would be taking the photos.

Let's just say that my plan was to finish this Alaska marathon and then run the Honolulu Marathon on Sunday, December 15, 2015, to finish my second time through my 50-state marathon journey. Also, I needed both states for a sub 4 four-hour marathon for the 50sub4 State Marathon Club.

So, on Sunday, August 16th, 2015 I ran the Big Life Wild Runs Marathon in 3:49:43. But wait, one of the miles I ran per my watch was around 3 minutes and a few seconds. I checked my Garmin and I noted that my mileage was off significantly from the course markings. So maybe the course markings are off I thought? Nope, I finished the marathon in 3:49:43 for clearly a sub-4-hour marathon but my Garmin had stated around 25.4, so I knew the course had to be short. I only first wore a Garmin watch because I obtained one free in 2011, so the Garmin confirmed my worst fear - the marathon course was definitely short in distance by between .7 to possibly as much as one mile.

Once I finished the race, I tried to tell marathon staff that the course was short only to be told that the course "was the correct distance." So maybe I did run a three-minute mile and I hadn't even noticed. I just knew that wasn't possible.

We were then informed by email that the marathon course was indeed short. The cone that we turned around at going out had been accidentally placed in the wrong spot. So, this marathon would not be counting for my 50 State Certified Marathon Club finish. It was a costly $1,500 trip to have a marathon not count towards my certified finish. No 50 State Marathon Club certified finish in Honolulu, Hawaii, would be happening in 2015.

My adjusted time still counted for my sub 50sub4 State Marathon certified finish but I didn't want that. I knew I would have to go back to Alaska for a third time. I needed an Alaska marathon certified finish to get my second time 50 State Marathon certified finish and I wanted an official marathon with an official Sub 4 Marathon time as well.

On Saturday, July 30th, 2016, I finished the Frank Maier Marathon that was in Juneau, Alaska, in 3:56:12. A marathon that would count not only towards my 50sub4 State Marathon certified goal but also for my second time Alaska marathon certified finish. So, I finished the Frank Maier Marathon as my marathon for my second time finish for the 50 State Marathon Club certified finish. Yeah!

Alaska was supposed to be my third time 50 State certified marathon finish, but now it was my second time certified finish. Hawaii then would become my third time 50 State Marathon Club certified finish state when I finished the Honolulu Marathon on Sunday, December 10th, 2017, in 4:38:16.

In a convoluted way I accomplished my goal of finishing a marathon for my 50 State Marathon Club with a certified finish in both Alaska and Hawaii. It just wasn't in the order I had been planning for five years, but I still accomplished my mission. A five-year mission, that turned into a six-year mission, but I still started my goal and I still finished my goal.

Reflecting back on that experience years later I know that I initially had a lot of anger and frustration with the marathon course being short and it not counting towards my certified marathon finish. Sometimes things happen in our lives that change our direction that we can't control and we need to be a little more flexible with how we approach things. That was one of the many learning experiences I have been taught during my 47-year running journey that the path we take might lead us on a detour that wasn't planned. We sometimes need to adjust to the detour and enjoy the new road we are traveling. My anger and frustration over not getting what I clearly wanted would have only been a hindrance to me moving forward. As Bobby McFerrin sang about just "don't worry be happy."

I have been back to Alaska multiple times since and have now finished the Anchorage, Alaska, marathon that is held in August five more times. This marathon has had several different names over the years, and I have paced this marathon numerous times as well.

I have several favorite memories of this marathon over the years, and one was in 2022 when I had the pleasure of meeting a runner that was from the Tulsa, Oklahoma area. He was finishing his 50 State Marathon journey on Sunday, August 21st, 2022 at the Big Life Wild Runs Marathon as I was pacing the 6-hour group and I finished in 5:59:58.

The runner known as "Slow Juan" would successfully finish his 50 State Marathon Club journey that day. No short course was going to be an issue for him. No black bear or a moose on the course was going to stop him that day. Note I actually did see both a black bear and a moose on the course that day, but neither impeded my running progress as I still finished the marathon and hit my marathon pace goal.

So sometimes in life plans go exactly as you plan them and other times not so much. It just matters that we start a goal and work around any obstacle that gets in our way to the finish of our goal.

Maybe I never would have made it to Juneau, Alaska, in 2016, to run a marathon. I don't believe I would have but who knows. Two things will always stick in my mind from the Frank Maier Marathon in Juneau, Alaska, and the first is eating the freshly grilled salmon when we finished. And the second thing is the legendary Bob Kennedy finishing in 4:00:03 as he wasn't able to break that sub-4-hour marathon mark that day. Luckily, he had previously run a sub-4-hour Alaska marathon to his credit. As the legendary actor Don Adams stated in the television show Get Smart, Bob Kennedy "missed it by that much." Bob, just "don't worry be happy."

John D. "Slow Juan" Points
Tulsa, OK
John's word for himself: Persevere

Mine is a simple and, perhaps, relatively uninteresting story. Rather than wax poetic about my own journey, I want to be an encouragement for you to undertake yours. I began running distance when I hit thirty years old, but not as a competitive endeavor. I just wanted to support my pizza habit, manage my weight, reduce stress and enjoy the social aspects of running. Marathons were a cheap and effective way to do that. My finish time was never particularly important to me and I haven't used the timer on my race watch in nearly three decades now. I know, without verifying, the older I get, the better I was.

Ten years ago, I was a hardened skeptic about the prospect of running a marathon in every state. I thought that it was a foolish, selfish, and expensive venture. But I also realized that age and gravity are not your friends and that if I was going to do this thing, I was rapidly running out of runway. At age 62, with only 24 states under my belt, I signed up under the encouragement of Steve and Paula Boone. They assured me that I could still, "go the distance."

The absolutely best thing about running the 50 States is that it will take you to places where you might not have otherwise gone. So, what will you see, what will you experience on your 50-State marathon sojourn?

Seek marathons in proximity to National Parks, Monuments, and Seashores. I treasure the races that took me to Acadia, Cape Cod, Denali, Glacier, Haleakala, Mount Rushmore, White Sands...

Don't miss the themed marathons: Hatfield & McCoy, Full Moon Marathon (Area 51) , Shamrock Marathon, Outer Banks, the Cowtown, Lost Dutchman, or the OZ Marathon in Olathe, KS (an annual favorite!) .

Appreciate and revere the marathons that honor the military: Bataan Death March Memorial Marathon, Air Force Marathon, Marine Corp Marathon, Soldier Marathon, or Tough Ruck.

Any marathon that takes you through a sports venue is not to be missed: Run the sidelines of Lambeau Field in Green Bay, roll in the outfield grass of Schwab Field in Omaha, trot around the infield of Churchill Downs in Louisville (*"I love the smell of manure in the morning..."*) , finish-with-a-football at the Marshall Marathon.

I "rewarded" myself along the way with visits to the local micro-brewery culture. So much good beer, so little time. Don't miss "Bad Martha's" on Cape Cod, "49th State" in Anchorage, "Atlantic Brewing" in Bah Hawbah, ME with a lobstah roll, "Dangerous Man" in Minneapolis, "Four Score Brewing" in Gettysburg, "Moby Dick Brewing" in Bedford, MA, "Kona Brewing" and/or "Maui Brewing" in Hawaii. I promise you; you will find your own favorites!

The great people and race directors you'll meet along the way: Steve & Paula Boone of the 50 States Marathon Club, Heidi Schwartz of Cowtown, Destiny Green & Tim Fisher of the Route 66 Marathon, Geneva Lamm - the G-Force behind the Little Rock Marathon, Mike and Katie Sohaskey of RaceRaves, and Tom Perri, Marathoning's Ambassador & Pacer without equal.

Go find your story!

Chapter 16: Everyone is Truly Special

Song: "The Gold and Beyond"

Artist: John Denver

Quote: "You can't put a limit on anything. The more you dream, the farther you get." - Michael Phelps, American swimmer and most-decorated Olympian of all time

Tiffany's word for me: Determined

The Athens Olympic Games first took place from April 6 to April 15, 1896. The Athens Games were the start of what would soon become known as the modern-day Olympic Games. For the inaugural games of the modern Olympics, they were unfortunately attended only by male athletes.

Helene de Pourtales was the first female Olympian to win an Olympic medal in sailing in 1900. Helene was a Swiss-American countess born in 1868 who was passionate about horses and sailing. That year was the first-time women were allowed to compete in the Olympic Games. That year, only 22 of the 997 total athletes were women. The sports they were allowed to participate in were limited but included golf, sailing, tennis, and croquet.

Mary Lou Retton then became the first American woman to win an individual Olympic gold medal in gymnastics at the 1984 Summer Olympic Games in Los Angeles, California.

Kerri Strug, American gymnast and 1996 gold medalist, is quoted as saying "the ones who are successful are the ones who really want it. You have to have that inner drive otherwise it's not going to work out."

No matter what your goal is you have to have an inner drive of *real* desire to reach that goal. You can't stop smoking if you truly don't have the real deep desire to do so. Losing weight won't happen by just talking about losing weight. Beating cancer takes an intestinal fortitude that you need to find deep within yourself. You actually have to put some thought and determination into your effort.

Jesse Owens, former American track and field athlete and four-time gold medalist, stated "we all have dreams. But in order to make dreams into reality, it takes an awful lot of determination, dedication, self-discipline, and effort" No one really shows up to the Olympics with a minimal amount of training and takes home a medal.

It was an incredible experience for me on Saturday, September 23rd, 2023, to run into the Olympiastadium for the finish of the Berlin 4KM Fun Run. Jesse Owens won medals there in 1936. Usain Bolt breaks a World Record in a time of 9.58 seconds to win the 100 meters in Berlin on August 16, 2009 on the newer track.

Even the former American figure skater Michelle Kwan, and two-time Olympic medalist, was quoted as saying "I didn't lose the gold. I won the silver."

Shalane Flanagan, American long-distance runner and Olympic medalist, is quoted as saying "in the midst of an ordinary training day, I try to remind myself that I am preparing for the extraordinary."

Not all of us are destined to be in the Olympics.

Before you can take home an Olympic gold medal you have to get yourself into the games. The odds of simply being an Olympic athlete is estimated to be about 1 in 700,000 and that is probably on the extremely low end of your chances.

If your dream goal is to win a gold medal the odds may be as high as an astounding 1 in 22 million.

"It's not about winning at the Olympic Games. It's about trying to win. The motto is faster, higher, and stronger, it is not fastest, highest, and strongest. Sometimes it's the trying that matters" states Bronte Barratt, Australian swimmer and 2008 gold medalist.

The athletes know that not everyone that goes to the games will win any Olympic medal. They simply do the best that they can do each and every day.

We need to be happy with our successes, and happy with our failures. As per the great Jean-Claude Killy, French ski racer and three-time gold medalist, "to win, you have to risk loss. We can't assume that everything in life will go our way. We will likely not win or be the best at everything, but we still try and try again."

Reality set into me with the Stage 4 cancer diagnosis, that much of my faster running days were gone.

I believe I can still compete and be a competitive athlete and runner. At the time of this writing, I can still get to the start line, but now the main goal is to *simply* finish.

I never ever had a desire for an Olympic gold medal. That was never my dream or lifetime goal. Maybe sometimes it is best to not have goals that are entirely not possible or within a reasonable realm of happening. Maybe we need to keep our dreams within reality for ourselves.

It was in the 1950s and early 1960s, when Eunice Kennedy Shriver saw how unjustly and unfairly people with intellectual disabilities were treated.

Eunice Kennedy Shriver, founder of Special Olympics in 1968, was a pioneer in the worldwide struggle for rights and acceptance for people with intellectual disabilities.

Eunice Kennedy Shriver saw the adjective "special" as a way to define the unique gifts of adults and children with intellectual disabilities. Eunice Kennedy Shriver wanted to focus on the athlete's abilities, not disabilities.

Special Olympics athletes are people who are at least 8 years old or older and who have an intellectual disability. There is no upper age limit, and in fact, nearly one-third of the athletes are age 22 or older.

Special Olympics is one of only two organizations authorized to use the name "Olympics." I think that is incredibly special.

Tiffany Carey
Brooklyn Park, MN
Tiffany's word for herself: Perseverance

Tiffany, can you tell us your story of how you became a supporter of six siblings who were known for their own athletic accomplishments and awards to finally becoming an Olympic champion, winning gold?

I was one of seven children. My identical twin sister and I were born six weeks prematurely. I was born with a rare genetic disease which left me with many physical and mental difficulties. It wasn't until I was seventeen that my life began to change when I joined Special Olympics! My mother has been my biggest advocate in my care and improvement. As time went, I slowly improved by getting stronger and more flexible. I began to like sports and because of the Special Olympics I started to participate in bowling and basketball where we were state champions coached by my dad. My dad would say that I'm determined and persistent. My mother is my hero because of all she has done for me. My father and mother are grateful for the Special Olympics for giving not only me, but the many thousands of people of all ages the opportunity to succeed and accomplish their goals!

Tiffany can you please tell us how it felt to win the gold in gymnastics?

I was so amazed and surprised. I was frozen in joy and I started to cry in awe of what had just happened, not only because all the training and hard work that paid off, but also for my coaches who helped me and encouraged me to do my best. There are so many people I have to thank for supporting me in reaching my goal, such as my whole family, relatives, teammates, and friends. I am extremely grateful for all those people, because I know that some of my teammates did not have that kind of support.

Tiffany, with all the hard training and hours you put in what did you do in the little spare time you had?

I love to watch Golden Girls with my mother.

Tiffany didn't simply wake up one morning and go to the Special Olympics World Games in Berlin.

She practiced and trained and then she practiced and trained again and again. Then again.

She worked hard. She never quit trying. She never gave up on her dream. She worked harder and harder.

If she failed or had a bad routine, she would just do it again and again. Then again. She didn't stop trying.

She never gave up on her dream.

She won five medals - including one Gold medal - at the Special Olympics USA National Games in 2006.

The trip to Berlin in 2023 to represent the United States at the Special Olympics World Games was from years of work representing Minnesota at the National level. Then patiently - sometimes impatiently- waiting every four years to go to the Special Olympics World Games.

Tiffany actually screamed really loud when she read the email that she had actually been picked and would be going to the Special Olympics World Games in Berlin. She cried a lot. Tears of happiness and not sadness.

"I just fulfilled my dream" as for 32 years I wanted to go to the Special Olympics World Games. Not only did she go, but she earned a Gold Medal in the all-around competition.

But wait, not only did she accomplish her goal, but she also got one Silver and two Bronze medals. So not just one medal won, but a successful four medal campaign.

What Tiffany liked besides getting her medals was meeting new people. People from other parts of the world - Canada, Germany, and Slovakia - to name a few.

Tiffany saw people competing in other events. Everyone trying so hard. Athletes giving it there all.

Tiffany says she will keep practicing and training to get to the next Special Olympic World Games. She will keep dreaming of being picked again for the next World Games.

In 2022, Minnesota won the bid to host the 2026 Special Olympics USA Games. Over 4,000 athletes representing all 50 states will compete in Minnesota, specifically in the Twin Cities area.

Simply dream big, and win a Gold medal. Mission accomplished.

Simply keep dreaming, and win another Gold medal this time in her home state of Minnesota.

That is what makes Tiffany extra special, don't you agree?

Trivia

The first Special Olympics Winter Games took place in 1977 in Steamboat Springs, Colorado, which introduced a host of new sports to the program. More than 500 athletes came to compete in 1977. Currently the Special Olympics Winter Games take place every four years.

Chapter 17: It's About to Get Noisy!

Song: "We Will Rock You"

Artist: Queen

Quote: "So early in my life, I had learned that if you want something, you had better make some noise." - Malcolm X, The Autobiography of Malcom X

Fitz's word for me: Persistent

Cancer:
Can - cer cancer 'kansarI
noun
1 a disease caused by an uncontrolled division of abnormal cells in a part of the body

How about let's all of us get the CER out of here! Just like Prince wants us to "Let's Go Crazy" how about every cancer patient remove the CER from cancer and become a CAN. No more I can't do this or that but that I CAN do this or that. Trade the word cancer for CAN and see what you CAN do.

We might not be able to overcome cancer. We might not be able to get our Stage 4 cancer into remission. But we certainly can decide to not let cancer dictate our lives.

No one wants to be told what we can't do. We all hate it when restrictions are put upon us that limit what we can do.

Cancer will definitely change you so you can't do certain things.

No one wants to be diagnosed with cancer. No one wants to do radiation treatments. No one wants to do chemotherapy. No one wants monthly drug injections.

"No one wants the word "cancer" to be part of who we are. Unfortunately, once you get the big "C" diagnosis it becomes part of you for the rest of your life.

Just don't ever let cancer tell you what you can still do. Be the best that you can be with what you are and have and can still do. You might have to make minuscule changes and other changes may need to be bigger. You can replace what you used to be able to do with something that you can now do.

On the days that my fatigue is bad I simply take naps to recharge instead of being out running. I know tomorrow is another day and tomorrow I will probably be able to run.

Instead of reading a book because I can't clearly think because of my brain fog I might watch an old TV show like "Gilligan's Island." I think about how lucky I was to be in Honolulu five times to run the Honolulu Marathon. I remember staying at the Hilton Waikiki Beach hotel and seeing where the opening scene of Gilligan's Island was filmed for the first season opening at the Ala Wai Yacht Club in Honolulu, Hawaii. I visual positive experiences and keep thinking about positive experiences. I replace negative experiences and thoughts with positive experiences and thoughts.

Change from cannot attitude to can do attitude. Adjusting your attitude will pay huge rewards in making yourself happy.

Note there is nothing wrong with getting angry about your cancer diagnosis. Just release your anger in appropriate ways. Maybe schedule a five-minute daily block of time to vent your anger and frustration over the cancer diagnosis. When your five minutes is up you focus then on what you are still able to accomplish and do.

The American Cancer Society has programs and services to help you during and after cancer treatment. Make sure to use available resources if you need assistance or help.

There is a 24-hour cancer helpline that helps with people dealing with cancer related issues that you can call at 1-800-227-2345. Use the resources available to you.

The cancer battle is best won when using *all* the resources available. Sometimes even talking anonymously to someone might put things into a perspective that you hadn't previously thought about.

You are not in this cancer battle alone. ACS CARES (Community Access to Resources, Education, and Support) is a new patient and caregiver support program that connects people with quality curated information and one-on-one support. Use these resources as that are what they are available for to assist and help on our journey with cancer.

Seriously, please don't be afraid to ask for help. To me asking for help is not a sign of weakness, but a sign of strength that you are successfully taking on the cancer battle.

If might be helpful to identify what you are good at in the battle with cancer and what you might need help with. Identifying your strengths can help you realize the areas you need assistance and help with.

For those of you out there that want to keep your cancer diagnosis private I can understand that. It was a decision that I made to be open about my Stage 4 cancer diagnosis back in March of 2020 when I did the Runners World article. I wanted to be open about myself to others. I felt I was expanding my support system when I did that. It was purely my choice and no one else's choice. I just hope that if you are keeping your cancer diagnosis private that you have a solid support system in place.

What I am telling you is that the more *noise* you make about your cancer the better you will be. The more that people can offer assistance and support. I hope you aren't feeling ashamed or guilty about having a cancer diagnosis. If you are then there are services and support groups available to help you.

I want you to be a CAN do person and not let the word cancer take over your life. Cancer is just a word.

I want you to find a positive word that describes you, so that you can work to become that word. Each person in this book shared a word that described me as well as themselves.

Ask your family, friends, or significant other for a positive word that best describes you. Then pick the word that you feel best describes you. Encompass that word and become that word.

The moral of this chapter is cancer is simply a word. Don't let that word cancer ruin your life. Become a word that clearly resembles who you are and what you are and then you will be showing to the world of how you are winning the cancer battle one positive word at a time.

Fitz Koehler, MSESS
Gainesville, Florida
Fitz's word for herself: Noisy

My Very Healthy & Noisy Cancer Comeback

Cancer should make you better. I know that sounds nutso, but when a doctor tells you, "You have cancer," all the nonsense in the world dissipates, and you're stuck focusing on one thing. **Life.** Not only length of life but quality. Cancer makes you focus on actual health - having a body that feels and performs well. It also challenges your mental fortitude in ways you didn't know possible. You'll have to make many challenging decisions to preserve yourself for the future, which can become a fantastic skill. It was for me.

In February of 2019, seven weeks after a crystal-clear mammogram, while standing naked outside of the shower during a race weekend, I randomly rubbed my underboob and found a lump. Within 30 seconds, I had my gynecologist on the phone. This set off a series of appointments, scans, and biopsies, which yielded that dreaded call from my surgeon. "I'm so sorry, but you do indeed have breast cancer, and it has already spread to several lymph nodes. It's moving through you like wildfire, so we must treat you immediately and aggressively." I was terrified.

I'm normally the most positive person on earth, but I couldn't help thinking, "I have the perfect family, the perfect career. I'm the perfect beacon of health and happiness as a fitness pro, race announcer, athlete, and speaker. I am DEFINITELY going to make the perfect tale of tragedy." Now, I don't usually believe anything about me is perfect in any way; however - at this point, I couldn't avoid thinking about the stories that would be told after my demise. "Poor girl did everything right … so cruel!" My true grief came at the thought of missing out on my children's lives, which was unbearable.

Thankfully, most of my dread was soon alleviated when my hematology oncologist confirmed that he had a plan to cure me. In fact, I think my survival rate hovered around 95%. I liked those odds a lot. My scheduled treatment would be brutal: 15 months of chemotherapy, 33 rounds of radiation, and surgery, so my focus turned to enduring the cure. It was around this point that I made some incredible decisions that benefited me greatly and, in turn, have benefitted thousands of other cancer patients and survivors through my three books. *My Noisy Cancer Comeback, Your Healthy Cancer Comeback: Sick to Strong* and the *Healthy Cancer Comeback Journal.*

Whether you do or do not have cancer, these four decisions that I made, and you can make as well, will help you live better and longer, no doubt - and that's what my brand Fitzness is all about.

Perspective should rule your world. Even though my cancer diagnosis was super scary and my treatment wouldn't be fun, I couldn't help thinking about the children and babies in the pediatric oncology unit at the nearby UF Health hospital. I was so grateful that I wasn't a kid with cancer, and more importantly, it wasn't my kid with cancer. Keeping those gifts in mind, I never allowed myself a pity party. Did I cry? You betcha. Quite often, I would sit in my car for 15 minutes and boohoo. Once I got it out, I would dry my tears, put on my big-girl panties, and soldier on. It's okay to be sad and scared. It's NOT okay to wallow in it. That only leads to depression and worse. Become a person who finds the bright side and looks for silver linings no matter what. Once you do, you'll never get twisted up over a traffic jam, red wine on your white carpet, or any other trivial irritations.

Passions are non-negotiable. Cancer care made me violently ill. I not only suffered from baldness and fatigue, but my poor digestive system was put through a cheese grater. I was sick in every way possible for a very long time, but I never sacrificed my career or special times with my kids. Though many fearfully suggested that I avoid travel and hide out at home, I knew better. I knew that missing out on the things and people that I loved would only leave me sad, lonely, and depressed. Instead, I boarded about 30 planes out of my hometown of Gainesville, Florida, during my treatment to zig-zag across America, presenting keynotes and announcing many of America's most iconic running events. Even though travel days were difficult, and I often slept on the hotel bathroom floors, once I stepped onto my stages to serve incredible organizations and people, I'd experience pure magic. Every single thing that was wrong with me would disappear. I wasn't sick, fatigued, or suffering in any way. In fact, in these scenarios, I had the temporary blessing of being full-force Fitz Koehler again, which was such a relief from the constant punishment I was enduring. The same thing happened when I showed up to watch my kids partake in sports, ceremonies, or shows. On top of being transfixed on something other than my suffering, the kindness of my PEOPLE, especially the running community, provided much-needed amounts of joyful juju and kindness. Lesson for you: no matter what happens, you absolutely MUST pursue your passions. DO NOT sacrifice the things that bring you joy.

Exercise is essential. What could bring focus onto your physical health more clearly than being told you have cancer? In reality, going into any sort of illness or injury, a fit body will be more likely to recover and rebound far more effectively than an unfit body. Is your body prepared to do battle? If not, it's time to get to work. Many cancer patients are told to stay in bed and rest full-time. So ignorant. Resting too much will cause loss of muscle mass, strength, stamina, flexibility, mobility and balance. Instead, work to keep your body as fit as possible by doing what you can when you can. I lost a ton of weight and strength during treatment; it was brutal. However, I never stopped making efforts. I would do leg lifts and bridges in bed, stretch in the shower, walk, and swim as much as possible. Even the smallest efforts paid off, and I was able to transform my skeletal and sick little body back into a strong and athletic machine that allowed me to run the Boston Marathon about a year after finishing treatment.

Some food helps, and some hurts. You know how many people gorge on vitamin C when they start seeing signs of a cold? It won't surprise you that food is powerful and can make your situation better or worse. Like many, chemo messed with my tastebuds and my digestive system. Eating wasn't always easy. However, I always aimed to find the best foods possible. Endless studies prove that exercise and quality nutrition can make a cancer patient far more likely to reach remission and less likely to have a recurrence. You don't have to be perfect, but you should choose more good foods than bad. Every extra chance of a long quality life is worth putting effort into.

Cancer was a nightmare, and I certainly suffered physically and emotionally. However, I refused to play the victim and controlled those things that I could. Those decisions benefitted me endlessly during treatment by giving me professional satisfaction, success and income, joyful moments with family and friends, and a body that was always less sick than it would have been without my efforts. They also continue to serve me several years out. I'm as healthy as ever, yet I continuously work to improve. I'm also even happier than

I was pre-cancer because I fear very little and let almost nothing upset me. Why? It's not cancer! I've pursued some new hobbies like guitar and dance because I know that life is short, and I want to experience and learn as much as possible while I'm here. Lastly, I've found so much satisfaction in helping so many others with my Cancer Comeback series books. They're the deliciously sweet lemonade I've made out of cancerous lemons.

It's been a true privilege to witness and celebrate Tom Perri as he's run several of the races I announce. He role-models hardcore, continuing to run marathons despite cancer. Don't wait for cancer to upgrade your life. Life is good. Life is short. Life is now!

Trivia

It was in 1965, in a University of Florida lab a team of scientists invented a sports drink to quench one's thirst. Gatorade was named for the University of Florida Gators where the drink was first developed.

Chapter 18: Climbing Mount Everest

Song: "Climb Every Mountain"

Artist: Richard Rodgers

Quote: "It is very tough to climb a mountain. However, it is not as tough as convincing yourself that you can climb it." - Bhuwan Thapaliya

Hank's word for me: Unstoppable

John Lennon and Paul McCartney were correct when they sang "woke up, fell out of bed dragged a comb across my head found my way downstairs and drank a cup." This song "A Day in the Life" was released as the final track of the 1967 album Sgt. Pepper's Lonely Hearts Club Band. However, had I been there with them and they were writing the song lyrics today in 2023, I would have suggested they maybe follow that line with "got in my car in seconds flat, made my way to pace the Twin Cities Marathon."

My last Twin Cities Marathon I ran on Sunday, October 3rd, 2021, in 4:25:30, as due to the COVID Pandemic pacers were not being used for the marathon. My 27th Twin Cities Marathon would be completed on October 1st, 2023, pacing the 6-hour group. It looked to be the hottest Twin Cities Marathon on record. This would be my marathon and/or ultra #663 in the books today.

I had just parked the car at 5:25 AM and then I read the text. I wish maybe I hadn't gotten out of bed and dragged a comb across my head. Per the email received at 5:30 AM "Today's10 mile and marathon races are cancelled due to EAS Black Flag weather conditions - Extreme and Dangerous Conditions. The latest weather forecast update projects record-setting heat conditions that do not allow a safe event for runners, supporters and volunteers." So, no #663 overall marathon or ultra today.

So, no marathon yet completed for October 2023. I would have to patiently wait until my pacing the Chicago Marathon on Sunday, October 8th, 2023, to hopefully have my first marathon for October of 2023. My 241 consecutive months of doing a marathon (note that April & May of 2020 were virtual marathons completed during the COVID Pandemic) would have to wait.

I was at 59 career races canceled without including the 40 COVID Pandemic races that were canceled and if you include the canceled races from the COVID Pandemic I had 99 total races canceled. So Twin Cities Marathon would go down as my 100th race that was canceled either before or after the race started, that stopped me from successfully completing the race. I will always remember the date of October 1st, 2023 as being my 100th career race canceled.

You can't control a lot of things in our lives. Some things are beyond our control. Sure, it is frustrating for a marathon or a race to cancel. You prepare to run a BQ (Boston Qualifying) or a PR (Personal Record) or simply your first marathon and your chance to run your marathon on Sunday, October 1st, 2023, is suddenly gone through no fault of your own.

You did nothing wrong. You did all your training. You spent multiple days out on runs in the rain, running when you would rather be resting, and running when the temperatures were colder or warmer than you would have liked. It just isn't fair you think that the race was canceled. You might be angry. You might be frustrated. You might be sad. Ironically, you might even be secretly happy that the marathon actually canceled as you weren't properly prepared.

That is the way with life. Things sometimes happen that you don't like or understand. Was it right to cancel the marathon? The people making the decision made the decision that they felt was the *right* decision. Not all decisions in our life that are made do we accept or agree with. The temperature I saw was 92 degrees that day for Saint Paul, Minnesota, at 2:20 pm with 50% humidity. That would have been approximately the time I would have been finishing with my 6-hour pace group that day, though I only checked one weather site. I didn't keep checking sites as the first site just told me they made the right decision to cancel the marathon with those expected weather conditions that would have affected almost one-third of the projected marathon runners.

I guess I trust the experts to make the right decision. I am not a meteorologist. I am not an expert at predicting what the potential feel like temperature or humidity could be. We have to put our trust that the right decision was made to cancel the marathon.

When I was told on December 26th, 2018, that I "likely had prostate cancer." I remember thinking is that really true? Could they be wrong in saying I might have prostate cancer? Do I then get a second opinion? How about a third opinion?

You do the bloodwork, then a biopsy, then some scans, and they confirm you have prostate cancer. Then you have a radical prostatectomy to remove the prostate. Then they tell you that you now have Stage 4 cancer. Do you believe the doctors and medical team with what they tell you? Do you get a second opinion?

Both times I sought second opinions. I wasn't sure what or whom to believe or who to trust.

Believe me when I say it wasn't initially easy accepting what they were telling me back when I was told I initially had cancer. I had just assumed my initial PSA (prostate-specific antigen) test was not valid or wrong because maybe I had an infection when told I initially probably had prostate cancer. Or they had my name on the wrong person's tube of blood, but the second test had nearly identical results which helped confirm the first test. I couldn't keep getting tested and getting more opinions, so I had to finally *accept* the Stage 4 prostate cancer diagnosis.

Eventually I accepted what was being said to me on my cancer diagnosis. I had to trust what they were telling me was in my best interest.

Just like I didn't like them telling me that the Twin Cities Marathon might be canceled, I didn't like the doctors telling me I probably had cancer - especially when told I had Stage 4 cancer. You see all the emails and news stories about the potential heat and weather conditions and then you keep monitoring the situation about the marathon being canceled during the week.

No matter what I did that week it didn't really matter. I was notified by an email that the Twin Cities marathon was canceled at 5:30 am on Sunday, October 1st, 2023, just 2 1/2 hours before the marathon was to start. There would be no Twin Cities marathon that day.

I wouldn't have to worry about running in the heat and humidity. I wouldn't have to stress if I was going to be able to handle the race conditions. I wouldn't have to worry about ending up in the medical tent. I wouldn't have to worry about hitting my pace. I hadn't been feeling the greatest since throwing up on the Berlin marathon course the weekend before - which I am still not sure why I threw up twice then - so I could just rest.

I simply accepted that the Twin Cities marathon was canceled and that nothing I could do would change that fact. I felt I had grown a lot since my frustration over the issue with Big Life Wild Life Runs on Sunday, August 16, 2015, in Anchorage, Alaska, when I was angry and frustrated over the course being .93 miles short. Then the marathon not counting as a certified finish marathon - for the 50 States Marathon Club for a certified marathon for the state of Alaska - after five years of planning seemed simply wasted.

Believe me when I say it was tougher trying to accept being initially diagnosed with cancer. Then it didn't get any easier accepting my Stage 4 cancer diagnosis.

I know in my heart and mind that there is the potential for me at any day and time to be sitting with my doctor and medical team and being told "you have terminal cancer and you have potentially days or weeks or months to live."

There is definitely a possibility at any time that I will get a terminal cancer diagnosis. But there is also the possibility that I could die in a plane crash when traveling to a marathon which is probably a one in twelve million chance. There is also the probability that I could get killed by lightning which might be around a one in twenty million chance.

But with all those odds against me in just those few examples it definitely won't make me stay sheltered in my house. I don't know what my statistical odds of being in my house and dying by some freak of nature happening. For instance, like having a meteorite fall from the sky and crush me, as I am not researching that probability because I definitely won't be sitting in my house.

Just because I did get a cancer diagnosis, it won't make me live my life angry and frustrated because of my cancer diagnosis. My Stage 4 cancer diagnosis won't make me stay seated on my couch just sitting watching life pass me by.

I will cherish every second and minute that I am alive and I will get off the couch and out the front door. I am not guaranteed tomorrow so I will live as best as I can today. If tomorrow doesn't come then at least I tried to do my best today. That is all one can ask of themselves to give their best each and every day.

I have registered for well over 3,200 career races and *only* 100 have canceled for whatever reason. So just about a 3% chance that any race of mine that I registered for would get canceled. I wasn't allowed to start at some and others the race was canceled during the event. Either way it was the same outcome - the race wouldn't count in my record books.

I will continue to plan and register for marathons and races at least 3 years in advance. Yes, I did say *three years in advance* because so far nobody has told me I definitely won't be around in three years.

I will continue my looking at 80 races a year and plan to register each year for the ones that best fit my plans and schedule. At the very least my goal is a minimum of 36 races a year to keep my 36 races a year intact. I am not sitting back worried what might or might not happen. I will make what I can happen.

I have made at least 36 years of at least 36 races a year happen. Is it all possible I could make 36 years of 36 races a year from July 30th, 2019, from when I was diagnosed with Stage 4 cancer to July 30th, 2055? That would make me 94 years old so I would likely be in 90 plus age category. I believe that age group will be competitive then so it is never too early to begin training. And of you youngsters out there reading this better be incorporating some speed work in your training, or you will be seeing me *pass* you during the race. You have been warned.

If by chance the race doesn't happen for whatever reason I am okay with that. I at the very least had the courage to sign up for the race and to take a chance that I would run the race. Whatever happens after I register happens, as some things I can control and some I can't control.

As the Prayer for Serenity states:

"God, grant me the serenity to accept the things I cannot change, the courage to change the things I can, and the wisdom to know the difference." We all need to find the wisdom to know the difference.

As Franklin Roosevelt so eloquently stated – "the only thing we have to fear is fear itself."

So don't be afraid or hesitant to plan or sign up for your next race fearing the race might be canceled. Have the initial courage to sign up for the race. Then you need the courage to start the race. Then you need the courage to finish the race.

If by chance the race provides a medal to finishers, you will be amazed at the feeling that you will have once you finish the race. The feeling of having that medal placed around your neck when you finish will be amazing. Wear your medal you earned with pride.

Hopefully I might pace you or see you at the race that day. If I see you later in that day and you are wearing your finishers medal all the better.

On Friday, October 20th, I received an email from Twin Cities in Motion stating that "Twin Cities In Motion is pleased to announce that you will receive a refund equal to your registration payment as compensation for your cancelled race on October 1. Also, the email stated "in addition to your refund, we are pleased to share that marathoners and 10 milers will receive exclusive guaranteed access to your event in 2024 at prices equal to 2023."

To me that is a class act and hopefully in 2024 you will get to experience the "Most Beautiful Urban Marathon in America" or "The Shortcut to the Capitol" as you originally intended. I hope some of you will join me as I pace the 6 hour of pace group. Let's do this!

We all have mountains to climb in life, just never fear taking that first step up the mountain. You can't finish climbing the mountain without taking that initial first step. Believe me when I say the feeling and view from being on the top of the mountain is a feeling like no other. We just need to enjoy and be patient with the climb up the mountain. Remember I never said it would be easy, but the feeling of success when you climbed that mountain is priceless.

Hank Lopez
North Berwick, Maine
Hank's word for himself: Resilient

It all began when a neighbor suggested running a local 5K race in May of 2010. So that's what a race feels like was the only take away from that event. Oh, and look at all the wonderful treats at the end of the race. This could be the start of something big.

Soon after there was another 5k and another 5k, it became a pleasant outing to run these races and continually meeting new running friends. I also decided to develop some nice and easy strength training. This was a huge success overall, but I still had not learned to run more than a 5K race. I still remember my first 5k double, a race on Saturday and a race on Sunday, this was epic! Once winter hit and things got cold in Maine, I would simply stop running from October thru April. I quickly realized this was not a good path.

I did find some winter activities, and focused on my favorite the Snow Shoe Races, as I quickly learned the strength training, I had been doing was an important part of this sport. Cutting through snow on single track trails in the cold was an endurance challenge in itself.

By 2012 I was up to running close to 100 yearly 5k distance races locally in New England. Then the opportunity to run a 10K presented itself and I almost did not finish making a note how challenging this race had been. By May 2013, I began to wonder why I was always the same pace as I could not get any faster at the races. I decided to come up with a goal and develop my own self-taught training plan. The goal would be to finish a 5K in under 30 minutes by my birthday which was at the end of October, 2013. First, I added not only getting a morning run but also a mid-day run. During these runs I used telephone poles to alternate run/walk. This interval felt great and was very easy to manage without any fancy watches or electronics. By the middle of summer, I added an evening segment and sure enough my 5k race times were getting faster at each race. How amazing! My race day on October 2013, I finished a 5k in 29:05 and I was in shock on my accomplishment. Another lesson learned that putting in the work yielded amazing results.

2014 started out like 2013, the company I was working for became a lead sponsor in a local race series. Race entries were plentiful, but very few of my co-workers were interested in running any of these races. One of the races was a half marathon in November. The race would become a small corporate team building activity! Just about all my co-workers were seasoned runners for many years. About a week before the half-marathon I was asked, what is your weekly mileage? Easy, I get in 25-30 miles a week. Soon into that conversation after I elaborated more on those miles, I was asked, exactly how do you put in those miles? Even easier to answer – "oh, I run about 3 miles a day." The look of horror engulfed the office! Sure, I had run a few 10Ks but that was it. The ultimate question was if I had ever run a distance over a 10K? The answer was a firm NO!

The week before my 1st half marathon, I ran 7 miles on Monday, 9 miles on Tuesday, 10 miles on Thursday and then the half marathon on Sunday. It was uncharted waters after mile 10. I really didn't finish that badly as I had a plan to run ¾ of a mile and walk for ¼ mile. The finishing touch was that I could not walk for a week after the race! So, it was finally time to learn how to really train for a half marathon!

After some real training and picking up some additional running knowledge and skills, I was finally enjoying the half marathon distance.

In 2016, I was introduced to USATF (United States of America Track & Field) specifically the USATF-NE chapter. The USATF New England Road Race Grand Prix, composed of seven USATF Championship events. Run all 7 New England races of all different distances, 5k, 5M, 10K, 10M, 15K, Half and Marathon then receive this amazing embroidered USATF jacket with the race names listed! I wanted this jacket!! In 2016 the marathon distance was the last series race in November. I procrastinated my way thru 11 months till race day, stating this was a crazy thing to do, but I wanted that jacket! My training was 2 to 3 half marathons a month with the occasional 30k. Race Day came and went and to this day it was one of my best races ever. Not knowing what would happen after mile 19 was a treat!

The only person, other than the USATF-NE team members that knew I was running this marathon, was my high school best friend. He had been texting me thru the race looking for a status, so I took a selfie at the Mile 23 marker and that became a thing at every marathon since then. My first marathon was a success!

In 2017, I decided on marathon #3 and #4 to be my first double, just like running two 5k races right, one on Saturday and one on Sunday? Well not exactly, and I had the best time ever completing that challenge I set for myself.

Goals for 2018 included marathon #5 which was the Philadelphia Marathon in November. It was after this race that on the 23rd step, of the movie Rocky steps that he trained on, that I declared I would run a marathon in all 50 states! Marathons, #6 - #9 Four Corners; (4 states; CO, UT, NM, AZ, 4 days, 4 marathons) in early December, then #10 at the Savage 7 in Ocala, Florida. This Florida race would also be my first 50K. At this time, I qualified to apply for membership to the 50 States Marathon Club.

The journey had begun! In addition to joining the 50 States Marathon Club, I also joined the Marathon Maniacs & Half Fanatics Club. This club had some interesting challenges for sure! In 2019 I completed the highest level;

SUN in Half Fanatics by running 52 half marathons in one year while also running the occasional marathon.

2020 put everything on hold. Once things began to get to a normal level, I made the decision; as I felt I was running out of runway, I want to get my 50 state marathons done ASAP!!! It would be an all out and get it done process.

It was a quiet and dark early morning that I met Tom Perri at the Hatfield and McCoy Marathon on Saturday, June 12th, 2021, at one of the remote parking areas ready to board a bus to the start line. We chatted on who knew, when and where and quickly determined we had several New England and National friends in common. I would not forget this visit with this individual who had run 100's of marathons as well as several times around the states.

On January of 2022, I completed my 50th Marathon State and hit one of the most major goals I have ever set eyes on, it was also my 64th lifetime marathon.

Then in April of 2022, I became the 23rd Marathon Maniac/Half Fanatic/Double Agent club member to run 30 Half Marathons and 30 Marathons in different states in 365 days. I had finally climbed Mount Everest.

In June of 2023, I completed my 200th lifetime half marathon.

Setting goals in an important part of life. When it comes to the running community this becomes an even bigger challenge to get to that start line and of course finishing the race. Life has challenges that you just don't know what is around the next mile marker.

I have never personally dealt with cancer, but the scare and series of events that transpired are very real to me. After my routine yearly physical in 2020, my doctor indicated I had an elevated PSA. It was not at any alarming level, so the recommendation was made to see the urologist. An appointment was made with a recommended urologist that some friends had used. Initial visit and blood work confirmed that further testing would be required. The next step was either an MRI or a biopsy, and the MRI path was taken. MRI results came back with no findings. It was recommended that the biopsy be the next step. After the very invasive biopsy was completed, the results also came back with no findings of cancer. What does this all mean is yet to be determined! The only choice I have is to keep a yearly watch on my PSA and remain motivated and healthy in my running career! Having been on a prostate cancer scare still weighs on my mind every day. This is something that I will have to keep a watch on for the rest of my life.

Running races has not always been about the quantity for me. The quality for me is in the people I have met. From the person running their first half marathon to the person running their 1000th and 2000th marathon. The relationships created has by far been the most rewarding part of this thing we call running.

Now I am on my way to 100 lifetime marathons and 300 lifetime half marathons, with the goal of finishing 50 states of round 2 for marathon and a round 1 for half marathons.

Chapter 19: Running and Walking with Cancer

Song: "Power of the Dream"

Artist: Celine Dion

Quote: "You beat cancer by how you live, why you live, and in the manner in which you live." - Stuart Scott

Benji's word for me: Persistent

"Anyone who runs a marathon is sick!" is a quote by a legendary marathon runner. Do you have any idea who said that famous quote? I will eventually tell you if you don't already know, so just keep reading.

Unfortunately for me I had nearly 500 marathons in before I did get sick. But it wasn't marathons that was making me sick, as it was found to be cancer that was causing me to be sick. To be more specific it was prostate cancer. The big "C" (cancer) was causing me issues that I had no idea in 2018 was the main reason I was struggling with running.

I was comfortably running mile races under 6:40 with no speed work. Running 5ks easily in the 22-minute range and under for the 50 to 59 Age Group or 55 to 59 age group.

I was just starting to work on my second time of a 50sub4 hour marathon in all 50 states. 18 states finished and I was working on my second round. But my energy level and legs weren't cooperating. What was easy a year ago wasn't so easy today. Was it age related? Did turning 58 years old mean my faster running days were magically over? I sure was hoping that wasn't the case.

Depending upon the day I can still run rather well. Some of the races I did were completed while having undergone a recent surgery, or when I was receiving radiation treatments, or recent drug or hormone treatment, or a combination of all of them. I even ran well one day when I was having an absolutely miserable day with bladder, bowel, and fatigue issues that made me feel like maybe I should have just stayed in bed all day. I was so glad that I made it out of bed that day.

The number one biggest challenge for me with any race is the fatigue factor. The longer the race the worse my level of fatigue. It is difficult to run for over 30 minutes without feeling fatigue. The faster I run the faster the fatigue happens. Three hours for a marathon is basically all I have in me to simply run. The rest of the marathon is all emotional and mental as there is basically nothing left physically in me. Like the song by Jackson Browne, I am "Running on Empty." But like the song says, empty or not, I am still "running on empty" which is be better than not running at all.

The second factor is how my bowel and bladder hold out. Some races I need to wear a diaper due to bladder and bowel issues. In fact, sometimes I need to carry a second diaper inside my belt or inside my water bottle holder. Some races multiple times I need to use the bathroom. I just never know until the race is started and until I finish how good or bad a day I might have. Honestly most days are not bad as I am continually learning to regulate what and when I eat and drink before a race to make it manageable.

One thing I can not recommend enough if you are exercising or running is to talk to a nutritionist about your diet.

Unfortunately for me I can't eat 13 hours before an event if I am running it. Meaning if I am racing a 5k or half marathon, or even a marathon that I am pushing my running pace, I simply can't eat before the race. If the 5k starts at 8am on a Sunday, then on Saturday at 7pm I simply stop eating as I need that 13 hours to hopefully completely empty my system. If I don't my bowels and stomach will unleash some unpleasant sounds and contents. I started at 10 hours of fasting before race start, and now 13 hours is the magic amount of time. If I am not racing or pacing a faster time, I will tend to have a very small breakfast for some energy race day morning usually three hours before the race.

It is also imperative that I watch closely what I eat during the race as well, and this is especially true for the marathon distance. Excess sugary substances can really upset my stomach like excess gels and even sports drinks. I take my own energy food and beverage with me on the course and supplement that with what is on the course. When I was doing radiation and hormone treatment combined my bladder and bowels were a mess, so I had to experiment with stuff on my training runs, or on a race I wasn't pacing.

One thing I will stress if at all possible is to not try any new diets or foods at least 24 hours before a race, and that is especially true of the marathon. What you put in your body that is new might have an interesting way of leaving your body. Just save the new beverage or food item for a day when you can take a chance when the next couple days you are not racing and you are just running.

If you are not familiar with the beverage/energy/food on the course I strongly encourage you to see about buying and trying the beverage/energy/food on a couple of training runs to see how you react to it. This is especially true for people working on their Six Star for the Majors or the 7 (now 8) continent goal.

It is imperative that if you are in active treatment that you need to watch your diet. Once my radiation treatments kept going the more issues I was having. You might need to experiment on what foods simply work for you and don't work for you and then keep track.

I personally went to a higher protein diet overall to better manage my diet and weight loss issues. I went to six meals a day diet to better regulate my nutritional needs when trying to exercise while in active treatment. Make sure you have someone that can help you like a nutritionist. One of my special meals during my combined radiation and hormone treatments was simply two White Castle sliders with simply ketchup and mustard and no cheese. I was able to simply digest this and it gave me incredible comfort with no stomach issues afterwards. Thank you, White Castle. Just find what food works for you and is potentially comfortable and enjoyable.

Keeping on the weight at times will be more important than anything else at times when dealing with cancer and its treatments. Note that my weight since my Stage 4 cancer diagnosis really varies as my lowest weight was 147 and my highest weight was 179. My weight tended to be lower when doing the combination hormone and radiation treatments, especially from November 2019 through January of 2020. You just need to accept that weight fluctuations will be part of the cancer process as well as part of the cancer treatment process.

I have multiple other issues especially with side effects, so each race is a new experience. However, I made it to the start line and I made it to the finish line, so in all honesty I really don't have much to complain about.

As mentioned all those issues are basically from the combination of the prostate surgery, bladder surgery, the three rounds of radiation treatment, and the drugs and hormone treatments.

Below are my fastest times in that particular race distance since being diagnosed with Stage 4 cancer on July 30th, 2019. Some of the races I was running when I was actively in treatment. I keep thinking that I will beat all those times below, so it becomes a motivating factor for me.

1 mile - 6:47
Anchorage RunFest
Anchorage, Alaska
8/21/2022 - Age 61
First place Senior Grand Master

5k - 22:20
Grandma's Irvin 5k
Duluth, Minnesota
6/17/2021 – Age 60
Second place 60-64 Age Group

5 Miler – 37:44
Des Moines 5 Miler
Des Moines, Iowa
10/16/2021 – Age 60
First place 60-64 Age Group

10k - 50:22
Little Rock Arkansas 10k
Little Rock, Arkansas
11/20/2021 – Age 60
First place 60-64 Age Group

Half-marathon – 2:04:15
Sedona Half-Marathon
Sedona, Arizona
2/6/2022 – Age 61

Marathon - 4:09:08

Grandma's Marathon
Duluth, Minnesota
6/19/2021 - Age 61

Ultra - 30 miler - 5:54:36
The Stuffed Turkey Endurance Race
Granger, Iowa
11/18/2020 - Age 59

One of the things I realized when dealing with an active Stage 4 cancer diagnosis is that it is a 24 hour a day diagnosis. By that I mean each and every second, minute, hour, and a day can, might, and may be unique. Rarely has any day been even remotely the same.

You will have a bad second or seconds possibly when getting a painful shot or having a biopsy taken. Believe me when I say having a prostate biopsy is not a fun procedure, but it is not ridiculously painful. Note that everyone has their own specific pain tolerance. I am a Minnesota sports fan so I know a lot about experiencing pain, but that again is a whole other book. However, with that being said if you don't like pain or do not have a high pain threshold. I would suggest then that you not be awake for the prostate biopsy procedure like I was. Nor is having a scope inserted into the penis for a look to see if there is a bladder stone issue or other medical issues a very exciting experience.

Just like the runner that experiences cramps during a race, in most instances it is a temporary discomfort or pain that I experience. The cramps, headaches, and stomach issues just happen and they eventually go away. Also, the hot flashes that I get seem to last longer and are more intense. The fatigue just keeps getting worse, unless I manage it with taking naps and reducing training on days it is bad.

One of the side effects for me of the one hormone treatment was insomnia. It is difficult enough to sleep all night when ever few hours the need to urinate wakes me up. On any given night that is two to five times a night. Naps of at least a 1/2 hour are needed almost every day.

However, unlike for the marathon runner whose pain is temporary and might dissipate when the marathon is completed, that may not be for a Stage 4 cancer patient. The Stage 4 cancer patient may have a real *constant* pain.

That is when we need to remember that we have 24 hours a day each and every day and not a minute more.

Take life one day at a time and do not obsess on the day especially if you are having a rough and tough day. Live to run another day!

If you are running a 6-day event you can't make it to day 6 without completing day 1. Once you complete Day 1 then you can move onto finishing Day 2.

Luckily for me I was rarely being seen, or in treatment, seven days a week, but there was multiple 5-day weeks.

I knew each time when I had to initially get through my 38 radiation treatments, that every time I completed one treatment, that it was one less day and treatment to think about.

If I am having a "bad day" I know that tomorrow is a new day. The severe fatigue that I am experiencing today might not feel so bad tomorrow. If the fatigue is bad today, I remind myself not be too hard on myself. I might take a slightly longer nap that day. I might skip going to the gym. I might not do my laundry that day. I simply go easy on myself.

We need to not be hard on ourselves.

Tomorrow brings me another day. Another 24 hours to experience another day in my life and no one knows what that tomorrow may bring.

A marathon is simply completed one mile at a time, with a little bonus .22 after mile 26 to finish.

A day is finished when every second, minute, and hour is completed to make it count for the full 24 hours and a completed day.

I can't promise you every second or that any day will be discomfort free or pain free and perfect. If you suffer from depression, I can't promise that each second of every day will be a happy day. What I can promise you is that if you make it through that 24 hours and complete the day, then you will have another day that you never experienced before.

It is no different for every person that has completed a marathon, or a 100 miler, or a 24-hour challenge. They get a belt buckle or medal or ribbon, or even in some races just the satisfaction of finishing the race.

A cancer patient is a" survivor" who handles life 24 hours a day. We don't get a medal for finishing that day, but we get the satisfaction that we simply beat cancer for another day.

We can only beat cancer tomorrow if we first beat cancer today.

Just like the great Dale Earnhardt stated that "The winner ain't the one with the fastest car; it's the one who refuses to lose."

We don't lose to cancer if we make it another day with cancer. We simply refuse to let cancer win. Keep running if you can. Your running may feel different but you are still running. Learn to love the run for the run itself.

I will end this by quoting John Bingham that "what distinguishes those of us at the starting line from those of us on the couch is that we learn through running to take what the days gives us, what our body will allow us, and what our will can tolerate."

The legendary runner that made that earlier famous quote is none other than Benji Durden after the Peach Bowl Marathon in 1974. Read on.

Benji Durden
Boulder, CO
Benji's word for himself: Persistent

Over the years last 58 years. I have finished countless races from 100 yards and up. I have finished 139 marathons winning 11 of them. I figure I have covered over 150,000 miles.

I started racing in 1965 because I wanted to be a competitive athlete. I tried swimming and was just ok and hated getting in the pool at 6 am. I wasn't big enough for football or basketball. Baseball was scary with the ball nearly hitting me head on more than one occasion (this was before hard hat protections) . That left track and field.

I was just okay, at first. In High School, I improved enough to be in the top 10 in the state as a miler, but my state, Georgia, wasn't a national power house. I ran for UGA in college, but was still nothing that special. I improved after college, running local road races even winning one, but not being national class by any means. In 1974 I started a marathon (Peach Bowl Marathon) and dropped out thinking that was a foolish thing to do. The next year I went back and finished the marathon I had dropped out of and ran 2:36:19 which at the time was decent, but not great. But now I was *hooked* on road racing.

By May of 1980, I had run 16 marathons, winning 3 of them, and improved my best time to 2:13:47. I went to the Olympic marathon Trials hoping to finish in the top 5-10. I surprised myself and others by finishing 2nd running 2:10:41 and making the team. But I wouldn't be going to Moscow because much of the Western world was boycotting the Games to protest the USSR's invasion of Afghanistan. It was just the way it was and I continued racing, reaching my peak in 1983 when I ran 2:09:57 to finish 3rd at the Boston Marathon. I also damaged my plantar fascia in that race and sadly never ran a marathon under 2:15 again.

As the 90's began, I made a brief surge as a Masters runner running 2 marathons winning one out-right. But within a year, I tore my other plantar fascia while running a half marathon and decided to basically retire from running marathons and most racing in general.

By 2003, I was around 175 pounds (my racing weight had been 145 pounds) and running at most 20 miles per week. I was rarely racing and had not finished a marathon since 1991. Our lives focused mostly on work. That spring Amie and myself went to a health fair being held in the CU Basketball arena. One of the tests I had done while I was there was my 1st PSA test. It was then that I began my journey into the land of cancer.

When my PSA test came back with a 4+ PSA, my GP (General Practitioner) recommended I get a second test which came back with a higher 4+ PSA. We were in a state of shock as we began deciding on my urologist to proceed with a biopsy and likely treatment for prostate cancer. We settled on Dr. Melouk based on his personality, since I would probably be seeing him regularly. He performed the biopsy (which wasn't as bad as I had feared) and the waiting began. In late July of 2003 I was timing a race when I got a call from Dr. Melouk with the bad news; it was confirmed I had prostate cancer. I wanted to get surgery immediately, but we had to wait 6 weeks because the prostate needed to recover from the biopsy.

While we were waiting, we began to think about mortality which leads to us thinking about our lifestyle. We realized that we were not enjoying life as much as we should. One thing Amie and I both agreed we were missing was daily runs and made it a point to get back out daily. I began to work on being as fit as possible for the upcoming surgery, losing 10 pounds in the process.

September 4th, 2003, I had my prostate removed, but the margins weren't clean. But my PSA was non-detectable. During my recovery from the surgery, I walked as much as I could, even doing small laps in our condo. As soon as I could, I began to run again both for my physical and mental health. That December, I raced a 5K as fast as I had in years and was believing cancer was in the rearview mirror.

Soon, Amie and I returned to frequent racing, eventually setting a goal of running a marathon in all 50 states, which we finished in 2013. During that adventure, we began going to Dallas to run marathons put on by Angela Tortorice. It was there that we met Tom Perri in 2014.

It was around then that I began to slow down in my marathons and figured it was just age. Actually, it was early signs of my next cancer, colon cancer. Jumping ahead to June 2016, I was struggling so much in the Manitoba Marathon, that Amie beat me, which was not a good sign since I was usually at least 30 minutes ahead of her in marathons. At home I was feeling so bad after eating that we knew something was wrong. With the help of my former GP, we managed to quickly get a colonoscopy and confirmed that I had colon cancer.

Surgery took care of the tumor, but the cancer was stage 3, so chemotherapy was the next step under the direction of Dr. Andorsky of Rocky Mountain Cancer Center. During my 1st session of chemotherapy, I was feeling a bit nauseous as well as needing to pee, so I got up and pushing my treatment stand I went to the bathroom. By the time I returned to the recliner where I sat for my chemotherapy, I was feeling better and I realized that movement would help me through this. I started with just walking as much as I could every day, especially when I was feeling bad. Soon I began interspersing short runs into my daily long walks. By the end of my 6 months of chemotherapy, I was fit enough to run a good half marathon the weekend after my last treatment. In April I returned to running marathons.

Once again, I figured I was through dealing with cancer. My PSA remained non-detectable, my follow-up CAT scans and other blood tests were good. I was running reasonably fast in my racing. But then came COVID and traveling to races stopped. I also missed going to my urologist for a bit which meant I wasn't getting my PSA checked. But in early 2022 I did get my PSA checked as part of my colon cancer follow-up. My PSA was 0.0107; a detectable level for the 1st time in almost 18 years. We figured it was a testing error.

Then one of the follow-up CAT scans showed a spot on my left lung. Another biopsy revealed lung cancer this time. Surgery in July, 2021, required removing the lower left lobe of my lungs. It was stage 1 cancer, and I was soon back to running.

August of 2022 I finally went back to see Dr. Melouk. He felt I should have another PSA test because it probably wasn't a test error when I was tested earlier that year. This time my PSA was slightly higher at 0.115 and it was time to find a radiation oncologist. We chose Dr. Richard at the Rocky Mountain Cancer Center. He felt we should wait until my PSA was 0.200 before starting radiation treatments. I reached that level in January, 2023. In February, I got a Lupron shot to block my testosterone production since prostate cancer growth is helped by testosterone. Then I started with my 35 radiation treatments.

Since radiation ended, I have had 3 PSA tests that were less than 0.01, or basically non-detectable. My testosterone is still very low but slowly rising. I am racing even slower, but I am still out there.

Running through all of these cancers has helped me stay sane and, I think, healthier. We are mortal, but being a runner helps with the quality of life while we have left.

Chapter 20: Indiana Wants Me

Song: "Hip to Be Square"

Artist: This is a song by Huey Lewis and the News, Sean Hopper, and Huey Lewis. It was released in 1986 as the second single from the multi-platinum album Fore!.

Quote: "As I look back on my life, I realize that every time I thought I was being rejected from something good, I was actually being redirected to something better." - Dr. Steve Maraboli

Josh's word for me: Legendary

The Kingda Ka is the fastest roller coaster in the United States and one of the fastest in the world. So, if going crazy fast is your passion, Kingda Ka delivers.

The year 2020 was definitely a roller coaster year replicating the Kingda Ka as COVID quickly became a major issue in everyone's life in 2020.

On January 17th, 2020, I had just finished 8 months of hormone treatment. On Thursday, January 23rd, 2020, I finished my 38 rounds of radiation treatment. At least 23 days into 2020 and I had had no surgery so things were definitely looking up.

So how do you celebrate finishing radiation treatment? You go home and take a nap for two hours. Fatigue from my cancer combined with my radiation treatments made nap time an important part of my daily routine. My daily naps to this day are an incredibly important part of my life.

Then when I woke up refreshed, I planned 40 races which were mostly marathons. These were races and marathons I was going to do once recovered from my treatment starting in April of 2020. Every day after one of my surgeries or radiation treatments I would plan a race to do in 2020. It was part of my process to focus on something good when something not so good was happening. I figured a negative event plus thinking and planning a positive event equal okay.

Why 40 races and marathons you ask? Because I had two surgeries and 38 radiation treatments so what better way to "honor" each of those days than with a race or marathon.

Also, I needed to keep my streak of at least 36 races a year completed. Cancer was not going to stop that yearly goal.

It was a confusing time for both the runners and all the Race Director's. Pacing gigs were disappearing faster than Chestnut Joey consuming hotdogs at the Nathan's hot dog eating contest on the 4th of July. The condensed version is ALL forty races that I had planned from April 1st, 2020, until December 31st, 2020, were cancelled.

It was incredible that I could pick a total of 40 races and marathons and not one single one would happen. My week in London pacing the London marathon wasn't happening. Pacing the Missoula Marathon wasn't happening. My pacing Grandma's Marathon and Twin Cities Marathon wasn't happening. My trip to go to Chicago to pace the Chicago marathon wasn't happening. My trip to New York City to pace the New York City Marathon wasn't happening.

Marathons like Fargo that I was planning on pacing tried switching their spring date to a fall date but it still never occurred.

My original schedule for 2020 had at least one marathon a month, to keep my monthly marathon and race streak alive through March. I had no idea that the Little Rock Marathon that I paced the 5:30 group and finished in 5:29:22 on Sunday, March 1st, 2020, would be my last real marathon until June 2020. How in the world would I have ever guessed that? Well, I didn't and a new major roadblock was before me.

I just finished dealing with my Stage 4 cancer for the past nine months and now COVID was here to present a new road block. The unique difference with this road block was finding out that very little of it could I control.

So, with all my marathons and races canceled in April & May of 2020 my only real option was virtual races. There were definitely a few races held that had a few runners in April and May that the Race Director did decide to proceed with the race regardless of COVID, but they were basically trail races. They were not taking any more runners due to size limit due to COVID restrictions. Travel as well was rather difficult due to quarantine issues if one was to follow the guidelines and protocols. I also wasn't sure how deadly catching COVID would be in my weakened state since my Stage 4 cancer diagnosis, surgeries, and all my treatments.

There was no marathon of substantial numbers of runners in either April or May of 2020 as it just wasn't

I completed 25 virtual races during COVID and my statistics for streaks have an asterisk by the months of April and May indicating COVID months. The virtual races do not count in my official marathon total being it was "not an official result and time."

It was wasn't until the Jackson Scenic Trail Marathon on Saturday, June 27th, 2020, that I would run a live in person race and finish in 4:48:07. I needed this marathon to continue my monthly marathon streak as some marathons had suddenly become available and I needed to continue my marathon streak. I needed and wanted my life and running life to appear a little more normal.

It was finally in September of 2020 that a lot more races and marathons were appearing and actually occurring as live events.

It was at the Fair to Square Marathon in Danville, Indiana, that I felt that races were proceeding a little bit more like normal. I guess it was "hip to be square" thanks to Todd Oliver, the Race Director.

Normal running felt awesome to me. I was missing my pacing a wide variety of races. It was rather strange to see races that I had actually planned on doing never occur. Races I hadn't planned on doing were happening, but pacing gigs simply were not happening. A lot it seemed depended on the actual size of the race and what state the race was held in for the marathon occur.

What I was missing was doing my usual pacing. It felt incredibly strange to me to be running a marathon or a race without a pacing stick in my hand. So, at various marathons I would be running and talking to various marathon runners to see how the marathon was going. I was particularly focused on helping the first-time marathoners successfully finish their first marathon. It was a way for me to keep my passion for pacing alive and well for the past forty-seven years.

On Saturday, September 12th, 2020, I ran the Fair on The Square Marathon in Danville, Indiana. It was a nice two loop course out on basically country roads. So not an incredibly flat and fast course, but those really aren't my marathon preference for courses. I really enjoy and like variations on courses so my leg muscles get a nice mixture of flat and inclines and hills.

If you get to know me, you know I find it rather difficult to run without talking to someone. I was missing my pacing gigs so I would try to talk to runners along the way on the course.

My heart has always had a soft spot for first time marathoners, so when I was running, I met Josh who was running his first marathon. I couldn't have a better runner to stay close to and talk with during the marathon.

I think that took me a little while to understand as a Pacer, was that over the years there are definitely runners that simply want to run by themselves. They want no one interacting with them and that they just want to be left alone. They might run *near* a pace group, but they don't want to be part of the group. I tend to rather loud at times and some people might find that annoying. It was just part of learning throughout the years how to be a more effective pacer.

I just stayed with Josh and when he basically "hit the wall" all I had to do was basically get him through that experience. Josh never gave up and I promised him at mile 20 three things: that we would definitely finish the marathon, that we would do our best to finish under 5 hours, and that somehow, we would find a cold beer at the finish.

We eventually did finish which was goal number one. Then we accomplished second goal as we did finish under five hours as we finished side by side in 4:50:29. Then we celebrated with a cold beer. All three goals successfully accomplished.

Cancer you can't ever take that experience away from me that day. I clearly beat you that day and will continue to try to beat you each and every day.

That was perfect for me as I felt incredibly lucky that after my Stage 4 cancer that I could finish my 500th career marathon and ultra in 2019. Now I was just going to try to reach 550 marathons and ultras. Just one marathon or ultra at a time and I made another new running friend along the way. Even with Stage 4 cancer and COVID Pandemic life my running was good as it gets.

Joshua Winograd
Orlando, Florida
Joshua's word for himself: Earnest

I was a second-year law student at Indiana University when the COVID lockdown began. I was actually on spring break and only meant to spend a weekend with my little sister where she lived in Georgia when I was notified that spring break had been extended indefinitely. My sister and I decided to lockdown together, rather than be alone. Suddenly, a weekend in Georgia turned into an open-ended question and a busy law student had plenty of time on his hands. Unwilling to sit still in my sister's apartment and unable to work out in a gym, I needed a way to get outside, stay in shape, and keep myself from going crazy. Although before COVID I was just a casual runner who had only ever run 1-3 miles at a time, getting serious about running checked all my boxes. So, I dove headfirst into endurance training, applying the same drive and commitment I was accustomed to in law school. I did my research and put myself on a marathon training plan.

It was not easy at first but eventually I found true happiness in the long run. I dedicated all my mornings to running around Georgia. I explored every park and trail I could run to. Afterwards, on my sister's couch, I had all day to recover and rest my legs. It was the perfect set-up. Before I knew it, I needed to book a race, but COVID stretched on and no races were happening. A friend of mine and fellow runner back in Indiana told me about a marathon in rural Danville, Indiana and I jumped at the opportunity. Keep in mind, I had never participated in a race longer than a 5K but I spent months training alone and I was eager to accomplish the marathon distance. I returned to Indiana and finished a brutally hot summer of training.

I arrived at the Fair on the Square Marathon in Danville nervous and unprepared. The downside to training alone is that I did not have the community of resources that one benefits from with a running group. There was so much I had not learned yet. In other words, I was still making rookie mistakes without someone to catch and correct them. Early on in the race I found myself running near Tom Perri, who struck up a conversation with me. We started with small talk but that grew to big talk. Tom shared his story with me, which is quite a powerful thing for a first-time racer to hear. We chatted for hours while running through long stretches of farmland in rural Indiana. After all the solo-running, I felt lucky at the time to have found a running buddy, and a legendary one at that, but I did not yet know how lucky I was to have Tom nearby.

Around mile 20 both of my legs seized. It felt as if I was hobbling on wooden legs like a pirate. I had not been watching my nutrition properly during the race and I had stupidly drained myself of electrolytes. My legs were shutting down and the sensation was incredibly painful. With 6 miles to go, I had sincere doubts that I would be able to finish. If I stopped or tried walking, my legs felt tighter and further immobilized. The experience was shocking, I had never cramped like this before. Tom explained to me the situation I was in and showed me the reservoir of salt packets he kept on himself during races. Tom made clear that I could not stop and that he would not leave me behind. At first, I could only hop with a hand on his shoulder for balance. Once I got my legs moving again, Tom and I ran the remainder of the race. He reinforced countlessly during the last painful few miles that I had what it took within me to finish. I dug deep, powered through, and we crossed the finish line together. I would not have finished if it was not for Tom's help. As an experienced veteran racer, he knew exactly what to do and say to pull me through.

I celebrated with a beer. Tom introduced me to some of his friends at the race. We took a few pictures. And I thought that would be it, a chance encounter with a stranger, and that it would end there. Instead, Tom did something I did not expect: he stayed in touch with me. I continue to receive regular updates on his health, treatment, travel, and races. My favorite updates are when he makes the news! Even more miraculous than making sure I finish my first marathon; Tom brought me into his inner circle and made me feel like family. I cherish that. All these years later, I am fortunate to have Tom check in on me and ask how I am doing. Tom is a truly a special person.

I still love endurance training! But I now focus on triathlons, with plans to do my first full Ironman soon.

Chapter 21: You Are Never Late to Start Your Running Journey

Song: "Born to Run"

Artist: Bruce Springsteen and E Street Band

Quote: "Age is just a number, and your talent will never fail you. It has no expiry date." - Madhuri Dixit

Gwen's word for me: Dedicated

Age is just a word. Your actual age is just a number. Over the years I have been running I have seen all ages and abilities of runners. The diversity of the runners in today's running world is forever changing. When I first started running, women made up a smaller percentage of the runners.

In today's running environment, women are frequently more than 50% of the runners for a race. While difficult to state the average age of a marathoner, it might be that the age is going in the slightly higher age range.

Marathons and races used to have age groups from 60 and above for the Senior Grand Master awards. Now it is not uncommon to see Age Group awards at bigger races having 80 to 84, and 85 and above, or just 80 to 89. I have paced runners as young as 4 running a 5k, to as old as 89 years. With marathons I have paced several eleven-year-old boys and girls, and several male athletes in their 80's. I have yet to pace a female athlete in her eighties, but that is only a matter of time before that will happen. I have not personally paced anyone runner under 4 years old, or 90 years and older.

I think it is likely that I will be pacing a male over 90 at a marathon, and a female over 80, within the next decade.

I have been asked several times about personally pacing runners as young as five years old for a marathon, and I have declined. This is just my opinion, but I don't feel it is in the best interest of a 5-year-old to run a marathon distance.

It was interesting to be part of the book "Running Past Fifty: Advice and Inspiration for Senior Runners" by Gail Waesche Kislevitz. As stated by the legendary Bill Rodgers, "it will give you advice, tips, and inspiration to run endless masters' miles."

If you are over 50, I strongly recommend this book for inspiration to begin or continue your running journey. Note that this book came out in October of 2018, so at the time I was included in the book I was *not* yet diagnosed with cancer. My cancer journey began on December 26th, 2018, shortly after the book was released.

Many of my running friends share their stories in Running Past Fifty that are mentioned in this book including Julian Gordon, Eddie Rousseau, and Kathy Waldron.

I am not honestly able to say how running at 60 years old is different from when I was running at 50 or 55 years old, due to all my treatments and my Stage 4 cancer diagnosis. My current goal is simply to still be running when I am 70 years old. Whether I will still be pacing marathons and races is still to be determined.

It has been amazing to see all the older runners doing and setting some amazing goals. As mentioned earlier age is just a word, and your actual age is just a number.

To all the especially older runners that I have paced and ran with I want to thank you for the courage to take that risk to get to the start line regardless of whether or not you successfully finished the marathon or race. I just want to say "thank you" for the memories.

I didn't get to where I am in my running and my running goals without seeing you older runners doing all your marathons and races. Many of us were old school with no watches, not using GPS, not using Strava, or any type of technology. We simply ran for the pure and simple joy that running is. Just listening to the sounds around us, and enjoying the scenery without Earbuds in our ears.

I feel honored to have met Gwen Jacobson early in her running career and journey. Gwen is a classic example of someone that started running later in life and has had an amazing running journey since her first step. Gwen continues to show by example that age is just a word, and your actual age is just a number.

Gwen and myself, share several passions besides running, and one of those is visiting breweries and microbreweries. I think to both of use there can never be enough races or microbreweries.

Gwen Jacobson
Rochester, Minnesota
Gwen's word for herself: Dedicated

I started running in January 2010 to train for a 5K race for a co-worker's husband who was battling cancer. I decided to continue running a race every month to keep me motivated and became interested in longer distances. I ran my first 5k on May 1, 2010, and haven't stopped running since!

A friend encouraged me to enter the lottery for the 2011 Garry Bjorklund Half Marathon and I was selected. I completed the Garry Bjorklund Half Marathon on June 18, 2011, with a time of 1:54:05. After that race I decided I was half way to the marathon distance so I wanted to run a marathon. The Twin Cities Marathon was sold out but my local running club, The Rochester Track Club, offered a training class that included an entry for the marathon so I signed up. So, my first marathon was the Twin Cities Marathon on Sunday, October 2, 2011. I finished in 4:06:46 and learned I had missed qualifying for the prestigious Boston Marathon by less than two minutes. Of course, I decided I could train harder and try to qualify for Boston.

My next marathon attempt was the 2012 Grandma's Marathon. I went into the race with an undetermined pain in my left hip. As the race progressed the pain became worse and by mile 13, I was forced to a walk/run. I finished with a time of 5:07:46 (my slowest marathon to date) and went immediately to the med tent and then to the hospital. I had suffered a femoral hip stress fracture and was sidelined from running for 7 weeks.

I recovered and resumed training and completed my first sub-4-hour marathon and Boston qualifying race at the 2013 Grandma's Marathon with a time of 3:58:42. I only ran 3 marathons in 2013 but all three were in different states and I decided to set a goal to complete a marathon in all 50 states.

I ran my first Boston Marathon in April 2014, the year after the bombing and it remains one of my most memorable races. The support for the entire city of Boston was overwhelming and crossing the finish line on Boylston Street was a proud moment for me.

I then finished a marathon with a time under 4 hours in 7 different states in 2014 including running 3 of the 6 World Majors (Boston, Chicago and New

York City).

While I was running the Georgia Marathon in Atlanta, Georgia, in March of 2015 another runner told me about the 50sub4 club. My goal then changed from just doing a marathon in all 50 states to completing a sub-4-hour marathon and run a Boston Qualifying time in all 50 states. I accomplished both of these goals at the Des Moines Marathon on October 20, 2019 surrounded by my family and running friends from around the country. When I finished the 50sub4 states in October 2019 I was the oldest female finisher at the time but since then another club member (Deborah Lazaroff) completed her 50 states at an older age than I was at the time of my completion.

Regarding trying to complete this quest, the state of Wyoming was my most challenging state to complete. When I ran the Jackson Hole Marathon in 2015 weather conditions ranged from rain to sunshine to hail. I also struggled with altitude sickness during the entire race. I tried to hang on to earn a BQ time but couldn't even manage that. My finish time of 4:14:48 is my second slowest career marathon. I redeemed myself when I ran the Jackson Hole Marathon in 2018 with a time of 3:50:42 and was the Female Masters Winner.

The Age Group record that I am most proud of is the Boston Marathon that was held on October 11th, 2021, where I won First Place Female Age Group 60-64 (3:23:08) just 8 days after running a personal best (3:20:41) at the London Marathon and earning third place in the inaugural Abbott WANDA Age Group World Championships.

I think I was first introduced to Pacer Tom Perri at the Med City Marathon in either 2015 or 2017. I do know that by 2019 Tom and I had run many races together in the United States and shared many

post-race beverages together. Tom knows so many runners and race directors and was instrumental in helping make my 50-state finish one to remember. When I told Tom I was going to finish at the Des Moines Marathon in October 2019 he connected me with Chris Burch, the Des Moines Marathon Race Director. Chris reserved Bib 50 for me and also included me as one of the athletes featured in the Spotlights section of the Souvenir Guide. Seeing Tom pre-race for a photo and having him join my friends and family for my 50sub4/BQ 50 State finish made the day complete.

Chapter 22: Brain Power - Using Your Mind

Song: "Dancing Queen"

Artist: Abba

Quote: "Nothing is impossible, the word itself says 'I'm possible'!" - Audrey Hepburn

Julia Khvasechko's word for me: Persistence

If you think you can, you likely can. Think you can finish a marathon? You definitely more than likely can finish a marathon. Think you can successfully get through radiation treatment? The more likely that the radiation treatments will be more tolerable.

If you think you can't finish a marathon, and you can't change or are not willing to change your mindset then you likely can't finish a marathon. If you think chemotherapy is going to be utterly awful, the more likely it will be utterly awful.

How about using your given brain power to adjust and change your mindset? You will be amazed at how this will make a significant difference in your life.

When using your mind then you have the most powerful component to create success in life. Our mindset creates who we are, who we will become, and what we will accomplish. The mind influences our physical well-being and our emotional state. Never underestimate the power of your mind and what it can help you accomplish in life. You can have incredible athletic ability, but without the correct mindset will you be the best that you can be? Highly unlikely.

"The mind is everything. What you think you become." Buddha

As mentioned, the word cancer is just that and nothing more. Cancer is simply a word. When you cut the word down the middle you have "can" and "cer." Let's get rid of the "cer" and focus on the remaining word "can." If you can accomplish in your mind this one simple concept you are on a successful journey in your battle with cancer.

Cancer certainly tells us what we can't do, but it won't tell us what we can do.

The word cancer is just a word that is a noun. Let's just then replace it with the word grit here - the word Julia in this particular story is choosing - and we still have a noun. The word grit's connotation here is firmness of mind or spirit; it is unyielding courage in the face of hardship or danger.

When you are given a diagnosis regardless of whether the news is good, bad, or ugly, you have been given a word or maybe a few words. For example, "you have cancer", or "suffer from clinical depression." The main emphasis here is that those are "just words." Don't let the "diagnosis of cancer" or the "diagnosis of clinical depression" become who you are.

What you need to do is to grab a word that defines you. If grit is your word, then become one with unyielding courage in the face of hardship or danger." Become that word. Live that word. Embody that word.

Don't let the cancer - or whatever diagnosis or word/s - stop you from leading your best possible life. I can guarantee you that the road you are traveling with cancer will definitely not be easy.

If you focus on positive thoughts and don't let the "negative thoughts" clutter your mind, you are on the road to a more successful journey with cancer. For any bump in the road that you experience, just let your positive thoughts keep you on a successful journey. There is nothing that can stop you.

So what word are you going to choose for yourself?

I suggest writing down at least a dozen words and see which word you feel connected to, or reaches out to you. Ask a dozen friends what word they choose for you.

I showed this by example in this book. I asked the primary story tellers to tell me what word I was to them. Then they choose their own word for themselves. It is very possible that a word that someone gives us today or themselves changes over time as we change and grow.

Choose your word and stick it on your refrigerator so you see it several times a day. Or write it on your training wall calendar to remind yourself that you are not just "cancer" or "depression or "HIV/AIDS," as you are so much more.

You are more than *just* a survivor. You are going to live your life to the best of your ability and enjoy your life no matter what is thrown at you.

Just like the ex-governor of Minnesota, Jesse Ventura, stated in the movie "Predator" that "I ain't got time to bleed." Let's move on from the diagnosis, that has negative connotations and become so much more. There are plenty of positive words in this book, or simply choose your own.

Become perseverance and not cancer. Become determined and not depressed. So many words to choose from. Use your brain power and your mind in your battles in life. Let me know what word you chose for yourself when I see you next.

On every run you do for training for the marathon (race) repeat to yourself "I'm a finisher." I strongly encourage you to take on the word "finisher" when you start your first marathon or race. Every mile on the marathon course when you see each mile marker say to yourself "I'm a finisher." The more you say it to yourself, the more you become that word "finisher" and the more that you will honestly believe you will be a "finisher."

Using the power of your brain and mind will definitely reap your rewards. You will then be forever known as a "*marathon finisher*" once you cross that finish line.

Maybe you might even feel like dancing when you cross that finish line, especially when that medal goes around your neck.

Julia Khvasechko LMT
NYC
Julia's word for herself: Grit

How did you overcome your medical situation to be become a runner?

In my 20's I started to have serious health issues with symptoms that couldn't be explained with predominately just being tired. In those days, I was working 60 hours a week in finance and going to school at the same time; and if that wasn't enough, my hobby was going to dance clubs with friends and dancing all night long several times a week. It was the 1990's and life in Manhattan presented plenty of opportunities; and as most young people do, I mistakenly believed that sleep was unnecessary for my body.

Looking back in hindsight, I had no idea where I found the energy to do it all, but I did have a ton of energy as I lived in the city that never sleeps. I was seriously burning the candle on both ends for a long time until one day, I had a grand mal seizure while at work. There was no denying that something was seriously amiss.

After visiting with many specialists, it was determined, that I had a brain tumor in my right temporal lobe. Going to grad school, working crazy long hours, partying in dance clubs on my free time, I was truly living a hectic lifestyle, and something had to give. My body's symptoms became too much to ignore, and I started seeking answers instead of anesthetizing my symptoms and explaining them away with not having enough sleep.

I had to change my life. The more research I did in the library about how a healthy young adult in her 20â€™s could develop a brain tumor, the more convinced I became that I needed to change my life with diet. I gave up anything that could possibly hurt me, anything that led me to have inflammation in my body, and that included animal products, sugar, alcohol, and all processed and highly refined foods. Then I added meditation along with visual imagery, acupuncture, and saunas. I left my stressful job on the trading desk and took a year off of school to focus solely on healing. Instead of dance clubs, I started going to kirtan and chanting. Instead of being a news junky constantly being stressed by my Bloomberg terminal, I stated practicing yoga and meditating regularly. I replaced my White Russians with green juice filled with wheat grass and barley grass and chlorella and moringa and made sure I got 10 plants a day into a smoothie in the mornings. While it didn't happen overnight, I worked on it diligently, giving 100% attention to my daily choices. The more I turned my life around, the more I used food as medicine, the more urgency I developed and took control of my health, the better I started to feel.

What made you decide to run your first marathon?

I was at MSKCC (Memorial Sloan Kettering Cancer Center) when I witnessed my first NYCM (New York City Marathon) . It was after my 2nd brain surgery, as I was there regularly for treatment. On a crisp day in November, there was a commotion on 1st Ave. I wheeled myself over to the window, like everyone else I stared transfixed at the people running outside. I watched the parade of runners for hours. I didn't know how long a marathon was, but I knew that everyone looked so happy and so healthy. I first thought we were watching a shooting of a movie taking place, since NYC is a sight for many movies. I remember thinking how lucky those people were to be able to be strong enough to run. I watched people of all walks of life, some were fit and young and looked like they were running effortlessly while others were older and out of shape and appeared to be struggling but they still were out there, still pushing their bodies along; some looked happy and some looked rather fatigued, but they were moving forward, and I was inspired by their resilience. I remember that a certain group of people got more applause than anyone else. I asked someone next to me who they were, ˝are they famous,' I thought to myself in my naivety. I learned later that they were running to raise funds for MSKCC, they were "Fred's Team" participants, and they were running for us. I was deeply touched to find out that people were raising money for my hospital and I thought that was so beautiful that I made a deal with God that day. If I ever got strong enough to leave my wheelchair, if God gave me a second chance at my health, I was going to run the marathon for Fred's team and give back to this very special place that I've called home for so long.

In my 20's I never thought about doing anything for anyone else before. This was my opportunity to give back, to change my life from being self-absorbed to being altruistic. This was the golden carrot I needed to start focusing more on regaining my strength. Little by little I learned to stand, I learned to walk, and I walked for a couple of years, and eventually, I learned to run.

My first race was a 5K that raised money for the National Brain Tumor Society, and I trained for that race for months. It gave me so much purpose. I loved raising awareness by talking to people about what I was doing but what I really loved was the training. I started with a one minute of walking; one minute run method. I hoped that I could get strong enough to run the entire 5K when race day rolled around. I trained for that one race as if it was the Olympics, and to me, it was. I gave it my all, as a survivor, I felt I needed to represent and show that I was able to run the entire distance.

When race day came around and the survivors lined up in our yellow shirts, I prayed that I could make it the whole way without stopping. That is the proudest I've ever been of myself, crossing that finish line, exhausted but exhilarated and I knew I was ready for more. It was after that race that I got the confidence I needed to sign up for my first marathon. I had no idea then that running a marathon would change the outcome of my entire life, I just knew I had to fulfill the promise I made to God at MSKCC.

What about the challenges of being a pacer?

After running marathons for 6 years regularly and completing 32 marathons, I decided to accept the challenge of being a Pacer. My best marathons were running with pacers, and I admired their ability to stay consistent. I used pacers at my best marathons to keep myself consistent until the last 5K, and then I decided to push it and took off like a bat out of hell to finish my best marathons in Chicago, NYC, and WDW (Walt Disney World) . I already knew I could go the distance, but I wanted to see if I could stay consistent throughout. In December 2011, I paced the 4:15 group at the LVM (Las Vegas Marathon) and Pacer Julia was born. I paced my next marathon two months later at the Cowtown Marathon in Texas and later that year, I started pacing half marathons for the NYRR and in the fall, I was honored with the opportunity to pace the famed NYCM. I was overjoyed to be able to give back to the race that started it all for me. I love pacing for so many reasons. Running for something bigger than yourself is giving back to the sport that has given me so much. It is tremendously satisfying, so much more meaningful and truly inspiring than to run by and for myself. Not to mention that when you are motivating and encouraging others to not give up and focusing on everyone around you, you find strength you didn't know you possessed. When that pacing stick is in your hands, you feel the magic, you find that fortitude that you normally have to dig deep for, in the darker miles, you seem to find it with a lot less effort. You seem to attain the grace and the raw energy you need to keep going. I feel both excited and honored when I'm pacing and when I'm helping someone achieve a PR or a BQ, I can honestly say that it's much more of a blessing to give than to receive. I get to feel those first-time finish line highs on a regular basis. I get to witness the ugly tears when you see the finish line, I get to feel those sweaty hugs after I help to make dreams come true. I am a natural cheerleader and I love to keep my pacer group runners motivated. I love to find out why they started running and when they need a boost, I tell them about my own story. I remind them that they are stronger than they think they are, and I assure them that we can do it together. Mile by mile I encourage others to not give up on themselves but to give it all they've got. When you find something that you love, you want to do it all the time. Suddenly it becomes habit and the habit becomes quite manageable and the seemingly impossible becomes merely challenging, the laborious becomes purposeful resistance; the once difficult loses its edge and is made beautiful by your progress. I am blessed to have found my passion and today I pace much more than I race. I love to share my passion with others. I get so much more out of pacing, than just racing for myself.

Since I tend to pace on the slower end, I usually have mostly women in my group, and I love giving them tips to better their running form. As a running coach, a yoga teacher, and a licensed massage therapist, I discuss their bodies and their ailments with them as we run. I usually get asked the same questions and I love sharing how I myself can run so many marathons year, year after year. I am 100% convinced that it's Whole Food Plant Based, anti-inflammatory diet which allows me to recover faster.

What is the roadblock that you personally overcame to accomplish your goal and what you ultimately learned from this experience?

My first marathon required the courage to start, as John Brigham said, "˜the miracle isn't that I finished, the miracle is that I had the courage to start." Once I knew I could finish the marathon, like everyone else who's ever run a marathon, I wanted to see if I can run one faster. This went on for four years where I kept brining my time down with each race. I set my marathon PR in 2009 and once I realized I wasn't going to get any faster, I needed a new goal to chase. My new goal was to run a marathon in all 50 states; it was an audacious goal for someone who worked full time and went to school at night but also exactly what I needed. I enjoyed going to new cities and making new friends for a few years. I was meeting amazing people along the way, and sharing the journey with like-minded friends, including some of my best friends today and my husband.

Once that goal was achieved in 2014, I set my sights on running an ultra-marathon in every state, and that led to me running my first 100 miler. The 100 miler that I chose for myself eluded me for many years, but I didn't let it stop me. What I learned from all my running goals is that there will always be roadblocks to anything worth achieving. But if we want it bad enough, if we are willing to put in the work, if we are willing to learn from our mistakes, then they can become your greatest teachers. Marathoning has taught me that there are no limits to what you can do. If you are willing to put in the hard training and the not so sexy work of running long distances on the weekends even when the temperature and weather is not ideal, then you can make your dreams and goals come true.

There are no short cuts to anyplace worth going and the more challenging something is, the sweeter the reward when you actually attain it. I learned to use the word impossible with caution; I learned that roadblocks are just steppingstones and I learned to see both victories and DNF's as lessons. I DNF'd a 100 miler called the 'Beast of Burden' 3X, the Beast of Burden is 100 miles in Lockport NY. But I also learned "not to take No for an answer." I kept coming back because I left a part of my soul on that course, and I had to go back to claim it. I kept fighting for what I wanted, I knew that if I kept trying, eventually victory would be mine. Running has taught me that no doesn't actually mean NO, it means not right now. No teaches me how badly I really want something. No might keep others out, those who don't really want it bad enough, but not those who are willing to work harder for it. I learned that when we really want something, the universe meets us halfway and helps us achieve it.

On the 4th time I lined up at the starting line of Beast of Burden, the weather was 20 degrees cooler than the previous years and that was exactly what I needed. Ultimately, I learned that I am much stronger than I ever thought I was, and I learned to believe in myself and the power of my dreams. I will never be able to articulate how much finishing that race meant to me. I can keep paying it forward and helping others achieve their own finish lines as I line up at each starting line as Pacer Julia and invite others to come along this beautiful journey of self-discovery with me and remind them that they are stronger than they will ever know.

I am not exactly sure when I met Tom first but I know it was somewhere between September of 2011 and September of 2012, and that year I ran 37 marathons! I was going for something that belong in the Marathon Maniacs call Titanium, which required running 30 marathons in 30 states in 365 days as one way of obtaining that status. I was traveling almost every weekend for either a marathon or a yoga retreat (continuing education and teacher training seminars) . It was such a crazy year. At one of those marathon states, (I was working on my first round of the 50 states) I met Pacer Tom. I recall him telling me he was doing his second round of the 50 states, and I was so impressed. I didn't think anyone would do more than one round in those days because it was so expensive, but now I'm working on my 4th round! I started seeing him all the time at events all over the country and we became friends. That year was very challenging for me since my boyfriend at the time, Shane (now my husband) was deployed in Afghanistan and I was beside myself with worry, so I wanted to keep busy, running races with friends or learning was my way of avoiding sitting home and crying.

Chapter 23: Ready or Not Boston Here I Come

Song: "Rock & Roll Band"

Artist: Boston

Quote: "Runner's logic: I'm tired. Let me go for a run." - Unknown

Amie's word for me: Relentless

The question of "Have you run Boston Marathon?" is without a doubt one of the most frequent questions I have been asked since I completed my first marathon at Twin Cities Marathon in 1993. The only other question that competes with that question is "What is your favorite marathon?"

Even when I was running my first marathon, I clearly remember people asking me about "What was your Boston Marathon experience like?" I am like "I have no clue as I haven't yet even finished my first marathon!"

I wouldn't have a clue what running Boston Marathon would be like for nearly thirty years *after* my first marathon. It is hard to believe but I wouldn't complete the Boston marathon until my 642nd marathon/ultra. I would run at least 16,800 miles at different marathons and ultras before I would even have a clue what running the Boston Marathon was like. There are probably a lot of Boston Marathon runners that have finished the Boston Marathon that have never ran nearly 17,000 miles in their lifetime.

I guess the assumption in my early days of running marathons is that if you are considered a faster runner and that you run marathons, that probably logically you have simply completed Boston. Or at the very least you have a BQ - which translates to one having a "Boston Qualifying" time so you could have done or could do Boston had you chosen to.

Sorry to be a spoiler here but Boston was never a "must do race before I die type marathon when I started running marathons. I really didn't care whether I completed the Boston marathon or not. It just wasn't a major running goal of mine in the 1990's when I started running marathons.

I am not sure how many times I have been to the greater Boston area but at least thirty times is probably accurate. I visited Boston to go to Fenway ballpark and was fortunate when I was attending a Boston Red Sox game to see the legendary writer Stephen King in attendance watching the game. Oh, and I won't even go into the pain of seeing David Ortiz being in a Red Sox uniform being a Minnesota Twins fan to see what he had accomplished. Remember the year 2013? "Big Papi" congratulations on your World Series Most Valuable Player award! I went and walked the Freedom Trail which to me is a must do bucket list item if you are in the Boston area. I have had multiple beers and clam chowder at The Warren Tavern which definitely is one of the most historic taverns in America as it is the oldest tavern in Massachusetts. It is fascinating to me that I was sitting at a bar and having a Samuel Adams 26.2 beer, which was visited by many famous individuals including George Washington and Paul Revere.

The Union Oyster House is the oldest restaurant in Boston and the oldest restaurant in continuous service in the United States as the doors have always been open to diners since 1826, and it is located on the Freedom Trail. You might have heard of a famous family with the last name of Kennedy that visited the Union Oyster House for years. Apparently, John Fitzgerald Kennedy, AKA J.F.K. loved to feast in privacy of the upstairs dining room. If you go, I suggest you try and ask to sit at his favorite booth which is aptly named "The Kennedy Booth" which was dedicated in his memory. If lobster stew is on the menu, then you can eat one of his favorite meals.

Then after eating a meal there, I strongly suggest dessert with a visit to Mike's Pastry shop for a different kind of lobster roll or a cannolo. We run, and then we eat and drink. Life is good.

For me the way to get too many of my east coast marathons was to fly into Boston Logan Airport as it is a major airport and has ample car rental options. Plus, all the major airlines fly there so one can compare multiple flight options.

Years would go by and slowly the mystique of the Boston Marathon would take hold of me. Remember I said slowly, as it wasn't until I did my first Abbott Major Marathon - the Chicago Marathon on Sunday, October 13th, 2013 - that the Boston Marathon would even start to slowly interest me. Had the pace coordinator, Paul Miller, not graciously accepted me onto the Chicago pace team I might never have started this journey to the Boston Marathon. So, thank you Paul for helping me to start on accomplishing this Six Star goal.

The reason I didn't start with the Boston Marathon in the Majors was because for the Abbott Major Marathon finish, the Boston Marathon was to be my Sixth Star finish marathon. My real motivation for when and why I would only do Boston Marathon was when I had finished all the other Major marathons. If I finished all of the five other major marathons - Berlin, Chicago, London, New York City, and Tokyo, - then I could do Boston. If the other five Major Marathons were not finished then no Boston Marathon. Pretty simple, right?

So basically, the Boston Marathon would become my Sixth Star Finish. This wasn't going to be an issue to get a Boston Qualifying time as I was still running 5k's in the very low twenties and my mile time was around a 6:25 minute mile with no speed work training.

I really didn't do any type of speed workouts and I have never had a coach. I was luckily born on the thinner side on the weight scale with relatively fast feet and a decent running form, so running 22-minute 5k's was still rather effortless once I turned 55 years old.

My first Chicago Marathon was completed in 2013 pacing the 5:25 group and finishing in 5:24:18, and then New York City Marathon was completed in 2016 pacing the 4:35 group in 4:34:43.

So, two major marathons completed and now four to go, when I was invited in January of 2019 to pace the prestigious London Marathon.

So off to London marathon I might go. Yes, I said that correctly off to London Marathon I *MIGHT* go.

When the invite came to pace the London Marathon, it was shortly after I was likely to be positively confirmed with a specific stage diagnosis of prostate cancer. I was waiting on some more scans and tests to positively give me a definitive prostate cancer diagnosis. It then was confirmed that I definitely had Stage 3 prostate cancer.

I would forever be identified as a "cancer" person moving forward. The word "cancer" would become a word that would forever be a part of me. The major question was whether I would be a cancer survivor and for how long.

The question enters my mind, "Do I agree to pace the 5:30 pace group at the London Marathon?"

Or do I state, "Sorry mates I can't Pace the London marathon as I am dealing with prostate cancer. I unfortunately won't be joining you to have a London Pride beer to celebrate with you after the London Marathon."

I have stated numerous times that cancer I know will and would tell me what I could not do today and, in my future, but it certainly wouldn't tell me what I could still do and would definitely do.

So obviously I accepted and agreed to the challenge of pacing the 5:30 pace group.

At this time in January of 2019, I had no idea what kind of impact the cancer diagnosis would have on me. Would my ability to simply run suffer? Could I even run at all? I had no idea.

All I knew was that I was going to be pacing the 5:30 group at the London Marathon on Sunday, April 28th, 2019. I didn't even honestly know if I would be even able to walk that pace if needed, yet alone *run* that pace.

So, I started planning my overseas adventure. Traveling to the United Kingdom required a mandatory passport, as that was one item I would not have to worry about as I was Passport ready.

So here I am planning this trip to London and going to multiple medical appointments. Spending countless hours on the phone making medical appointments and getting second opinions. Sometimes even a third opinion. Talking to my insurance company took up a significant amount of time.

I feel very fortunate looking back on this experience as this was about exactly a year before the COVID Pandemic would change almost everyone's life.

I wasn't going to let a cancer diagnosis deter my goal. All along the process I was making sure to keep my medical appointments and schedule future appointments. Nothing would be scheduled regarding all my medical appointments during my short trip to London of six days and five nights.

I planned the London Marathon trip by myself as I didn't want anyone going with me. I knew this trip would be an emotional rollercoaster ride for me. In hindsight I regret not going with a running friend or friend on the trip to keep me company. At the time I really didn't understand how hard it is for runners to get into the London Marathon. Thus, a major reason why none of my running friends were doing it in 2019. If you're from the United States getting into London Marathon is probably the hardest of the six major marathons to simply get into.

The one thing that I hadn't really planned on was that right before I was to leave for the London Marathon, I was basically being asked about what treatment option route I wanted to take for my battle with my prostate cancer.

So, my treatment team consisted of my General Practitioner, a Urologist, a Radiation Oncologist, a Physician Assistant, a Nutritionist, etc., This would be a team decision, however with me having the final say with what my eventual treatment would be.

I was still going to London and thinking and worrying about my treatment options would happen regardless of whether I was in Minnesota or the United Kingdom. I could debate about the effectiveness of having a radical prostatectomy - which is the main type of surgery for prostate cancer - in a pub in England drinking a London Pride beer as easily as I could be at my favorite bar Malone's in my home city of Maple Grove, Minnesota, and drinking the monthly featured beer.

One *important* part of this that I didn't realize was that in the pubs in England I would be sitting by myself watching football which ironically to me looked a lot like a sport I called soccer. I certainly couldn't enter into an intelligent conversation with my new pub mate about which team I thought was better Liverpool or Everton. Or about mistakenly thinking I could discuss which team was better between Manchester City and the Manchester United. So had I been sitting having a beer at Malone's, I likely would have had friends or Malone's staff to me company. We likely would have been talking about the Minnesota Wild being in search of a Stanley Cup or the Minnesota Twins chances of making the playoffs. Likely I would have seen AJ, Jess, or Junior, to name just a few of the staff there.

I also had to find out specifically if anything special was needed for my trip. As mentioned, this was my first time overseas, and my first big trip with a cancer diagnosis. Would anything be different? I certainly was clueless as to what I needed to potentially be bringing with me.

Eventually nothing was different for my adventure and trip. I wasn't leaving with any medication and no surgery had yet been scheduled to worry about. I would be leaving the United States to go to London with Stage 3 prostate cancer and I would be returning to the United States six days later with Stage 3 prostate cancer.

Then I found I had a co-pacer as well for the London marathon for the 5:30pace group. Would this make my pacing and running the London Marathon more stressful or not? Luckily for me I was fortunate to have a marvelous co-pacer, Francesco. We paced the 5:30 group and finished in 5:29:15 so we successfully succeeded in hitting our marathon pace goal.

So, Chicago Marathon, New York Marathon, and London marathon are completed. I still needed Berlin and Tokyo marathon before Boston.

I hadn't looked at doing the Berlin Marathon in 2019, so I was hoping for 2020 to do the Berlin Marathon. Hoping was all I could have realistically done because the COVID Pandemic wiped out any chance of me doing the Berlin Marathon in 2020.

No Boston Marathon would be happening for me in 2021 as I still needed the Berlin and Tokyo Marathon. I would not be getting my Six Star finish before I turned 60 years old, which iron was my original plan to get my Sixth Star after I turned 60. The bigger question now was could I get the Boston Marathon in before my Stage 4 prostate cancer stopped my running?

So patiently I had to wait until the COVID Pandemic slowed down and then I finally did the Berlin marathon on Sunday, September 25th, 2022, finishing in 4:30:36. I can always say that I was at the Berlin Marathon when Eliud Kipchoge, then set the men's marathon World Record in 2:01:09. I seriously hope Eliud Kipchoge didn't look back for me thinking I might catch him, because he was finished well before I even probably crossed the 10k timing mat.

So then that meant Tokyo was up next, so to make this as simple as possible and to hopefully guarantee my admittance to the Tokyo marathon I applied to the charity Gold Ribbon Network. Gold Ribbon Network (GRN) is a non-profit organization dedicated to supporting children with cancer and their families. In Japan, approximately 2,000 children are diagnosed with cancer every year, so I thought this was a perfect charity for me. My application was accepted and so off to run Tokyo marathon. I simply paid the donation amount and I was then able to register for the Tokyo Marathon.

The Tokyo Marathon in my opinion is the most complex and trickiest of the Six Star marathons from application to getting officially to the starting line to getting back to your accommodations after you finish. Part of the issue was that Tokyo was still surprisingly dealing with issues related to the COVID Pandemic in 2023.

Tokyo was one of my best marathons of the six majors with just meeting and connecting with other runners. Highlights of the trip included meeting Juan Castillo for the first time. Also seeing many 50sub4 state marathoners including Gwen Jacobson and Kasey Kuker. It seemed wherever I went in Tokyo I would somehow literally run into Gwen. Also, Carrie and Paul Miller, were staying at the Hilton Hotel where we stayed at in Tokyo as they were finishing their Six Star journey. If you do see Paul Miller, I strongly encourage you to ask him," So how did your Cribbage game go with Amie when you were in Tokyo?" Inquiring minds want to know.

On Sunday, March 5th, 2023, I finished the Tokyo Marathon in 5:14:04. So, my fifth major marathon was successfully completed.

One finisher highlight from the 2023 Tokyo Marathon was that a new Guinness World Record was set for the most people to earn a Six Star medal at a single marathon. Apparently some 3,033 runners completed the race to earn their Six Star Medal, smashing the previous highest total set in Tokyo in 2019 of 732 and establishing the first official world record for the Six Star program. Incredibly among them, 40 runners were completing the journey for a second time; five for a third time, and one runner was going round the series for an incredible fourth time.

One aspect that I did not like about the race day experience with the Tokyo marathon was the bathroom situation. Note that when you have cancer - especially with Stage 4 prostate cancer and after all the drugs and treatments - your bowel and bladder simply do not function properly. I need to know before the race starts what the bathroom situation is going to be like on the course. The Tokyo marathon was challenging due to not only the long bathroom lines, but the location of where the bathrooms are can be challenging. Just note that a bathroom visit can *easily* add fifteen minutes to your marathon time. This is especially important as Tokyo marathon has a tight cutoff to finish the marathon. You must be ahead of the cutoff time at certain spots along the course in order to successfully complete the marathon. Just be careful with your bathroom visits and bathroom visit time if you are concerned about officially finishing the Tokyo marathon.

So finally, Boston marathon becomes my Six Star finish. Sadly, for me Stage 4 prostate cancer wasn't letting me unfortunately get my Boston Qualifying time. My best chance for a BQ time was at Grandma's marathon in 2021 as there would be no pacers so I wouldn't be pacing this marathon. So, I had this marathon open to simply just run. On my 27th Grandma's Marathon on Saturday, June 19th, 2021, I finished in 4:09:58. I was under 2 hours at the 1/2 marathon timing mat, but fatigue just would not let me run any faster after mile 17. Mile by mile I was simply getting slower and slower and there was absolutely nothing I could do about it. If you think I was disappointed I didn't BQ that day that would be a "yes." But the disappointment fades quickly as I was incredibly happy that I could still even run *remotely* close to a sub-4-hour marathon after all I have been through since being diagnosed with cancer.

So, with no BQ, I reached out to Boston if any exception could be given to me due to having finished over 600 marathons, a 6th time 50 state certified marathon finisher, and a 50sub4 State certified marathon finisher. Even with those numbers and statistics no exception was given.

My only option was to enter Boston by a charity. I had reached out to several charities, and finally the American Red Cross had an open spot. I quickly took the open spot and my fundraising goal was $10,000. I did go over my goal as I hit $10,400. Thank you to everyone that contributed by donating to help me reach my goal of $10,000. I know a lot of people donated anonymously, so I wasn't able to personally thank them. I just want to clearly make sure everyone that donated knows how much I appreciated the donation. Especially if you are by chance reading this book that is an added bonus, so thank you!

When I began my running journey it was really the mystique of the small-town races that would attract my interest. It was the local 5k that all the locals would run, or walk, that I enjoyed running the most. It was partly how I accomplished my 549 career overall wins and/or age group awards in a wide variety of races. I still love running the 5K distance and still frequently run 5ks to this day. My marathon total completed - or any other running race distance - will never exceed my 5k races completed.

So, the Saturday before the Boston Marathon I completed the inaugural Article Fifteen Brewing Veterans 5k Beer Run held in Rockland, Massachusetts on Saturday, April 15th, 2023. This race was created by Veterans in the hopes to raise money for the Rockland Veterans, however I never heard how much money was raised. One part of running in these small-town races that I absolutely love is that it is usually a "benefit" for someone or some group. The second part I like is that some small towns are struggling to keep in existence and I feel by visiting them I am contributing to their very survival by spending money in these towns. That can be from simply buying a beer at a bar or local brewery, to eating at a restaurant, or buying gas at the local gas station.

The field for this race was rather small and I don't know if they ever reached the 75 participants for the limited t-shirt. I ran 23:25 finishing first in the 60 to 69 Age Group. Not bad for a 61-year-old male with a Stage 4 cancer diagnosis.

The Boston Marathon date was Monday, April 17, 2023. The day was a little chilly with a steady rain while waiting for the race to start. There was intermittent rain at times throughout the marathon. I had run part of the marathon course on my many visits to Boston, but this time I was an actual registered runner running during the actual marathon.

Regarding the Boston Marathon it should be noted that almost all the Boston Marathon course is not actually in the city of Boston. In fact, you could probably call it "Boston under three miles" as it isn't until the final 5k that you are even in Boston.

The three highlights on the course for me was hearing it get louder and louder as you approach mile 12 as you get closer to Wellesley College and go through the Scream Tunnel. There I suggest you stay to the right if you want high fives, pictures, hugs or kisses, and tons of positive words shouted at you. Also, try to read some of the posters and signs as they will definitely make you smile. This is definitely was the funniest part of the course for me.

The second part of the course that I loved was the infamous Newton Hills, which is a series of climbs that ends with the notorious Heartbreak Hill.

Then obviously the best part on the marathon course is when you take a left on Boylston, for the final 600 meters of the course. You are approaching a spectacular finish as you will soon be finishing one of most prestigious marathons in the world. I was trying to take it all in, as I finished in 4:58:23. My Six Star finish was complete.

I finished the Boston Marathon successfully and I obtained my Sixth Star.

I still haven't totally given up hope for getting a Boston Qualifying time. In fact, I probably set my own World Record having the most marathons ever completed before successfully getting into the Boston Marathon without a qualifying BQ time as I finished my 642nd marathon/ultra that day.

Currently if I was 65 years old, I would need a 4:05 or faster marathon time to BQ, so that might well be a feasible goal when I turn 65. That would also make it nearly 7 years since my Stage 4 cancer diagnosis. I suggest you don't even think about betting against me either on making it 7 years with my Stage 4 cancer diagnosis or eventually obtaining my BQ time.

In 2023 the Boston Marathon would record its highest ever total of Six Star Finishers with over 700 Six Star finishers. The previous high in Boston was 582 in 2019, the same year the Six Star Hall of Fame passed 5,000 finishers. The grand total now stands at well over 11,000 Six Star Finishers.

My current plan is to raise my $10,000 again for the American Red Cross so I can run the Boston Marathon again in 2024 as a charity runner. Since I cannot qualify for Boston at this time the American Red Cross will be having me raise hopefully over $20,000 for them since I began my Boston Marathon journey. I am glad that an obstacle that I have helps to make better another situation better. So, congratulations to the American Red Cross for benefiting from me not being able to BQ. This helped turn a negative into a positive.

It was at the Berlin marathon expo on Friday, September 22nd, 2023, where I finally saw my name displayed on the runner Wall of Fame Six Star Finishers. I needed 4 Major marathons to complete this goal while dealing with my Stage 4 cancer issues and I successfully completed all four.

It wasn't an easy goal but it was well worth it. Neither my initial cancer diagnosis, nor my Stage 4 cancer diagnosis, nor the COVID Pandemic could keep me from my goal. Another goal accomplished by not letting any obstacles get in my way.

There is a rumor that a Seventh Abbott Major Marathon will be added soon with it likely being the Sydney marathon. I guess I will possibly have to do that marathon in the future. On second thought, being it is a second thought, I guess I might eventually have to do the Sydney Marathon twice. Go figure, as me doing something twice seems to be a common theme.

One significant part of my Six Star marathon experiences was me running with a lady that I met at the Med City Marathon on Sunday, September 12th, 2021, pacing the 5-hour group. She was running the 20-mile race to get in a long training run for her approaching Fargo marathon. Her goal was to try and run a sub 5 hour at Fargo Marathon as it would be her first marathon in 6 years.

I had no idea how that chance encounter would eventually change my life. Maybe that will be shared more in my book when I turn 70 years old when I talk about my "60 years of Running!"

Amie Benson
Splits her time between Conroe, TX, and St. Michael, MN
Amie's word for herself: Courageous

From 50-pound weight gain to Boston marathon & Six Star finisher!

If I had to think back to the first time I had ever heard of or paid attention to the Boston marathon, it was probably 2008. That is the year I ran my first marathon and was participating in various running events. I remember seeing and running with people wearing that iconic blue and yellow jacket with a unicorn embroidered on it and thought someday, that will be me.

It all started in spring of 2007, when Weight Watchers (WW) was offered at my workplace. I was overweight since having my second child in late 2005. I joined and would weigh in once a week and attend a meeting. After successfully reaching my weight loss goal in the fall of 2007, I thought I was done. Not the case. The WW instructor asked me know what will you do? I thought what do you mean, I have to do more? She meant what will you do to stay active and maintain your weight loss? I was sedentary and had no activities per say. As I pondered this question, my friends at work encouraged me to run with them. I thought I hated running. I would only run if I was late or if someone was chasing me. I had coincidentally run my first 5k in Becker, MN with my sister in the summer of 2007. It took me over forty minutes and was very challenging. A few runs later and a few months later, I signed up for Grandmas marathon to take place in June of 2008. I paced myself to finish in 5:57:32, just under the 6-hour cut-off required to get my medal and my finisher shirt. I did it! The next six years I did many runs coming within 10 minutes of qualifying for Boston. Boston was always in the back of my mind, and I knew my qualifying time but it didn't happen. I shifted focus and did my first Ironman in Madison, WI in

215

September, 2014.

At some point in my busy life, my running faded, along with any thoughts of Boston, and other priorities took over. Fast forward to December, 2019. The day after Christmas, miserable with how I felt physically and emotionally, I knew I had to do something. I drove to my local WW to weigh in. I had gained almost 50 pounds in five years! The WW person wrote my weight on the card and that was my calling card to get moving and make changes my lifestyle. I made some progress losing weight and then COVID hit and my weekly in-person weigh-ins for WW stopped. The in-person weigh in was a big motivator for me. I was upset these would no longer happen and there was no date set to resume. I was on my own. I bought a scale and started using it in January of 2021.

That year, my older son asked if I wanted to join him for the Fargo marathon taking place in Sept, 2021. It was his first marathon. I agreed! I was excited and thought it would help me to focus getting back into running and lose a few extra pounds in the process. I ran Fargo on Sept 25, 2021, in 5:02:35.

My 20-mile training run leading up to Fargo was at the Med City Marathon held on September 12, 2021. This race had always held 20-mile training runs and the timing was perfect for Fargo marathon being 3 weeks out. I convinced my son to do it with me. I lined up at the start and ran with the 5:00 hour pacer and finished my 20 miles on pace.

During this run, I mentioned to the pacer that I wanted to qualify for and run the Boston marathon. It was my goal. Since I was turning 50 in 2022, my qualifying time would drop five minutes to 3:55:00 to run Boston on April 17, 2023. Qualifying time goes by age on the day of the race. The pacer responded to me that a ten-year goal for qualifying for Boston would be realistic. I knew in my head I wasn't going to wait ten years and I thought this guy doesn't know what he's talking about. What he said made me a little angry and more motivated to meet my goal. I'm not a patient person and I certainly wasn't going to wait ten years to run at Boston! I was determined.

I knew I had my work cut out for me to go from a 5:02 marathon to 3:55. And 3:55 was just to qualify. Boston has a cut-off time each year and it had recently ranged from 0 to 7:00+ minutes. I wanted to give myself a 5-minute cushion, really needing to run closer to 3:50. Was I really going to be able to shave 1:10:00+ off my marathon time? I needed a training plan, and a fast race. I would self-coach and follow the Run Less Run Faster plan by Bill Pierce, Scott Murr, and Ray Moss. It was a book I had on my shelf and 3 days of running with 2 days of cross-training each week sounded reasonable to me. Now, for the fast race. I scoured the internet for best BQ marathons. I considered CIM (California International Marathon) , but the date didn't work. Then I saw the Mesa/Phoenix marathon. I love the Phoenix area and thought I would really enjoy the race. I had just over 14 weeks to train.

It was the winter of 2021/2022 in Minnesota. It was miserable…freezing temperatures, snow, ice, you name it. When it came to my running, I had four choices: Run on the treadmill in my basement, run somewhere else indoors, run outdoors in Minnesota, or go somewhere warm to run outdoors. I did all of these over the next 14 weeks. I came to love my treadmill, which I previously dreaded. I especially liked it for short, fast runs, although I ran twenty miles on it more than once. I found a few places to run indoors in the winter in the Minneapolis/Twin cities area, but I didn't really enjoy the experience of running in circles on concrete or on turf. I tried running outdoors and it didn't go well as I had a hard time with ice and slippery surfaces but also with the cold in general. My favorite was traveling to a warm climate to get in a long training run. I got four of my key longer runs in by traveling to Nevada, Florida, and California. I timed the getaway to runs I needed at specific points in my training in December and January.

My final 20-mile training run was on the Santa Monica strand on January 23rd. It was a few minutes from my brother's place in Culver City and a perfect excuse to visit him. It was fantastic weather and a fun, low-key "half-marathon" that I extended to 20 miles. The best part of the race was the race organizers were waiting for me at the finish with TWO medals and a box of bananas and waters. They told me I won the half marathon for women and they gave me the left-over goodies! I hit my pace for the 20-mile run, felt great, and was pumped! The days leading up to the run weren't great. I had a hip bursitis that had been bothering me and knew it would take everything to finish, let alone, at my marathon-pace of 8:46/mile. I had given myself some rest but not too much as the race date was approaching. Somehow, the pain in my hip magically disappeared. Perhaps I had rested just enough.

I toed the line at the start of the 10th anniversary Mesa marathon that Saturday morning behind the 3:55 pacer. I didn't want to push my luck with starting any faster. We were off at 6:30 AM. I ran with the pacer the first 20 miles. Nobody was left with the pacer at that 20-mile point but me. We were ahead of pace. I felt good. I decided I was going to pick up my pace and leave the pacer, hoping she wouldn't end up passing me later. Around mile 25 I saw my younger son (he came with me to Mesa) on a scooter on the side of the marathon course. I yelled to him to meet me at the finish! He said I was running fast. I ran my last mile in 7:40. I finished in 3:50:07. I felt great, no cramping, and no issues whatsoever. I even hiked the hole in the wall rock trail later that day with my son. I did it, I qualified for Boston! Now, to get in.

After I returned home and registered for Boston, somebody mentioned NYC marathon. I knew New York was a stricter qualifying time than Boston, so I thought there was no way I'd get into NYC marathon. I googled NYC marathon and read the qualifying time for my age on the day of the race and it was 3:51:00. Unbelievably, I qualified for NYC too (by mere seconds) . Of course I applied.

I was accepted into the Boston marathon for 2023 with a "zero" cut-off time and I was accepted into the NYC marathon. 2022 and 2023 was an epic journey traveling to London, Berlin, New York City, Tokyo, and finishing with Boston to complete my final 5 of the 6 major world marathons. I am now the proud owner of a Boston jacket with the unicorn on it. A dream at one time, had become a reality.

So how did I do it? 100% focus. I looked at my training plan and followed it daily. My book was tattered with pages falling out by the end of my training. Some days I couldn't make the distance or the pace but I always tried, and commended myself if I could accomplish even 75% of a tough workout. I never "skipped" a workout or made an excuse that I had something else to do. That was also true with my cross-training which I did on my Peloton cycle 2x/week. Anyone can do it if you make it a priority. If I'm questioning my ability or confidence to set out to achieve a challenging goal, I look back at what I accomplished with my BQ goal and reflect on what I did. There is always a way. You just need to decide if something is your priority, and if it is, act on it. Happy running!

Trivia

Boston Marathon is held on the third Monday in April which is Patriot's Day. It's a state-observed holiday only in Maine and Massachusetts that commemorates early battles fought in the area during the Revolutionary War.

Also note Bobbi Gibb was the first woman to run the Boston Marathon incognito in 1966. She is recognized by the B.A.A. (Boston Athletic Association) as the pre-sanctioned era women's winner in 1966, 1967, and 1968.

In 1967 Katherine Switzer, who registered for the race a KV Switzer was almost thrown of the course by the race director, Jock Semple, when he saw that she was a female. Her boyfriend blocked Semple from grabbing her and she was encouraged by the men to keep running. She finished but her time was not recorded.

In 1972 females were allowed to officially register and race. Nina Kuscsik was the first official female to win Boston. Marathon that year.

Chapter 24: My Marathon Journey: A Day to Remember

Song: "I Won't Back Down"

Artist: Tom Petty and The Heartbreakers

Quote: "Always believe in yourself and always stretch yourself beyond your limits. Your life is worth a lot more than you think because you are capable of accomplishing more than you know. You have more potential than you think, but you will never know your full potential unless you keep challenging yourself and pushing beyond your own self-imposed limits." - Roy T. Bennett

Yvonne's word for me: Compassionate

I remember running my first marathon in 1993 and several of my running friends told me flat out "if you walk during the marathon, you technically have not run a marathon."

I am sure that I am not the first person to suggest that progress is impossible without change. I truly believe that those that cannot adjust or change their minds are less likely to change anything. Change can be good and it can be beneficial when done for the right reasons.

My first experience with pacing using specifically the run and walk method was the Cincinnati Flying Pig marathon in 2023 on Sunday, May 7th, 2023. I was co-pacing the 6:30 pace group using the Galloway method using a 30 second run and a 30 second walk. We finished officially in 6:46:51 as we had lost time sheltering for coverage during the storm. It had been twenty years since I had first completed this marathon on Sunday, May 4th, 2003, in 4:18:21.

The marathon started in pouring rain and the rain continued to come. We were just getting started when we were informed to take shelter due to a storm delay. Some runners continued on past, but we sought shelter near a parking ramp. We waited about 15 minutes before we continued on the marathon course.

This was my first time officially using the "Galloway method" in pacing a marathon. I was surprised how easy the marathon went, obviously minus the pouring rain and weather condition.

It wasn't until a couple of days after the marathon that I noticed significantly less soreness in my legs. Pacing a marathon using the Galloway method for the runners and myself was a success.

When the cancer forced me to pace marathons and run marathons at times in the 6 hour plus range the run and walk method proved to be a useful method to accomplish the pace goal.

The biggest learning curve for me as a Pacer was motivating and running with runners that were doing different intervals for their run and walk pace. Some used 30 seconds- 30 seconds, yet others used 60 seconds - 30 seconds, and some others used 60 seconds - 60 seconds. There were other variations as well for times for the run and walk that runners were using.

What I was noticing in the runners that were using the run and walk method is that they definitely seemed to be enjoying their marathon experience more, regardless of whether it was their first marathon or 100th marathon. In fact, it seemed the more experienced marathoners were mainly using the run and walk method at the slower marathon running times of over a 6-hour marathon finish time.

Since my Stage 4 cancer diagnosis I am now dealing with significant fatigue issues, so I incorporate walking breaks into my runs. My legs are significantly less sore two days after I have finished a marathon regardless of whether I did one marathon on a weekend or two marathons during a weekend.

It has been since my Stage 4 cancer diagnosis that I have more readily seen the value of the run and walk method.

The two definite advantages to the run and walk method that I have seen and experienced are: 1) easier and faster recovery after a marathon/ultra; and, 2) less wear on the body means potentially less chance for an injury.

Change can be good and I can readily admit that the Galloway method can be used successfully for races. Also, I clearly know now that when one walks during a marathon, that it clearly does not mean that one "has not technically run a marathon if one walks during any part of the marathon."

One important part is that you are definitely listed in the same marathon finisher results regardless of whether you walk or run the marathon. Also, you do get the same finishers medal.

Tip:

When training for your first marathon, especially if your overall goal is to "just finish" I strongly suggest incorporating walking breaks into your training.

It was around 1973 when Olympic Marathoner Jeff Galloway started using walk breaks for marathon training. Jeff created what is now known as the Galloway method, which is basically instead of continuously running for a given distance, you alternate it with periods of walking.

I strongly encourage you to visit Jeff Galloway's website for further explanation and for further exploring his running and walking method.

Yvonne Leaf
Negaunee, Michigan
Yvonne's word for herself: Kind

My Marathon Journey: A day to remember

It was Saturday, September 2nd, 2023, and the "Marathon Day" was finally here! I was excited like a little girl anticipating Christmas. Awaking at 5 AM, I could hardly wait to get out of bed! I quickly dressed in my black running pants and hot pink tank top. My race number was 28. Going through my pre-planning race routine, sunscreen, cap stretches, breakfast, and coffee felt great. My excitement continues to build.

I was surprised to see my husband Bob, son Ryan, and daughter Rebekah (Bex for short) greet me with matching red shirts that said, "My legs hurt just waiting for you." We all had a good laugh! I loved their humor, and their unshakable support was heartwarming. From the beginning, Bob has supported my goal of training for a marathon and has been there for me each step of the way. I love this man and his team spirit. Before leaving the house, he prayed for all the runners in the marathon and their safety during the day.

In Ishpeming, I was greeted with the energy of music and the sight of other excited racers. I was also so happy to see my other daughter Rachael and grandchildren coming to cheer me on! They were also dressed in red matching T-shirts! I was smiling from ear to ear! After group pictures, we said our goodbyes till later.

I quickly found the 6-hour pacer that I wanted to keep pace with. I placed myself slightly ahead of him. There was excitement in the air, and my heart was pounding to the cheers as the crowd began to run. I was overwhelmed with joy. The day I had trained so hard for was finally here. It was hard to believe this was actually happening. Right now, at this very moment, I felt prepared and ready.

I was taking everything in, my senses were keenly aware of my surroundings. Heading towards the heritage trail were groups of people cheering for us. I love the heritage trail. The canopy of trees gracing the trail was beautiful and offered additional coolness to the overcast morning. I was enjoying my run. My thoughts quickly traveled to a previous memorable run in Cornell, MI, through farming country. On river J-5 lane, I was greeted by a doe and her two baby fawns. They just stood and stared at me before darting into the woods. Another mile down the road, I spotted a bald eagle flying effortlessly through the sky. Such beauty in the U.P! On this same run, I was also mooed at by a cow and barked at by dogs. I was truly blessed to have seen God's beautiful creation and his handy work on this early morning long run.

My daughter Bex met me every 3-4 miles along the race route with a fresh bottle of Tailwind electrolyte mix and scratch gummies for my waist belt. She has been my cheerleader this entire journey saying, "You got this, mom!" Ryan and Bob waited eagerly for me with their cheers at all the spectator checkpoints. Seeing and hearing their support was music to my ears.

My running goals were to run 4 miles and walk 2 minutes, enjoy the journey, and finish the race. So far, this was working for me, but I was starting to feel the heat of the day. Around mile 8, the pacer caught up to me and asked, "How was I doing?" I admitted that I felt hot. We exchanged names and where we were from. I also told him this was my "first" marathon. From then on, when other runners passed us and greeted him, Tom would tell them this was "Yvonne's first marathon." They usually shouted back encouraging words, which spurred me on.

Tom was a delight to run with. I couldn't figure out how he knew trivial things about me, such as the month I was born, my favorite food, etc. When I asked him, he replied, "I'm psychic!" (I learned after the marathon that he had spoken to Bex) LOL! Conversing with Tom made miles tick away quickly. He was reluctant to share too much information about himself. He did reply when

I asked, "this evening when you are bored, look up the name Tom Perri as I had no idea who he was! I even asked if he was famous. In the course of our running, Tom introduced me to his method of running for this race. He suggested running 1 minute and walking briskly for 2 minutes. I was thankful for this information, his encouragement, and his kindness. Around mile 16, I had GI issues and needed the bathroom quickly!

On My Own

Tom was in view as I could spot his lime green T-shirt and pacer sign just ahead. I practiced what he had taught me with success. I was thankful to have the rocks out of my shoes that I had traveled with while running on the gravel trail. There was a gentle breeze that felt good to me on this hot day. As I neared mile marker 20, I noticed my hands were beginning to swell, I think my legs were too. They felt like wooden pegs moving stiffly. I was no longer able to run. I chose to walk the remaining miles briskly. I was determined! I would finish if I had to crawl!!

Walking towards South Marquette, there is so much beauty to enjoy. I am always in awe when viewing the cool waters of Lake Superior. There were several runners ahead of me and behind me. Some had already made the South Marquette loop and were heading towards Presque Isle. We exchanged encouraging words of affirmation, and then they were gone. After reaching Presque Isle, Bex walked with me at a fast pace for a distance. She said, "Mom, if you want to finish strong, you need to pick up the pace." So I did! With her cowbell ringing behind me, spurring me on once again.

The Dome in Sight

I could see the Superior Dome as I continued on this journey. I was pushing hard to finish. It was so hot! The heat from the sun as well as the heat from the trail, was draining. I was so close! Keep pushing, I repeated over and over to myself. A few yards ahead, I spotted Tom, a welcome site. He was walking towards me. We greeted each other, and he gave me some recovery tips to help with soreness after the race. I was grateful and marveled at how he knew so much about running.

The Finish Line

Crossing the finish line was surreal! I was greeted by family members and friends; their loud cheers, expressions of happiness, and all their hugs were priceless! I will always remember these precious moments. Receiving my medallion, and a group picture with my family and Tom, was like the icing on the cake! I had finished!! My heart was full!

An Unexpected Gift

On the way back to our car, Bex gave me Tom's pacer sign flag showing the 6-hour pace time. I was surprised and once again touched by his kindness to myself and other runners. His thoughtfulness brought tears to my eyes. This keepsake, along with my medallion, pictures, and memories, I will always cherish. After driving away from the parking lot, I regretted not introducing him to the rest of my family and inviting him to our post-race celebration at our home. Maybe next time?

(NOTE: If you are in the Marquette, Michigan, area for a marathon or craving some Italian food I strongly encourage you to visit Marquette, Michigan's first original Italian Cuisine restaurant the Barbiere's Villa Capri Italian Cuisine. It has been in operation since 1967.

I feel fortunate to have dined at the Villa Capri with Chris Carpenter and his family several times during the Marquette Marathon weekend.

I think I truly come to Marquette, Michigan to see the Carpenter family and dine with them at the Villa Capri. Oh, then I just run the marathon because I am in the area that weekend and I like pacing marathons.

I am drooling just thinking about the Villa Capri's garlic bread.)

Chapter 25: It's All About Our Attitude

Song: "Let's Go Crazy"

Artist: Prince and The Revolution

Quote: "Too often in life, something happens and we blame other people for us not being happy or satisfied or fulfilled. So the point is, we all have choices, and we make the choice to accept people or situations or to not accept situations." – Tom Brady

Tina & Jeff's word for me: Empowering

Minnesota on May 11, 1858, became the 32nd state and is the 12th largest state. Minnesota has a large number of lakes, and is also known as the "Land of 10,000 Lakes". If you take active water lakes of 10 acres or more, then at last count Minnesota had 11,842 lakes. That seems similar to saying a marathon is 26.22 miles and when you finish your GPS shows 26.44.

Prince Rogers Nelson was born on June 7th, 1958, and he sadly passed away on Thursday, April 21st, 2016. One could easily argue that Prince was one of the greatest musicians of his generation and is arguably one of the top 100 musicians of all time.

Prince and myself, had three things in common with the first being both of us were born in Minnesota.

Secondly, we shared the same birthday of June 7th, yet Prince was three years older than me.

In 1980, the United States led a boycott of the Moscow Summer Olympics.So, in 1984, when the event moved to Los Angeles, the Soviet Union returned the favor.

In 1984 a man named Alex Trebek moved behind the podium in a show called Jeopardy.

In November 1984, Mondale would not just get beaten by Ronald Reagan, he was absolutely crushed. Ronald Reagan took 49 out of 50 states, with the exception of Minnesota which was Mondale's home state. Apparently, there was a joke about what Ronald Regan wanted for Christmas in 1984, as he mentioned "that Minnesota would have been nice."

Also, in 1984 came the release of the film and album Purple Rain. The lead single, "When Doves Cry," arguably had the most lasting impact.

"Let's Go Crazy" also was a song by Prince and The Revolution from the album Purple Rain.

If was finally time for Minnesota to "Let's Go Crazy" thanks to Prince and The Revolution.

The song begins with:

"Dearly beloved

We are gathered here today

To get through this thing called "life."

No one said that life was going to be easy. No one ever really says a marathon is easy - it is still 26.2 miles no matter whether you run or walk the distance.

The thing Prince taught us in 1984 that no matter what happens in life, that when going through life let us have some fun along the way. Make sure to get a little crazy now and then.

There are plenty of creative and different marathons out there. Not all races' we do have to be competitive or must have ourselves going for a BQ or a PR.

Note that I am approaching 300 different marathons, and well over 1,200 different races, but there are still plenty of marathons and races I have not done and unfortunately can't comment on.

I will mention a couple of them with being the Hatfield-McCoy Marathon as I have paced this race several times. Besides the marathon being a little challenging as well as fun the marathon can count for either Kentucky or West Virginia, as the marathon starts in Kentucky and ends in West Virginia. The Hatfield & McCoy feud started all about the disputed ownership of two razor-backed hogs.

I also love the Route 66 marathon as this marathon is for serious marathoners as well as for those marathoners that just want to have fun. If you have no issues with alcohol on the course, then this might be the ideal marathon course for you. Having paced this marathon, I get to see all the smiles on the runners and volunteers faces.

You can't help but not love Grandma's Marathon as on a beautiful day, Grandma's marathon is an incredibly scenic run along the North Shore. The infamous "Lemon Drop hill" is just a minor speed bump along the way to the finish line and gently gives your leg muscles a little variation.

Another marathon that you need to try is the Little Rock Marathon. Not only do you get to run right by the state capital but you can get one of the largest finisher's marathon medals of any marathon. The Little Rock Marathon staff put on an awesome race and race weekend.

The Missoula Marathon can be three days of running if you want it to be starting with a free Beer Run of three miles on Friday evening, which also gets you a free token of appreciation and a free beer or beverage when you finish. Free, free, and free is something we all can afford.

Then you do a 5k on Saturday morning, and then you can pick between a 1/2 marathon or marathon on Sunday. Then when done with your Sundays run you can pick up some extra bling for completing all three races.

There are plenty of other different and fun marathon and races out there. You can find races of distances from one mile, to an ultra distance up to 100 miles, as well as 12 and 24 hour runs and beyond. For fun I truly suggest trying a different distance for fun if nothing else and don't worry about your time and just enjoy and love the new experience.

One of my favorite things I used to do on a Saturday before I started doing all these marathons is traveling to some area or city I hadn't been to before and running a 5k or even a 10k if I wanted a little more of a run. Most of these 5k's would be an easy 30 minutes to three hours drive from my house so frequently I would leave my house race morning.

Regardless of whether you are fast or slow at smaller races always check the race results because you may have won an Age Group award. Doing a local race helps you get in a workout as well as helps support another community. You benefit and the community benefits, so everyone is a winner.

One of the things I love to do with runners is catch up on local trivia for a race that I am pacing. I will check out fun facts that some local runners might not know as well as runners that have travelled to do the run. An ulterior motive is that I can potentially use that knowledge on local trivia nights. So, one per mile trivia question I have been known to use to see how much the locals and other runners know about the area. It also takes a few minutes of time per mile to help the miles go by.

One important part of one's life is to have fun. Life can and will be stressful so have some fun with life.

If you can incorporate running and races into your life you get two incredible major benefits. You can get all the benefits of the exercise from the running. Then you get to rid yourself of all your stresses with your running when having fun with your run.

Laugh and enjoy your running each and every day. We are not guaranteed tomorrow. I hope to see you on a run or at a race soon.

As Prince so aptly stated:

We're all gonna die
When we do
What's it all for? (What's it all for?)
Better live now
Before the grim reaper comes knocking on your door.
Have fun and enjoy life.
Yes indeed, let's go crazy!

Prince and myself, enjoyed being a little crazy and so should you.

I strongly encourage everyone to have fun and challenging goals in life, regardless of whether it is running related or not. So, I went a little crazy on this running challenge. I decided that I would run a race of one mile or longer on all 366 days of the calendar, which meant that I was including February 29th for Leap Year.

I had no idea when I started this goal how challenging this goal would become. Many days were easy to accomplish as I had specific races that I wanted to do like Texas Marathon, which I have done several times, for January 1st in Kingwood, Texas. The Red, White, & Boom 1/2 Marathon on July 4th in Minneapolis, I had paced several times. I have done so many Memorial, Thanksgiving Day, and Labor Day runs that I covered multiple May, September, and November dates.

I simply challenged myself to find and complete 366 events. It took me over 16 years to complete this goal, but it was well worth it.

I suppose I really could have made this goal more challenging by doing a different race for all 366 dates. Maybe I could have made it all 5k's, or all 1/2 marathons, or even all marathons. The challenges and goals are endless that one can create for oneself.

All I obviously wanted was a goal that I could have a little crazy fun with. I set a goal and year after year I went out and ran races to accomplish that goal. Sure, it took me over 16 years to accomplish this goal but it was well worth the wait.

So, let us go crazy and pick a goal that is challenging and lots of fun.

Let's decide to live now.

Attitude is everything.

Jeff & Tina Hauser,
Carlsbad, CA
Jeff and Tina's word for themselves: Blessed

It all started with a bathrobe. Halloween flurries gave way to a blustery morning on Saturday, November 1, 2014, in Indianapolis, Indiana, where Jeff & I were in town to run the Indianapolis Monumental Marathon. The temperature was hardly arctic, but 17mph winds made 30F feel like 18F and we were in no hurry to leave the warm confines of our hotel room that conveniently overlooked the start area. As the 8am start time drew closer, we watched the corrals slowly fill up with runners. They were bundled up and huddled together, wearing all manner of cold-weather gear.

"Gear" in this context includes much more than accessories such as arm sleeves or wind-proof gloves made specifically for protection from the elements. Runners are incredibly creative and resourceful in their quest for inexpensive, disposable methods of staying warm before a marathon. Rather than wallow in the misery of the moment, we see an opportunity to have fun. Among our favorite pre-race whimsy is the basic lawn and leaf trash bag, upleveled to superhero status with arm holes and duct tape.

Finally, at 7:45am, 15 minutes before the race start, we could procrastinate no longer and knew it was time to brave the elements. I looked longingly at the down comforter on our bed and for a moment considered how I might sneak past the hotel staff with it draped over my shoulders. One disapproving glance from Jeff later and I abandoned the comforter, and we headed out in search of our start corral, not knowing that our repertoire of cold-weather gear, and our marathon journey, were about to change forever.

It would have been difficult to not meet Tom that morning in the start corral. Not because he was a pacer, but because the crowd surrounding him was larger and more boisterous than we had experienced until then. Tom wasn't just randomly chatting with a few runners loosely forming a group who would begin the marathon together. He was holding court, tossing out trivia questions, asking about individual race goals, and previewing the course. Until suddenly, he wasn't, when his attention abruptly turned to an attractive woman wearing a very extravagant bathrobe. As quickly as this moment began it was over; most runners probably didn't even notice that it happened. But Jeff & I did, and we took full advantage of the opportunity to tease Tom. And with that, an enduring friendship was born. (We also added bathrobes to our list of pre-race gear, albeit a more basic style prioritizing form over function.)

At the time we met Tom, Jeff & I had been running for only a few years. My journey began in 2009 with a DNF (did not finish) at Grandma's Marathon. Untrained and with no experience at shorter distances, I had no business toeing that start line much less thinking I had could finish. Then again, as an infant, I largely bypassed crawling and, after a brief stint going backwards, went straight to walking. That foreshadowed my approach to most of life; I just leap and grow my wings on the way down. Not to be denied a marathon medal, I returned to Grandma's Marathon in 2010 and finished. It was neither fast nor pretty, but it marked the beginning of what remains my greatest journey so far.

Except for a 10k in the mid-1980's, Jeff was not a runner either. When 2009 rolled around, he was happy being the best race supporter he could be but insisted there would be no running in his future. To his credit, he continued to hone his skills as a spectator for a couple of years until he finally gave in to temptation at Team Ortho's Get Lucky 7k in 2012. It didn't hurt that friends were running in addition to me, and traversing miles together became a very social event. By then I had run a few other shorter distances and finished my 2nd marathon in Chicago.

That spring of 2012 was when my journey came into focus and Jeff started joining me at races. If there was no marathon, we would run the half marathon together. Race weekends became events, complete with hotel stays, dinners out, and impromptu meetups with our growing circle of running friends. As my marathon count and trek towards 50 states continued its march towards double digits, Jeff finally gave in to the temptation and decided to join me for 26.2 miles. The 2013 edition of the LA Marathon coincided with St. Patrick's Day and was also Jeff's hometown race. When he signed up, he emphatically stated that it would be his first and last marathon. While it would certainly always be his first, the chances of it being his last were slim.

The two years spanning 2013 and 2014 remain among our favorite in our running journey. Race weekends were the rule, not the exception, and we ventured further and further beyond our comfort zone. By the time we met Tom in late 2014, we had run a few more marathons and I was fully committed to finishing a marathon in all 50 states. There were hiccups along the way including a broken toe halfway through a trail marathon and our first cancelled race. We quickly learned to roll with what the race gods gave us, adapt, and move forward. Attitude became everything, and as long we committed to crossing the start line, our race experience would largely be up to us.

In fact, some of our favorite memories grew out of things not going as planned. The Little Rock Marathon had been on our radar from very early on. It is known for its annual theme, oversized medals, and fabulous post-race experience. For us, the 2015 running is also now known for the ice storm that preceded it. We planned to fly from Minneapolis to Little Rock but due to flight issues, ended up driving. Tom was already in Little Rock, and thankfully was able to retrieve our race packets and even some expo swag. He also stayed in touch for the duration of our 17-hour trek, ultimately getting our things dropped off at our hotel. The drive was slow and nerve-wracking, but we made it and would not let the stress detract from our grand plan: to surprise Tom in bathrobes at the start line. Our race bibs were appropriately named "Bathrobe 1" and "Bathrobe 2." In turn, Tom surprised us with a giant pile of light bulbs he obtained at the race expo and hoped could hitch a ride home with us since we were driving. We of course still talk about the epic drive and how crazy it was at the time, but to this day, our Little Rock memories are dominated by bathrobes and light bulbs.

Meetups with Tom evolved from coincidences to planned events. His encyclopedic knowledge of marathon options in each state was invaluable as we got more intentional with our schedule. Some states had very few options, while certain weekends would require choosing one race over another. Soon, we were planning for 9-12 months in advance and eagerly awaiting the next trip where we would see Tom. What could have been overwhelming and stressful became something we looked forward to. Our shared love of craft beer meant that race weekends often contained afternoon diversions to local breweries. We were fortunate to be able to turn those trips into experiences that transcended the race itself. The running was just one part of conquering each state, and for that we are incredibly grateful. Our 50 states goal truly became more about the journey than the destination.

Jeff abandoned half marathons in favor of marathons in 2015, which meant we were often together for at least a portion of the race. Those portions were not always when I was at my best; it turns out I have a fear of being left behind. A giant phobia that is the reason I like to go out in front. It's less about winning and nearly all about not being last. I have no idea where this comes from and perhaps one day, I will figure that out. However, what's important is that running marathons helped me tackle it head-on. There's a big difference between not being last and being left behind. I got better at both! Jeff never left me behind. If he caught up to me during a particularly tough run, he would stay with me for the remaining miles no matter how good he felt or how much more quickly he could have finished. I learned to trust that I would not be left behind, even in my lowest, most raw moments.

Then, in 2017, Reno happened. Our options for Nevada were growing slim based on our schedule, so we registered for The Downtown River Run. Despite being large enough to qualify for a registered 50 state marathon finish, it was a smaller event run mostly by accomplished, local runners used to the hills and heat. We were confident about our ability to finish the double out-and-back within the strict, 6-hour limit and took a measured, conservative approach to the first half. Not too far into the second half, the 6-hour pacer caught up to us. By my watch, we were still well ahead of the time limit, so I freaked out. The pacer reassured me that my timing was correct. However, when I asked her why she was with us if that was the case, she cringed and said she was also the sweeper. In other words, we were last. Dead last. I freaked out even more than I did thinking our timing was off. It was getting warmer, and all my fears were coming home to roost. I wouldn't be left behind because Jeff was right next to me, and I even had a sweeper! But we were going to be last. It was time for a gut check. Did it matter? If we finished, another state was done. We would get the same medal as everyone else. I had no sooner achieved acceptance than the magic happened. A trio of motorcycle cops pulled up behind us. They kept a respectable distance but were there to open the course as we cleared checkpoints. It was time to have some fun. If we jogged, they sped up to maintain their prescribed gap. If we slowed down, so did them. Suddenly, being last meant it was all about us! We had a pacer to chat us up and motorcycles that would roll at our pace. Childish? Perhaps. But also, a lot of fun and a great way to distract me from counting miles. In the end, we finished with almost 10 minutes to spare, received credit for the state and proudly donned our medals. I slayed some demons that day in Reno, all thanks to changing my attitude.

We completed our 50 states journey in January 2020 and ran the last of the 6 Abbott World Marathon majors in October 2021. Epic adventures that left us with so much more than 2 big achievements. We ran through pain, dealt with adversity, and tackled personal demons. The common denominator is attitude. We were in full control of how we chose to react to each challenge. In hindsight, there are some we could have handled better, some perhaps differently, and some I still have no clue how we did it. Either way, we chose to find the silver linings, learn, and grow. This was never more evident than in Maui, our 50th state. It was hot, hilly, and windy; after a first half run to plan, the second half fell apart, and I struggled mightily just to put one foot in front of the other. What better time to channel everything learned up to that point? Not only did I do that, but I also sent Jeff up ahead and ran the last mile alone. I was not afraid of being last or being left behind. When you embrace your moments of struggle, they will make you strong.

So, how would I describe Tom in one word? Empowering. Tom believed in us even when we didn't. He made complicated problems simple. And he never left us behind. We are forever grateful and indebted to Tom for his role in our running journey. We are even more blessed for the gift of his friendship, which we wouldn't trade for anything.

Chapter 26: Making a Bad Day into a Good Day

Song: "One Moment in Time"

Artist: Whitney Houston

Quote: "You have to remember that the hard days are what make you stronger. The bad days make you realize what a good day is. If you never had any bad days, you would never have that sense of accomplishment!" - Aly Raisman

Heather's word for me: Strong

The Kalakaua Merrie Mile is the Saturday the day before the Honolulu marathon and a great way to get a quick shake out run the day before the marathon. This is a very flat and fast course if you want to challenge yourself for a fast mile time, or simply run along the ocean. Unfortunately, they do not give top three for Age Groups in the Kalakaua Merrie Mile where in 2022 I finished in 6:51 for third place in the 60-64 Age Group. The same two people finish ahead of me as well in 2021 when I finished in 6:54.

I still have one remaining goal with the state of Hawaii and that is either winning or getting an overall Age Group award in any race from the one-mile distance and up. Hawaii is my last state to accomplish this goal. It is particularly difficult and tricky because I can't just hop in the car on a Friday evening and drive from Minnesota to a race on any island in Hawaii.

It was at the Kulia Marathon that was on the Big Island on Saturday, March 9th, 2019, that I completed my 1,000th pacing assignment. It was a fun marathon that day meeting and pacing Marta Mixa and several others in my 4:20 pace group. Yes, that is the correct spelling of her first name "Marta." Michelle (Roma) Krok paced the 3:50 group successfully that day as well.

I felt like this was a "friends marathon reunion run" as seeing Glen Marumoto and Glen Anderson that are also 50sub4 club members, as well as Karen Murray.

We all have bad days and good days in life and especially when we are running races. Sometimes things happen that are beyond our control before the

239

race or during the race. No matter how much we run and train sometimes a bad race day happens.

However, a bad race for a marathon is significantly different than say a 5k. On a 5k if you have a bad mile, or even two bad miles, you are just about done anyway. With a marathon you can have "several bad miles" or even a "dozen bad miles" and have potentially 15 miles or more still to finish.

Especially for first time marathoners it is particularly important to note that the marathon should be looked at as a "mile by mile experience." Obviously, the goal is that all 26 miles of the marathon will go well, but occasionally a mile will go bad. It could be anything as minor as a rock in one's shoe, or an untied shoelace, or maybe needing some petroleum jelly (Vaseline) to help with chafing issues. All of those usually can be simply fixed in just a few seconds or a couple of minutes.

Other times we might need a little medical assistance for a muscle cramp. Or if having stomach issues when spending excessive time in the bathrooms. Here is where I will politely *warn* you first time marathoners that if by chance you see race volunteers at Aid Stations holding tongue depressors with what "looks like a slimy gel stuff on it" that is not an energy gel to be eaten. It is likely petroleum jelly to apply to your crotch or underarms to avoid serious chafing. Believe me when I say that you really don't want a glob of petroleum jelly in your mouth. Note that is not from my personal experience, but by hearing from various runners on the course that have mistakenly tried to ingest the petroleum jelly.

Then the other thing that can make a marathon increasingly difficult is when we are just not "feeling it" that day overall emotionally and mentally. We have all the running and training completed but we just skipped past "Race Day Marathon Mental Training: 101."

You start out running well and by a few miles on the course you feel like giving up on either your marathon goal time or even feeling like you simply want to finish the marathon.

Emotionally and mentally, you are feeling exhausted and frustrated. The miles seem to be getting longer than the actual 5,280 feet per mile. Doubting yourself and negative thoughts start to enter your mind. Those thoughts get worse as the marathon goes on.

Sometimes all it takes is a person - most frequently a pacer - to help give you an "attitude adjustment." I am not really referring to the Hank Williams Jr "Attitude Adjustment" song if you are familiar with it, but that is also a song you might want on your song playlist while running. It can be someone simply saying "you are doing great" or "keep going you got this" to help you complete that one mile, so you simply can get to that next mile.

This is where crowd support and friends and family can be so helpful on the course. Possibly a volunteer on the course saying "good job." Basically, someone saying something encouraging and positive to you.

Through all my years of pacing races I have been amazed at how a person can simply *change* their doubting and negative thought pattern when you *simplify tell them a single positive word or two.*

"You're a winner for a lifetime if you seize that one moment in time make it shine" is a lyric from the song One Moment in Time by Whitney Houston. For me it was helping a fellow runner Heather that day on Sunday, December 13th, 2015, at the Honolulu Marathon. I didn't run any part of that marathon for Heather as Heather ran the marathon with her own two legs. It just took a little effort and time and a few positive words, on my part, to change what was looking as impossible to a "100% possible."

When I met Heather on the course that day, she was rather dejected and depressed around mile 11 or so. She thought all her planning for her 50 Sub 4-hour marathon finish was slowing disappearing. All I simply did was give her a few positive words of encouragement. We replaced thoughts such as "there is another marathon I can do in Hawaii next year" to "you can still get your Sub 4 marathon today."

I am a numbers guy, so it was relatively easy to figure out her projected finish time in my head. When I saw her, she was still on pace for about a 3:58 to 4-hour finish. Remember I am trying to figure the time difference from her time from when she crossed the start mat to when I crossed the start mat. So, I thought a Sub 4-hour marathon goal for Heather was still achievable, as I was trying for around a 3:55 marathon to "safely" achieve my own sub-4-hour marathon goal for myself. Note that I didn't ever say it was going to be easy for Heather, just that it was achievable. I just want to make sure that distinction was noted as those are two *very* different concepts.

But I bet you didn't know that the #1 thing that helped Heather achieve her goal was because of a failure. Yes, I said that correctly as her GPS device had stopped working as that is what failed her. Her mind hadn't failed her as it just needed to be changed from a *negative* mind set to a *positive* mind set.

When we started running, I told Heather that we were running closer to a 9-minute pace. See I was glad her GPS watch wasn't working as we were actually running slightly faster than an 8:50 pace. Okay, maybe you need to add the song "Little Lies" by Fleetwood Mac to your song list, as I wasn't 100% truthful with my pace time with Heather. However, had I told Heather we were doing an 8:45 pace I think I might have heard potentially a few sailor words from her. Come to think of it, maybe I should have to have increased my vocabulary for when I play Scrabble, but those words usually aren't playable words.

I kept that up the nearly eight miles we ran together. Heather had no clue I was slightly "pushing" her pace. I knew she still had a hill to climb on the course coming by Diamond Head and my fear was that if she walked any part of that hill, she wouldn't make her sub 4 goal. Diamond Head is a volcanic cone and is considered the most popular Hawaii State Park and well worth a visit if you visit Honolulu, but I suggest you not do the park and climb to the top the day before or the day after the marathon as you do climb some steps, as it is about 2 hours for the roundtrip hike.

A 4-hour marathon is about a 9:09 minute pace mile but that would have cut her finish time too close for a sub 4 finish so I couldn't take any chances.

It should be noted that when I pace a marathon, I try for a 30 second to a 1-minute finish below my official scheduled pace time to have some wiggle room at the finish if needed. Without knowing her precise start time as mentioned when she actually crossed the start, I had to do my best guess estimating her finishing time needed.

So, we ran together past the 19th mile marker, and I simply tell Heather that "if you run a sub 9:50 pace the rest of the way to the finish you will get your sub-4-hour finish time." Heather actually *smiled* then and it was priceless. Something that seemed impossible less than two hours ago was now possible. I told Heather that I would be right behind her the whole way. If she needed me again the last few miles, I would be there for her. So, I checked in on another sub-4-hour marathon runner. Then I actually lost sight of Heather as she took off ahead of me. By now she was probably two minutes ahead of me and approaching a potential sub 3:55 marathon. When I finally was finishing, I could see Heather up slightly ahead of me.

Heather's sub-4-hour marathon was completed in 3:55:29. Her certified 50sub4 hour marathon finish in all states goal was accomplished. Sadly, though I would be missing out on learning a few sailor words had Heather probably not made her goal, but Heather was happy and that mattered more to me.

Funny, but I didn't feel terrible for not letting Heather not obtain her sub 4 marathon goal so she could leave the cold of Chicago in the winter months of 2016 to get a sub-4-hour marathon at another marathon in Hawaii.

I finished the Honolulu marathon that day in 3:56:20, but that is a side note to that day.

I couldn't have been prouder of Heather. Congratulations Heather on your amazing accomplishment. This I believe will always be my all-time favorite pacing moment. However, I am truly hoping for many more pacing moments during my running journey.

Sometimes things happen in life that were never planned, and they turn out to be the best memories. That was just one of those days on December 13th, 2015.

I hope you find a moment in time, and you make it shine. If we each day we daily make a difference in one person's life I truly believe the world would be a much better place to live. That would be an ideal "circle of life" where everyone helps one another and hurting another person no longer happens.

Heather Zeigler
Woodridge, IL
Heather's word for herself: Fun

I clearly remember my first mile that I ever ran. It was my senior year of high school when we had to do the required mile in PE (physical education.) I thought that it would be a good idea to actually run the whole thing because I was going to go into Navy ROTC in college. I did it! Then I spent the summer doing the training that was recommended by my Navy ROTC unit so I wouldn't die when I started running in college. It helped a little, but I definitely would not have considered myself a runner in college. I would fall out of our battalion runs nearly every time and I hated running.

This feeling pretty much continued throughout my time in the Navy and it wasn't until the end of my 4 years in the Navy that I found the love for running. I had my daughter in December of 2005. I was finishing up my time in the Navy in San Diego and had a flexible job, so this allowed for me to start running more often.

I began to run along the silver strand at lunch every day and before I knew it, I started to lose a lot of weight! What's not to love about that? I lost all the weight that I had gained during my pregnancy and eventually lost over 30 pounds more from where I was before I got pregnant. That's what made me realize that running was great!

I continued running to maintain the weight loss and in 2007 a high school friend asked me if I wanted to run the Chicago marathon with her and her sister. At the time, I lived in Jacksonville, Florida so I trained in the heat of Florida. It turned out that this was the best thing for me because the Chicago marathon was extremely hot that year and I was able to finish before they black flagged the course! It was such a fun experience for my first marathon, and I was in love!

I moved to the Chicago area in 2008 but because of life, I didn't get to run my second marathon until Chicago 2009. Once again, I loved it! By the next year, I decided that I wanted to have a goal to keep up my motivation and to maintain my weight loss. I made the goal of running 50 marathons before I was 50. At the time, I had only run 2 marathons and I was 30 so I thought a few marathons a year was a reasonable goal. I remember telling a few people about this goal at a race in September 2010 and they sort of laughed at me. They made me realize that my goal was very obtainable. It was people like them that led me to doing marathon more frequently. They were so easy-going and encouraging and I wanted to be around people like that! Before I knew it, I was planning race after race and ended up reaching that goal way before I turned 50. I'm only 43 now and I have run 288 marathons!

The people that I have met along the way and the travel is what led to me doing more frequent marathons. I have made so many friends around the country and it has now become my main hobby. I have also learned that if I run at least one marathon a month, I don't have to do any long training runs alone.

I prefer the comradery of a race so I would rather do that any day!

Eventually I made a goal to do all 50 States and as I began to do that I also began to get faster. My first marathon was around 4:30 but by 2011 I started to break 4 hours regularly. I met a few people that were in the 50sub4 Marathon Club, and they inspired me to add the extra goal of completing a marathon in all 50 states under 4 hours.

One of my favorite memories with Tom Perri was at the completion of my 50 states under 4 hours. It was at the Honolulu marathon in 2015. I live in Chicago and it is pretty cold in the Chicago area in December. I knew as soon as I stepped off the plane in Honolulu that the heat in December there was going to be a huge challenge for me. I was so nervous about breaking 4 hours that I cried at the start line. I also made the *rookie mistake* of not fully charging my watch so a few miles into the race, my watch died. Luckily for me, I bumped into Tom around that time. Tom was so encouraging! He offered to pace me the rest of the race. This was the best thing that could have happened for me because I had no idea what pace I was running, and I let him do all the thinking. With his help, I got there and managed to finish the 50 states under 4 hours. I couldn't have done it without him!

After I finished that goal, I changed my focus on time and began to give back and pace others just as Tom paced me. I have found that helping others has been so rewarding. From helping people get their first sub 4 marathon to helping people get their first Boston qualifying time, the experience of pacing has been so rewarding. If I am not pacing these days, I am just running for the fun of running. It has been the best stress reliever and has helped me continue to enjoy life and all the fun experiences along the way!

Trivia

Annual Chicago marathons were held from 1905 to the 1920s, but the first race in the present series occurred on Sunday, September 25, 1977, under the original name the Mayor Daley Marathon, which drew a field of 4,200 runners.

The 2023 Chicago Marathon field had more than 48,500 finishers for the 45th running of the Bank of Chicago Marathon, the most in race history.

Since the inaugural race in 1977, over 1 million participants have crossed the Chicago Marathon finish line.

That includes the event's millionth finisher, Allison Naval of Evanston,

Illinois, competing in her first marathon and finishing in 4:23:13.

Chapter 26.2: Stage 4 is Just a Diagnosis

Song: "Stronger (What Doesn't Kill You) "

Artist: Kelly Clarkson

Quote: "Life isn't about waiting for the storm to pass... It's about learning to dance in the rain." - Vivian Greene

Natalie's word for me: Tenacious

DetermiNation is the American Cancer Society's event endurance program, spanning a variety of sports including running. The collective efforts of the dedicated athletes who use their endurance and strength to help raise funds to take down cancer are nothing short of stupendous.

Susan G Komen, or often referred to as just Komen, is a breast cancer organization in the United States. Their race is a 5k run or walk raising money for breast cancer. The first race occurred in Dallas, Texas in 1983, with approximately 800 participants.

Breast cancer is the most commonly diagnosed cancer for women. Approximately 13% of all women in the United States are going to develop invasive breast cancer in the course of their life.

Breast cancer accounts for about 30% of all new cancer cases in women each year in the United States. Breast cancer accounts for 12.5% of all new annual cancer cases worldwide, making it the most common cancer in the world. Approximately 15% of women who get breast cancer have a family member diagnosed with it. There are currently more than 4 million women with a history of breast cancer in the United States.

The more prominent risk factors for breast cancer are being a woman and getting older.

A man's lifetime risk of breast cancer is approximately 1 in 850. For men the two most prominent factors appear to be aging as well as breast cancer risk is increased if other members of the family (blood relatives) have had breast cancer, as about 20% of men with breast cancer have a close relative, male or female, with the disease.

I think it is imperative that with any daunting diagnosis that a critical component is surrounding yourself with positive people. Positive people create positive energy.

Do you hear what I am trying to tell you? We all know of negative people, and we all understand how negative comments or remarks can affect our mood. It can be incredibly hurtful when you are already down and suffering with any cancer diagnosis.

If you are hurting and down you might need to get someone to act as your advocate - whether it is a relative, your spouse, significant other, or actual patient advocate.

When I was going through my second surgery in 2019, in less than four months after my prostate surgery, I had to reprogram myself to thinking that I was going to make it to the end of 2019 with no more surgeries. I thought initially one surgery a year, but when I needed a second one, then I needed to start thinking no more surgeries after October 23rd for the year as I needed to get started with my radiation treatments.

When I had 38 radiation treatments scheduled it became more of a countdown game for me. Each day that I had radiation I thought positive thoughts that I only had so many left. The process of cognitive reframing certainly doesn't change my situation with radiation treatment.

I am having radiation treatment regardless of whether or not I am thinking negative thoughts or having positive energy. I knew I had 38 radiation treatments ahead of me with 25 for the lymph nodes and 13 for the prostate area. When I was down to 13 radiation treatments left, I wasn't "woe is me as I have had 25 treatments." Instead, I was thinking "only 13 more treatments and I am done being an object of radiation." The situation in reality never changed for me except for the way I thought about my 38 radiation treatments.

When you get a Stage 4 cancer diagnosis it is highly probable that taking drugs, surgeries, radiation treatment, or any combination of those is likely to occur. So just try to be as positive as possible during this time and begin a count down until a treatment or process has been completed.

It is like counting down the 26 miles on a marathon course and knowing when you are done with 26 miles you just have just .2 miles to the finish. In most cases just like the crowd's energy and support can help you finish those last .2 miles while struggling, hopefully you have a support system in place to get you through your final treatments. Nobody said it would be an easy experience and journey, but once you are done you showed your endurance and how tough you are.

Always remember that no one should battle a cancer diagnosis alone. Please don't be afraid to ask for help. Be strong in your cancer journey. *No one should ever be in the cancer battle themselves.*

What I hope you have seen in this book is that running is of the best medicine for what might ail you. The running community just becomes that booster shot that adds another level of medicine to help alleviate what ails you.

Also, since the COVID Pandemic more and more stories are talking about how lonely people are. Loneliness can be deadly as it can lead to depression and isolation and progressing even as far as suicidal ideation.

I can't guarantee that going for a run or doing a race will increase your level of happiness, but it certainly won't hurt. If you do a race or join a running group that will certainly help with your feelings of isolation and loneliness.

Hopefully you will eventually agree that running was the "booster shot" that you needed. Then you will realize for yourself that *running is definitely the best medicine.*

Natalie Uyeno
Clovis, Cain
Natalie's word for herself: Strong

I first got into running while I was playing ice hockey in 2016. I was coming back to the bench winded between shifts and I wanted to add some cardio to my workouts. I started running 1 mile or 2 a couple days a week, then I gradually worked my way up to 3 miles 2-3 times a week while I was training for 5k races.

I did a handful of 5k races in 2016 and I liked the medals so much that I set a goal to do at least one 5k a month in 2017. I ended up finishing that year with 39 5ks, 3 10ks, one 5.5k, one 5-miler, and one-half marathon (my first) ! I never expected to run longer than a 10k, but I set higher goals for 2018 (at least 1 half marathon per month) .

I ended up registering for a lot more half marathons than I planned to in 2018. I also registered for my first marathon in March of that year (knowing that I would have a whole year to train for my first marathon in 2019 at age 50)

. Since I had completed 16 half marathons by the end of October 2018, I decided to add a few more so I could finish the year with 24 half marathons for the year.

2018 was also the year that I became a member of Half Fanatics, an international running club for people who love the half marathon distance. In Half Fanatics there are different levels that you can achieve by running more half marathons in a short time span. The highest level is Sun Level with 52 half marathons in a 365-day period. My goal was to complete 52+ half marathons for 3 consecutive years so that I could be inducted into the Half Fanatics Hall of Fame.

My totals for 2019 were 52 half marathons, 4 marathons, and several shorter distance races. 3 of those 4 marathons were completed in 90 days to qualify for Marathon Maniacs, the sister club to Half Fanatics. I had also completed my first World Major Marathon with a personal record by 10 minutes at Chicago in October of 2019.

I hit my goal of Sun Level in December 2019 and was well on my way to my second consecutive year of 52 plus half marathons in 2020 when the pandemic hit and cancelled all of my races after March of that year. My last race before the world shut down was on March 15, 2020 and I wasn't able to find another race until June. I had almost 3 months of races to make up to ensure that I could hit my goal for 2020. I began traveling to other states to find races and I was slowly starting to rack up new states towards my 50 states half marathon quest. By the end of 2020 I had completed half marathons in 18 states and was at 138 lifetime halves.

By 2021 things were starting to open up again and I was able to find more races. I was working towards my Half Fanatics HOF (Hall of Fame) goal while I was also knocking out new states towards my 50 states goal, but I had a *major* setback when I got diagnosed with breast cancer in September of 2021. I immediately cancelled my out-of-state travel for the rest of the year and I held off on registering for races in 2022 because I was uncertain how the chemotherapy would affect me.

I discovered a lump in my breast, but since I had lost my job and I didn't have health insurance, I wasn't able to get it checked out right away. I was first diagnosed as Stage 2B in September 2021, but 3 months later (when the doctors got all of my scans back and they saw that the cancer had spread into my bones) they re-diagnosed me as Stage 4. I was in shock! A range of emotions including depression, anxiety, anger, denial, frustration, and sadness were my new normal for the next few months. Chemo was debilitating, but I was disappointed that they quit chemo after only a few rounds and they cancelled my surgery to remove the tumor!

I was so taken aback by the news that I couldn't even share it with my immediate family for several months after my Stage 4 diagnosis. Only a couple of close friends and a couple of cousins knew the extent of my cancer. It took months to work up the courage to share with my mom, stepdad, and brother. I have since decided to share my journey with as many people as possible because I want to help bring awareness and encourage people to get checked regularly for cancer. I don't want anyone to have to go through what I've had to endure.

The medications have taken a toll on my body. First, I lost a lot of weight when I was undergoing chemo, then I gained it all back (and then some) after I went off chemo and into hormone therapy. It has taken over a year to lose some weight, but I'm still not back to my pre-cancer weight. I'm much slower than I used to be and I suffer from chronic fatigue and chronic pain, but it's manageable.

I am thankful that I was able to keep my streak of doing at least one-half marathon per month going even during the chemotherapy. I had to walk a few of those races, but I still got them done! 2022 was a bounce back year after undergoing chemo in late 2021. I started walking a couple times a week and I gradually worked my way back to running and run/walk for the longer distances. I even ran my first ultramarathon (32 miles) in May 2022 at age 53 because a friend gifted me the race registration! I'm thankful that I have been able to regain some of my endurance!

Now that I'm Stage 4 there is more of a sense of urgency to complete my 50 states quest! I have knocked out 12 new states for half marathons & 1 new state for marathons in 2023 year-to-date. I am hoping to complete my 50 states goal and hit 300 half marathons by 2024.

I recently underwent 10 rounds of radiation in July/August 2023, so that set me back a bit, but the running brings me so much joy and it gives me goals to keep striving for. The running community is so supportive and encouraging and is truly like family. As a single person, with no children it's important to stay active and positive and not succumb to depression and anxiety. I'm trying to stay strong for my elderly mother's sake and I am making it my mission to spread awareness about early detection and getting regular check-ups! Cancer is a horrible disease that has taken many of my friends and family members and I don't want to see anyone else I know have to suffer! Please don't be afraid to go get checked out! It's better to find out early!

Most importantly, DON'T GIVE UP! People with cancer can still run marathons and can live somewhat normal lives! Race companies like Mainly Marathons that have no time limits make that possible for slower runners like me! I'm grateful for the awesome running community and the hope and inspiration that it gives me! I have met so many amazing, inspiring runners of all ages from all over the country (and a few foreign countries too) ! These people keep me going!

I first met Tom Perri at the Anchorage RunFest in Alaska in August of 2021. We were both on the pace team. I didn't know Tom very well at all back then, but I knew that he was a fellow Marathon Maniac and he was also in the 50 States Marathon Club because I had seen him at races before we officially met wearing the club gear.

I hadn't been diagnosed with cancer yet when Tom & I first officially met, but I had a lump in my breast that I was planning to get checked out when I returned from my trip. I got diagnosed with breast cancer a couple of weeks later (in September 2021) . When I discovered that the cancer had metastasized into my bones 3 months later and I was Stage 4, I was shocked and devastated! I didn't share the Stage 4 news with hardly anyone for several months while I was still processing this news myself. In March 2022 I saw a mutual friend of Tom's & mine post something on Facebook about Tom having Stage 4 prostate cancer. I immediately reached out to our mutual friend Jun Ulama (who is also a Minnesotan like Tom) to ask for Tom's contact information.

I reached out to Tom shortly thereafter and I asked him all kinds of questions after sharing my Stage 4 diagnosis with him. He was very open and helpful.

Tom & I have seen each other at several races since then (a few of which we were on the same pace team) and he has become a good friend, mentor and confidant since then. I am thankful to have someone to vent to that truly understands what I am going through. Tom is such a positive, inspiring person who has become a real blessing in my life!

Chapter 27: Pet Therapy 101 - with Otto - My Best Buddy

Song: "Martha My Dear"

Artist: Paul McCartney

Quote: "All his life he tried to be a good person. Many times, however, he failed. For after all, he was only human. He wasn't a dog." - Charles M. Schulz

Otto's word for me: Constant

One might easily argue that one of the most endearing songs about dogs is "Martha My Dear," by Paul McCartney. That was the name of Paul's sheepdog - Martha. As Paul so eloquently stated "we're meant to be for each other."

I honestly don't remember that first day we met Otto. When I asked you when it was you simply cocked your head to the side and gave me a silly grin. I am sure you could care less about the day and date we met. Dogs know stuff like that isn't really important as what is important is that I have the *memory.* I am sure Otto, you find me humorous that I try to remember such crazy stuff, when you are simply trying to remember where you hid your last dog treat. Or maybe where you last left your big bone. The truly important stuff in your mind.

On one of the first few days we meet, we just simply connected. We formed a special bond. Maybe because you probably saw a "softie" that would be good for extra treats. You didn't even know then how good Uncle Tom's breakfasts could be.

I will always treasure that day when I was trying to decide what to do with my cancer diagnosis. Treatment or no treatment? If treatment then what type? Chemo? Radiation? Drug? One of those days in my life that was the absolute worse. When my fear and stress were so high because of the decisions I needed to make.

You didn't give me advice that day. You didn't tell me what to do. Incredibly you just came up and simply curled up into a ball and simply took a nap on my lap.

You simply napped. I made my phone calls and set up all my appointments and planned my drug treatment and surgery. You kept me calm and comforted me. You were like "Uncle Tom don't worry about it. We just need to rest. We just need our nap time." Otto, you showed me the importance of "rest when stressed."

That was the moment that I knew you were teaching me that we would be having lots of naps in the future together. You knew that when experiencing fear and stress that taking a nap might not solve my problems, but a nap would help me become more relaxed and think clearer. It would calm me.

I remember when you wouldn't eat your breakfast some mornings. But you would eat it when I spent time training you to do tricks. You caught on to "high five" and "lay" easily. You never got the concept of "roll over" and "catching" was definitely not your strength.

Otto just like I struggle in life with issues with pronunciation and relationships, you struggle with learning how to roll over and play catch. We all have our "Achilles heel," but when you have a best buddy at your side it makes our struggles less of an issue. We just enjoy life and play and continue on to the next day.

When I came home from the hospital on July 4th, I had a catheter in me. You simply didn't care. Nothing had changed after my surgery. You were still "my best buddy." Your love for me was totally *unconditional.*

You knew when I was sitting on the couch that we still needed to get our walks in. You would go to my front door and simply bark once. You knew we both needed our exercise - just a simple neighborhood walk

Our run time would have to wait for now. Uncle Tom had to get better. You didn't push me to go on runs with you. You didn't make me play chase with you. But you certainly made sure you got your daily treat and your walk treat. You were definitely going to make sure I wouldn't forget that. Treats are important as it shows you are enjoying life and are happy.

On July 30th, 2019, I received my Stage 4 cancer diagnosis. More drugs, surgeries, and treatments would be needed. When you saw me for the first time after that initial Stage 4 cancer diagnosis you just ran up to me and wanted me to pet you. You were so happy to see me. You made me smile. Stage 4 cancer meant nothing to you because you were just simply happy being together with me.

Otto, you had our daily routine set when you would come over. We needed to eat lunch as close to 11AM as possible. If I was on the computer and working you would run upstairs and bark once at me.

Then twice you would bark if you thought I didn't understand that lunch was late. Lunch was very important to you as it was our special time together.

Your number one lunch preference is chicken. You don't care if fried, grilled, or rotisserie chicken - you just like chicken. Yummy chicken.

Then when 100% positive there was no more chicken or lunch left to eat you went upstairs. That meant "our nap time" was happening. Depending upon the temperature and weather, you might cuddle right up next to me.

Of course, Marty is never very far away. Your stuffed toy - Marty - that you cherished as a puppy and still to this day. It crinkles and squeaks and you can carry it around if needed. Also, Marty has been well known to have a treat or two on him, or by him, after our walks that you would have to go find.

I think one of my favorite memories is when I first placed treats in an old white tube sock. I remember clearly how frustrated you were initially trying to get the treats out of that sock. But you figured it out that by swinging the sock most of the treats would come flying out. Then off to go find which treats you would readily eat and others you would leave for later. When the treats were close but not out of the sock you would get your head into the end of the sock to get your treats out. Otto you always seem to figure out a solution to every problem.

Otto I couldn't have said it any better than Paul McCartney – "we're meant to be for each other." And as Paul McCartney also states, "you have always been my inspiration."

I remember the first time you had to wear the "cone of shame" because you had to have that boy surgery that boy dogs get. We got through that together with you at times proudly wearing your cone. You were so happy when you didn't have to wear the "cone of shame" anymore.

Then unfortunately you were just having fun and relaxing and another dog bit you. So, you needed stitches and then you had to wear the "cone of shame" again. My heart went out to you when I saw you that first time, as nobody hurts my best buddy. But we got through it and the "cone of shame" was again gone.

When I was back again into a catheter, our running was limited. The medication I was placed on to keep my need to urinate frequently wasn't working. I was retaining urine, so a catheter was put in me again to get the urine flowing again.

I remember the first time I took you for a walk with my catheter. As John Hiatt states in the song "My Dog and Me" - the line "how many times can one dog pee." Otto you might never answer that mystery question for me. When I was a kid, I always wanted to know with certainty "how many licks does it take to get to the center of a Tootsie Pop?" I guess Otto with you I will never really know "how many times can a dog pee."

I felt terrible the day I had to rush you to the vet. Because you weren't feeling good and you were throwing up. I noticed some blood in your vomit and was worried about you. Maybe I overreacted that day, but I couldn't afford not to overreact. I just didn't like the feeling of leaving you alone at the vet. You don't just abandon your best buddy. I wanted to hold your paw through all of what you had to go through. That is what best buddies do for each other.

Your surprise appearance at my 600th Marathon party after the Fargo marathon was priceless.

You're running towards me in the meeting room at the Homewood Suites Hotel was priceless.

Two best buddies connecting again. I can't thank you enough for making my day extra special with your attendance. The photo of you in my lap became a classic photo and would eventually be seen by millions of people.

You quickly became a celebrity. You didn't really care. You were still the same goofball Otto. Uncle Tom was still picking up your poop, so all was good and that part will never change.

Otto, you have appeared in multiple articles, including in the USA Today. People know you from your appearance on the Today Show back in September of 2022. Al Roker I know would have loved to have been interviewing you instead of me. You're just so lovable Otto.

Not sure if your celebrity status brought out more lady dogs seeking a chance to meet Otto. You have so many lady dog friends to begin with that you have gotten to know over the years. From Frieda, to JJ, to Sierra to name just a few. You definitely attract the lady dogs with your handsome looks Otto, especially after a nice bath or grooming session. You used to have just about a pitch-black coat, and now you have a sophisticated touch of gray.

Otto, you have seen me through three surgeries, multiple drug injections, and some 46 radiation treatments, and you are still my best buddy. Nothing has changed with us. Our connection and love for each other runs deep.

We have both lost people near to us due to cancer. I lost my friend Rick to cancer. You lost one of your dog buddies, Reggie. I think Reggie taught you how to pee like a boy dog. Reggie loved his pork. Rick loved running and ended his running career with 2,845 races.

Otto you never cared that I had cancer. Otto you couldn't care less that I had Stage 4 cancer. Otto you could care less whether I wore a diaper or not. Otto, you didn't care when I had hot flashes.

Otto you never a made a comment or treated me differently when I lost weight. Otto, you just still loved me *unconditionally*.

Otto, you knew the days I struggled either emotionally, mentally, or physically. When I was having a bad day or struggling Otto you would still come over and lay by my side or on my lap. In fact, the worse day I was having the more attention you gave me.

You would get irritated when I would be reading a book or doing a Sudoku puzzle. I thought it was funny that when I was reading Dean Koontz's book the "Watchers" that you would come up and basically tell me with one look – "put the book down and pet me." You had to have all my attention. So, Dean Koontz was correct when he said "dogs are one of those things that make you happy and make you wonder." I'll probably never have a fair chance to read all of Dean Koontz's books Otto, as you will be always asking for and demanding my attention.

Remember our first "guys night" Otto? The first time you were staying over at Uncle Tom's? I had pictured us staying up late and having lots of crazy fun and eating lots of treats. Instead, after you ate dinner and we went out for a walk, at 7pm you were on the landing barking at me that you wanted to go upstairs to go to bed. What Otto? I finally convinced you take a nap on the sofa by me and at 8:30 pm I carried you upstairs to my bed for nighttime.

Then I had to get up and pee and you would give me "the look." Believe me when I say you don't want Otto to give you "the look." You were not happy that I interrupted your sleep. You woke up and moved away from me and curled up tight and went back to bed. You mustn't have stayed mad at me long though, because when I woke up you were laying right next to me just like nothing happened.

We have something that so many people need and want. We have *unconditional love for one another.*

As Gilda Radner so eloquently stated: "II think dogs are the most amazing creatures; they give unconditional love. For me, they are the role model for being alive."

I can't thank you enough for all you do buddy.

Whatever happens with us I know we will always have each other's back.

As Erica Jong so clearly stated, that "dogs come into our lives to teach us about love. They depart to teach us about loss. A new dog never replaces an old dog, it merely expands the heart."

Otto
(Otto's story is told by his mom Nora Jaster)
Crystal, MN
Otto's word for himself: Companion

I was looking to get a dog in 2018 that I was going to adopt but it wasn't going anywhere. I had been looking for quite some time and had submitted several applications to different agencies with no luck. Nothing. I didn't have a fenced in yard. I was living alone and had to rely on other people to help me if needed. I didn't have another dog for a companion. It just seemed that the list of denial reasons was endless.

Finally, a coworker of mine knew someone that had puppies for sale. I was one of several people that was interested but because I was a referral, they had *picked* me. Yeah! I was finally getting a dog!

My mom said I had to wait through all the rejections to get to Otto because he was meant to be with me. As soon as I brought Otto home, I knew he was a fantastic choice. He was a fast learner and listened, well for the most part he listened. He followed me everywhere from the beginning, like he knew I was his Mama. I just knew this was the right dog for me.

Tom initially offered to let him out while I was at work if I ever needed help. Having a dog lover as a neighbor, like Tom, would definitely be beneficial to Otto and myself. But would they get along is always a good question with dogs? Time would certainly tell.

Tom started to let Otto out during the day, just a couple times a day. Just basic walks so Otto could get some exercise and go potty and poop. But it seemed something magical might be happening.

Then before you know it, Tom would simply sit with Otto. Then he brought Otto a toy to play with. Then maybe a few more toys and some new treats. Then before you know it, they were hanging out every day I was at work. Two guys just hanging out together and enjoying each other's company, but it was far beyond that.

I have never seen a bond like I have between Otto and Tom. They started out as friends but quickly became best friends. I feel as though Otto was meant to be so he could be in my life and in Tom's life. Otto is always on the lookout for Tom, if he hears Tom's garage door open at the townhome, he lives in he expects Tom to come visit. When our garage door opens, Otto will jump excitedly at the door to greet him. When Otto is on a walk and sees a car that looks like Tom's he wants to see if it is Tom. Otto never wants to miss an opportunity to see Tom. He will give Tom many kisses, sit on his lap and *demand* to be petted.

It is priceless to watch Otto when he knows his visit with Tom is ending as he will not look at Tom. He will accept affection but will avoid *any* eye contact because he is mad that Tom is leaving him. He always wants to be near Tom. They simply love to spend time together and it shows when you see those two together.

Otto acts differently when he comes home from his time with Tom depending on how Tom feels. Otto acts sad when he comes home if Tom is having a bad day. I think he feels that he should have stayed with Tom longer to give him more support. I will never forget when Tom was first diagnosed. He came home and Otto just sat with him on the couch, like they were processing the news together. Otto was saying it's okay best buddy, I'm here to help you through it.

Otto surprised Tom at his 600th Marathon party at the Homewood Suites in Fargo, North Dakota. Otto didn't tell him he was coming as he wanted it to be a surprise. Tom was happily surprised as he was with holding and seeing his best buddy. The picture of Tom holding Otto that day even made it on the Today Show in September of 2022. Two best buddies just so happy to be with each other. Priceless.

Seeing the value of what a dog can do and mean to someone with an illness is amazing. Otto shows the meaning of what pet therapy is really all about. Simply unconditional love.

Well, okay not always unconditional love as sometimes Otto likes a treat. Well, let's just make it two treats.

A major bonus for me is that I have another important dog in my life.

Maggie Benson, Conroe, Texas, AKA "Pretty Girl", on running and your feelings and thoughts on your mom maybe getting a new puppy?

1) Maggie when did you come into your mom's life?

11/30/14 is when I was born. I got to my new home on 1/15/2015.

2) Maggie what is the longest you have run with your mom?

10 miles! When I simply had enough running, I would sit or lay down on the road and not move until we turned around to go back home.

3) Maggie what is your "nickname" and how and why did you get it?

"Pretty girl." My mom thinks I'm pretty. And Tom thinks I'm pretty.

4) You love sleeping in beds and comforting people when they are resting, please explain?

Yes, I like cuddling with humans. I'm very affectionate.

5) Rumor is there might be a new puppy in your life soon, any thoughts on that?

I think I'll grow to like the puppy as long as she doesn't eat my food/treats or take all of Tom's doting away from me. Super big grin here!

(Note: Just for clarification purposes, Maggie did not actually respond to these answers. Maggie's mom, Amie Benson, responded to these questions for her. Amie is solely responsible for the content contained within the answers.)

My Final Postcard

"How Do I say Goodbye"

Dean Lewis

When I started my initial quest to run a marathon in all 50 states back in August of 2002 one of the most important components of accomplishing my goal was making sure my mom was able to follow my progress. It is a very simple equation: mom happy = son happy.

Even though email communication was initially started in 1971, it really wasn't a main form of communication until the early 2000's. The cell phone craziness hadn't yet started as well, so back then not everyone had a cellphone to take pictures, talk, and text.

My mom wasn't computer literate so sending emails wasn't a viable option as this was just starting to become a major form of communication between two people. Sadly, I couldn't even text her photos of my marathons and travel adventures.

In 2002 I started sending my mom a postcard from a marathon that I had completed in each state. The goal was simple - my mom would eventually get a postcard from all 50 states that I would have completed a marathon. This seemed pretty simple at the time, but it did become more challenging every year since I started on this goal for many reasons.

Postcard stamps were just .23 apiece back in 2002. It was relatively easy to find a postcard at almost any airport store, drug store, or hotel I stayed at. I would carry a book of postcard stamps on me as those were not as easy to find.

I would buy a postcard, put on the stamp, and then once I successfully finished the marathon, I would complete the postcard. Frequently I would mail the postcard right from the hotel where I was staying or at the airport. It was at the Omaha, Nebraska, marathon on August 25th, 2002, I ran a 4:34:49 marathon on a hot and humid day. I felt no need to push the pace as visiting the medical tent or getting an IV after the marathon was not something I wanted to accomplish.

The Omaha marathon was a smaller marathon with just 258 finishers that year. However, that marathon had at least four marathoners from Minnesota that would include Frank Bartocci, Peter Butler, David Holmen, and myself.

I had no idea that day that the four of us would become the top four people from the state of Minnesota with the number of marathons/ultras completed by 2023. I don't think anyone would have guessed that in 2002. It took me many years to pass Peter Butler. I am still currently chasing Frank Bartocci who has at least 1,017 marathons or ultras. Yes, that is the correct number 1,017 marathons and ultras. I would have loved to have a photo of the four of us that day, but cell phone cameras were not yet an everyday item. Had I likely taken any photos back then it was usually on a disposable 24 shot Kodak camera. Looking back at photos from that weekend I sadly wasn't able to find any of the four of us together that day.

Here are the approximate number of Marathon/ultras for the four of us as of the writing of this book in 2023:

Frank Bartocci - 1,017
Tom Perri - 665
Peter Butler - 580
David Holmen – 500

The combined total for the four of us is 2,764 marathons. Or another way to look at it is nearly 72,500 miles ran between all these marathons and ultras. Amazingly there are only two marathons in Minnesota – Grandma's Marathon and Twin Cities Marathon - that have more marathon participants than the total of our marathon/ultras.

That marathon also had other notable marathon legends by the names of Norm Frank and Henry Rueden. In my opinion Norm Frank, should have been the first person in North America to hit 1,000 marathons. I believe he ended his lifetime marathon career at 965. That goal of 1,000 for a North America marathoner - regardless of being male or female was first accomplished by Jim Simpson on 1/1/13. It would be just over nine years later that Angela Tortorice would become the first female to run 1,000 marathons on April 2nd, 2022. Henry Rueden would be the third male in North America to reach the goal of 1,000 marathons.

It was also that day that I met several marathon runners that I would share multiple marathon experiences with. I had no idea when I completed that marathon on a Sunday in Omaha, Nebraska, that completing that marathon would change my life. Anyone noticing a theme here how running a marathon can your life? I sure hope so.

A postcard from Nebraska was the first postcard my mom received starting in 2002. She had received a postcard from my Disney Marathon in 1995, but that was well before I started on my 50-state marathon goal. Then came a few others but the big one in 2002 was Hawaii when I finished the Honolulu Marathon on Sunday, December 8th, 2002. My mom loved getting the postcards as they would frequently arrive to her before I had actually returned from my trip. When she received the postcard that was my confirmation that another marathon state was completed.

Back in 2002 and the early 2000's doing a marathon in all 50 states wasn't a very easy goal to accomplish. I am not just talking about just running the marathon, but the logistics and planning it takes to accomplish the goal. What made it even more complex was trying to find a marathon I could do in all 50 states. Some states maybe had only one or two marathons, while states like California, Florida, and Texas seemed to have a marathon, or a longer, distance race every weekend.

My initial goal was to get 12 states a year, but as mentioned with some states not having a great selection of marathons to choose from it took longer than planned to complete my 50-state marathon goal the first time. So instead of completing in four years, it took just over five years to complete the first time.

I had just finished the Charlotte's Thunder Road Marathon on Saturday, December 9th, 2006, in 3:58:51. I had already mailed my mom a postcard in 2005 when I had completed the inaugural Charlotte Thunder Road Marathon, so no postcard after that particular marathon in 2006, but in hindsight I wish I had.

That Sunday after returning from my flight from Charlotte airport I went out to see my mom and dad. My mom truly loved hearing the stories of my marathon travel adventures. She never understood my allure to running marathons but she loved seeing the finisher medal and my marathon swag which was usually a simple cotton t-shirt.

I still think to this day that my mom still loved it best when I would bring the local newspaper from the city that I had just visited, so she could read it during the upcoming week. She was always intrigued by the cost of a gallon of milk or a loaf of bread in a different city and state. My guess is that was from being alive around the time of the big depression.

On Wednesday, December 13th in the early evening I had received a call from my brother-in-law that my mom had taken a fall. Okay, so she had fallen before and had broken her hip and then she had hip surgery. So that is what I initially thought that happened again when she had fallen. However, this time I was told that she had apparently stumbled down the stairs and had hit her head. She had sustained a serious head injury.

Sadly, the next day at around 10am on Thursday, December 14th, my mom passed away at 83 years old.

My Catholic upbringing kicked in and my immediate thought was "remember that you are dust and to dust you shall return."

My mom was buried on a cold day on Monday, December 16th, 2006. She would never see me complete or hear about me completing my 50-state marathon goal. I had two postcards yet to send to her as I still needed marathons in the states of New Hampshire and Oregon.

Unfortunately for me, I was never in a real rush to finish my 50-state marathon goal. It was just assumed that my mom and one of her favorite actresses - Betty White - would both be going strong into their 100's. But as I had mentioned earlier there are no guarantees in life. Unfortunately, neither one of these made it to their magic 100th birthday.

So, I completed the inaugural Eugene Marathon in Eugene, Oregon, on Sunday, April 29th, 2007, in 3:40:02. The course is a very flat and fast course, and you get to finish on the Hayward field track. So, the postcard that was usually sent to my mom was now sent to just my dad.

So, 49 states completed and just New Hampshire left to complete, so at least one parent could see me achieve this goal. If you read an early chapter, you would remember that on Wednesday, August 1st, 2007, at approximately 5:36 pm I crossed over the I-35W bridge that goes over the Mississippi River into Minneapolis, Minnesota. I missed the bridge collapse by approximately 30 minutes. I put my goal of doing a marathon in New Hampshire into high urgency mode so I could get it done.

I also remember in another chapter telling you that life sometimes doesn't go as planned. Sadly, my dad died on Tuesday, September 18th, 2007. I truly believe he lost his fight or reason to live when his wife of 58 years had passed away before him. He also had significant health issues which was a contributing factor.

I never had the chance to sit and chat with my mom or dad and tell them about my finishing my goal of running a marathon in all 50 states. I am sure they were looking down on me on Saturday, September 29th, 2007, at the New Hampshire Marathon in Bristol, New Hampshire, as I struggled emotionally during this marathon finishing in 4:24:46. A rare race for me to emotionally struggle. This marathon was being run for one goal only and that was to simply finish the marathon.

I remember taking my time running this marathon and taking pictures along the course. When the sun peeked through the clouds, I knew that my parents were looking down on me. I had no doubt that I would successfully finish this marathon.

However, after I had time to ponder the significance of my accomplishment I needed to get cleaned up and move onto my next marathon the very next day - Sunday, September 30th, 2007. I completed another marathon in New Hampshire at the Clarence Demar Marathon in Keene, New Hampshire, in 3:57:46.

This was planned due to three reasons, with the first reason being just in case I had any travel issues getting to the race on Saturday I then had a New Hampshire marathon back-up plan for Sunday. Second, if any issues with the Saturday marathon not happening or getting canceled for whatever reason I was covered. The craziest third reason I thought at the time was if I ever did complete the 50-state marathon goal for the second time, I didn't want New Hampshire to be my final state again for my second time finishing the 50 States. So, by doing the Clarence Demar Marathon I immediately eliminated that from happening.

It was on a cooler fall day in October 2007 - the exact date I can't positively remember- that I sat at the grave site and simply talked about my 50-state marathon finish to my mom and dad. I was graciously granted a second marathon finisher medal that would eventually be placed on their gravesite that day at Fort Snelling cemetery. I finally was able to show my mom the medal and t-shirt that was of my final state that I needed to do a marathon in to accomplish my 50 State Marathon certified goal.

My niece Kristen Fjerstad, my Godchild that did a Question and Answer for this book, was mailed that final postcard from New Hampshire.

My 50 postcards were eventually all mailed so I accomplished my original goal. A total of 48 to my mom and dad. My dad then saw 49 of them. And Kristen received one of the postcards which was the final postcard.

Now as I deal with the emotional and physical side of Stage 4 cancer, I wonder what I would want to write on my final postcard. What do I want to be my final thoughts to be in a world that is forever getting more complex.

On my final postcard I think I would simply write:

"I never lived the perfect life that I so desperately wanted to live. I made many errors and mistakes, but I also did some amazing things right. Like everyone, I tried to overcome personal obstacles to make myself better in the bad times and good times. If I hurt anyone or disappointed anyone I truly apologize. If I made you laugh and smile at least once then I led a successful life. Please don't remember me by my running numbers and statistics. Please remember me for trying my best to make you have fun when you ran with me. If you remember me for my infectious desire to have everyone complete at least one marathon in their lifetime then I did okay, because I know a marathon can change one's life."

It is never too late to run your first marathon. Just saying.

Also, if you follow the "circle of life" with trying to make a difference in one person's life every day then you are living a life with meaning and purpose.

How you handle the personal obstacles in your life will say a lot about the legacy you leave behind and how people remember you regardless of whether you are still alive or dead.

What will your final postcard say?

How do you want to be remembered?

Final thoughts

Here is some basic information and numbers from just the 27 people stories including myself:

1) Approximately 11,000 races completed.

2) Approximately 3,100 marathons/ultras completed.

3) Approximately 900,000 miles ran.

Here is some basic information and numbers from all people that I gathered information from including myself:

1) Approximately 23,000 races completed.

2) Approximately 4,500 marathons/ultras completed.

3) Approximately two million miles ran.

Questions and Thoughts for individual or Group Discussion

For fun, see how your individual goals or running club compares to everyone's total in the book.

Did you beat us in any or all three categories of races completed, marathon/ultras completed, or miles ran?

Running is supposed to be about fun challenges and goals, so see what you can accomplish either individually or together with your running club.

Which new race distance or new running adventure will you now look forward to trying?

Which Chapter in the book did you relate to the most and why?

What new goal did this book inspire you to achieve?

What can I do in my daily life to make my community and the world a better place to live and run in?

Best piece of advice for a runner:

Always enjoy your running. - Benji Durden

My best advice for any runner is to enjoy where you are with your running. In other words, live in the moment of being healthy enough to run. Goals can be great motivators and at the same time it may lead you into over training. So why not enjoy each run for what you really need from it. Only you can decide what you really need from today's run. – Teresa Ferguson

Include intervals, hill repeats, and tempo runs in your training plan if you want to get faster. Strength training at least three times weekly helps to build endurance. Cross training such as biking or swimming also helps to prevent injury, you must stay healthy! – Gwen Jacobson

Learn to find joy in the pain of the effort. There will be a time when you cannot run and you will miss it. - Brock Jenkins

No matter your time, a mile is a mile. All that matters is that you finish!! ALWAYS finish what you start! - Joyel Kautza -Barnard

Enjoy, believe, and stay positive! Attitude is everything! - Danny Ripka

Recovery and diet are as important, if not more important, as the workout itself. All the effort you put into training, you need to equal that effort toward recovery and diet. Otherwise, you will face obstacles that will take even more effort to overcome. - Josh Winograd

For a runner that is training for their first marathon. Runners are notorious for telling people how difficult a marathon is to run. It is not that tough if you set reasonable expectations or people would not keep doing it. I have met a lot of runners, and I only know one person that has completed only one marathon. A marathon is a long distance that your mind cannot fully grasp at the start of training. Ever heard "I can't even drive that far" by a non-marathoner? Training is progressive with manageable increases per week. Contrary to popular belief, marathoners do not run marathon-like distances every day. Focus on no more than a month's worth of training to set a positive framework for your mind. Finally, when you get to the race, start at a slow and comfortable pace. Focus on a slower pace rather than how you feel. It is easy to feel great at the start and run too fast with all the excitement and anxiety. If you start even seconds per mile too fast at the start, you will slow minutes per mile and feel miserable at the end. You have run the perfect marathon if you think "I could have run faster" when you cross that finish line. Your priority should be to finish that first marathon. Practically no one in your circle is going to ask your finish time but will express sheer awe of the accomplishment. - Kathryn White

You are not in this by yourself. There is invisible and visible support waiting for you at the finish line. Whatever you are facing as you train and as you race, someone else also has been through it and made it. You can, too! - Kim Zabel

Must have race day item:

Sunglasses. - Amie Benson

Cute skirt. - Angel Brock

Get into my zone. - Tiffany Carey

Must have toilet available before race. - Steve DeBoer

My shoes. - Benji Durden

Sweat band. - Yvonne Leaf

GPS Watch. - Hank Lopez

As much orange as possible. - Tina Hauser

My music. - Joyel Kautza -Barnard

A reason WHY to run that race. - Steve Mura

Band-Aids or nip guards for nipples. - Tom Perri

My race bib! (Note that if doing more than one race that day/weekend, verify that you are positively wearing the correct bib for that race.) – Tom Perri

Sunscreen and race cap. - John Points

Electrolytes. - Natalie Uyeno

Sunglasses. - Kathryn White.

Banana and peanut butter bagel sandwich. - Josh Winograd

Banana. - Heather Zeigler

Must have race finish item:

Something COLD to drink. - Amie Benson

Banana and water. – Maggie Benson

Chocolate milk. (Note: I want my medal so I am assuming I am already getting that.) - Angel Brock

Comradery of my teammates. I am a good teammate! – Tiffany Carey

Fruit (watermelon favorite in the summer) ; something salty if 15K or longer. - Steve DeBoer

Must have finish item is the perfect medal picture!

It must be representative of the race or area. (Bonus points if it is on the course.) - Emily Enyeart

A cold beer with Tom. - Jeff & Tina Hauser

An ice-cold beer, no matter the distance, and no matter the time of day! – Linda Juretschke

1 Beer and 1 Bloody Mary. - Joyel Kautza -Barnard

A very big smile and the ability to have a celebratory jump! – Hank Lopez

Community. - Steve Mura

Lots of treats. - Otto

Positive memories. - Tom Perri

A great burger at a local micro-brewery. – John Points

Chocolate milk. - Cade Remsburg

Coke and salty chips. – Danny Ripka

Medal. - Natalie Uyeno

Sunglasses and a finisher's medal. -Kathryn White

Ice cold beer. – Heather Zeigler

Questions & Answers

Mike Andreen, from Brooklyn Center, MN on his past marathons and actively donating blood.

1) What was the deciding factor to register for your first marathon?

I was an avid hockey player in the fall and winter and chose training for a marathon as a way of staying in shape. Also, my friend, Bob Youds, had a goal of running Grandma's Marathon 20 consecutive years and his 11th time running Grandma's was my 1st marathon!

2) How many marathons have you completed?

10 – Grandma's Marathon

2 - NorthShore In-line Skate

3 - Metrodome In-line Skate

3 - Saint Paul In-line Skate

3) What was your deciding factor when you first registered to donate blood?

I really got a little bit of a push from Byron Van Dake (Charter Member of the Twin Cities Marathon who completed it the first 22 years) as he was so dedicated to it that he inspired me to start giving

4) Do you remember when you first donated blood?

It was in the early 1990's and I also organized blood drives while I was working for Centex Homes in Minnetonka.

5) How many gallons or pints of blood have you donated?

My next donation will be ten gallons.

6) Any advice for someone that is not sure or possibly a little afraid of donating blood that they should just donate?

The idea that you can save 3 lives with one donation just makes you feel good and once you get by the whole "needle" thing it's really painless.

7) One last question, is what retired Minnesota Twins player did you used to

play baseball with when you were younger?

It was Tim Laudner the 1987 Twins catcher. I played Babe Ruth baseball and High School baseball with him. He won't admit to me striking him out!

Braden Benson, Green Bay, Wisconsin, on his running journey and his first marathon experience.

1) When did you first start running and why?

I started running when I was about 13. My mom had got me into it at the time since she was running a decent amount.

2) What was your significant running accomplishment during your Senior year in High School?

My senior year of high school we had a pretty good 4x800 relay team. We kind of surprised ourselves at state when we were able to win with a relay time of 7:52. That was definitely a fun experience and helped make my decision to keep running in college.

3) What made you decide to run your first marathon and which marathon did you complete?

I ran my first marathon in September of 2021 in Fargo. I was done with college running at that point and decided I would try running one. A few of my college friends that had recently graduated were doing some marathons at the time as well.

4) What is the one thing you would have done differently regarding training for your first marathon?

Training for the marathon was somewhat difficult since I was usually running alone, which was a lot harder when you are used to running with a team. I was only doing about 30 miles a week during training. Doing a bit more miles would have probably helped with the race.

5) Any tip for someone running and training for their first marathon?

For someone running their first marathon I would just say find a training plan that works for your skill level and try your best to stick to it. As far as race day don't take the first one too seriously. You're either going to love it or hate it. If it doesn't go so well you can always do another one.

Diane Bolton, Nashville, Tennessee, on her marathon journey and being the North American Coordinator for the World Mega Marathon Ranking.

1) What fascinated you about the marathon distance to try to run your first marathon?

I thought females had to be not only fast but young, skinny and small chested to complete a marathon. The day I volunteered at a local marathon finish line that vision changed. I was sharing tears of joy with the athletes that crossed that finish line as I placed a medal around their neck! I encountered a multitude of ages, shapes, sizes, and pace times. They not only moved me with tears of joy for each athlete, THEY inspired me.

2) What is your best tip for someone running their first marathon?

DON'T…. WARNING: this can become addictive. Kidding aside, train, listen to your body & embrace the moment. Smile big as you see that finish line and smile BIGGER as you reach that finish line! There are so many cameras all around to capture your milestone!

3) How many marathons have you completed, as well as which marathon have you completed the most?

I have completed over 395 marathons or ultra marathons. After thinking more on the questions, I realized the marathons I completed the most are ones closest to Nashville where I live. I have a tie. Blister In The Sun Marathon, which is a hidden gem of a small-town low-key event held during a terrible month for running conditions here in Tennessee in August! In April we host the Country Music Marathon which also provides a fun tour of our city highlights.

4) Why did you decide to become the North American Coordinator for the World Mega Marathon Ranking?

Nearing the completion of my 300th marathon I was excited to know I would be eligible to join the World Mega Marathon Rankings. This achievement was incredible to me as like many, I thought I would be a run 1 and done. At the finish line of my 300th marathon was our North America

World Mega Marathon Ranking Coordinator, Walt Prescott and his wife & Kendel. They not only congratulated me on my race finish but welcomed me into the World Mega Marathon. It was such a beautiful moment for me to see them both present at this milestone. As we spoke more Walt said he was hoping I would consider accepting his coordinator position as he wished to pass on his title to one who would honor the integrity for which it was intended. To have the rectitude, trust and honesty endorsed by not only Walt Prescott but Tom Adair who is the founder of the World Mega Marathon Ranking is the highest compliment for me within the running community. It is an honor and privilege to uphold the integrity for which these rankings serve.

5) How and when can you join this club and is there any cost?

One can be added to the World Rankings once they achieve 300 marathons or ultra marathons that meet the criteria for the North America Mega Marathon Rankings. The criteria in which The North America Mega Marathon Rankings follow is that of the 50 States Marathon Club:
http://www.50statesmarathonclub.com
Upon verification that the races meet the criteria, I will ask for a list of these races which can be sent directly to me via email:
NorthAmericaMegamarathon@gmail.com
Tom Adair established these rankings for the purpose of fun and challenging oneself. There are absolutely no fees collected. I thank the vision and integrity of Tom and Walt in the achievements as we continue to maintain these rankings in the spirit of which they are intended to be.

6) Are you a Grandmother?

Hahah! I certainly am! Allows me to act like a kid again and get away with it!

Frank R. Campbell Ph.D, LCSW, C.T., from Baton Rouge, LA, Executive Director Emeritus, Baton Rouge Crisis Intervention Center and Founder of the, National Suicidology Training Center on fund raising and creating a charity run.

1) Do you remember the first time we met and what big item I bought at the live auction that final night of the conference way back in 1993, some thirty years ago?

I remember meeting you at the Annual AAS (American Association of Suicidology) conference. I did that Auction for over 20 years and it has been 20 since the last one and I am not able to recall the answer. I just know I liked you from day one and have been very proud of your accomplishments over the years I have known you.

(The auction occurred at the 25th Annual AAS conference in Chicago in 1993 which was my first time presenting at a National conference. I was lucky to get two items during the live auction with the first item being a Blackhawks signed hockey practice stick. The big item was a Michael Jordan signed basketball that I bought that I gave to my nephew as a high school graduation gift.)

2) You have a natural talent as an auctioneer, any special reason why?

I was lucky as a kid to know and run the reel-to-reel tape recorder for the auctioneer at the state 4H club event here at LSU (Louisiana State University) for several years. He was a natural and I guess I picked up some of his style. I'm a functional introvert so it is exhausting to do the auction as it forces me out of my preferred state of solitude. I did enjoy it and we raised a lot of money for the AAS board to use over the years.

3) You helped create a 5k fun run that was raising money for a charity that ran through what prison, please explain?

We were raising money for the Baton Rouge Crisis Intervention Center and someone came up with the idea to have an "Angola Break In" run. The money went to paying off two buildings we had purchased to run our 24-hour crisis line and survivors of suicide loss services. I had also created the LOSS Team model of Active Postvention and some of that went to help with any expenses we had going to the scenes of suicides.

4) You always can make me smile no matter how I am feeling that day, what is your secret power?

I wish I knew the answer and I am glad I can make that happen. I do have a unique ability to put humor into presentations on suicide and it is probably the most common feedback I get from my evaluations. I want people to relax and hear the information that can be hard to hear, I guess that has become part of my personality and it helps me be more at ease in social settings when I get others to smile when I notice something I think is funny or odd.

5) What is one thing you would say to someone struggling in a race and wants to give up to keep them going to finish the race?

I hear from folks like you who do marathons that what sustains them is a kind word from a person along the route that gives them water or encouragement to keep going. We all need those moments of support especially from friends and family. I know illness can run folks away from anyone battling cancer or any life stressor. We want to help and, in the moment, we pull back when a small gesture could not only be important to the person in need of support but to the person who offers that help. The Golden rule of "do unto others what you would want them to do for you" is golden for a reason.

Our loss team work has shown us that being the best part of someone's worst day makes a difference and provides the installation of hope that the newly bereaved will survive this indescribable manner of death. So being a small part of bringing hope to the hopeless is monumental to me.

Steve Cirks, from Champlin, Minnesota, on your running journey and your Boston experience in 2013.

1) Your favorite Minnesota Marathon and why?

My favorite Minnesota marathon is Twin Cities Marathon because it was my first and I have done fairly well there every time I ran it. I do have a love/hate relationship with Wild Duluth 50K (the course is tough but like that I finish it)
.

2) What year did you run the Great Wall of China Marathon and what was your biggest challenge running it?

Great Wall was spring of 2012 in China. I was running really well through 20 miles (first time up steps and hills didn't get me) after you get your pink wristband at 20-mile mark you head up "the goat path" it was referred to, steep terrian and ropes to help you get up (or down if going the other direction, I guess) . You could say I left a little bit of me over the wall in China and the Swedish Red Cross gives great IVs after the race.

3) What was your Boston Marathon experience like in 2013? I clearly remember talking to you that evening when you were at the hotel.

2013 Boston I was a late scratch with planter fasciitis, but went to support Eric, Jay and Joni to name a few. I was waiting for Joni at the finish (she was just finished for about 5 minutes and was in bag drop) when the first bomb went off. I was about two blocks away (one block past finish and one block over so I never saw the blast) . It wasn't until the second blast that we knew something was wrong. Then all the cops, firemen and first responders' radios went crazy and they tried to clear the streets. I avoided them long enough to see Joni and head back to the hotel. Pretty crazy not knowing what was going on and no cell service for hours. Also, sadly the hotel ran out of booze later in the day.

4) Have you been back to run the Boston Marathon since 2013?

I have not been back to run Boston, not due to bombings but I had been there 3 times and it wasn't on my important "to do" list anymore.

5) Your best advice for someone running their first marathon?

First marathon I tell everyone it should be no pressure, just finish at your own pace. The second marathon becomes tougher because you now have a time to beat which ratchets up the pressure.

Tom Daniel, from Maple Grove, MN, on being a great friend for nearly thirty years and your incredible softball career.

1) Do you remember when you played your first competitive game of softball?

I was 10 years old. Played around Memorial Park in St. James, Minnesota. My coach was Ab Stromen.

2) You are still playing competitive softball at what age and when do you plan on stopping?

I am playing competitive Senior Softball with the 85-year-old team. Called Team Rehab. I will keep playing as long as my body will let me.

3) How many softballs World Series have you played in and how many World Series rings do you have?

I have played in 25 World/National tournaments. I have a total of 22 rings for which 13 are Championship rings and 9 are Tournament rings. Also, one ring from USSSA (United States Specialty Sports Association) Hall of Fame.

4) How many years have you been umpiring softball games?

I have been umpiring for 50 plus years for both men and women slow pitch softball, as well as high school fast pitch.

5) What is the biggest challenge you had to face in life?

Sadly, the suicide deaths of my two sons.

Beth Davenport, from Sante Fe, New Mexico, on her marathon journey and being the "certifier" for the 50 State Marathon Club.

1) What was your deciding factor that made you want to run your first marathon?

I decided somewhere during my first 5K that I'd run a marathon someday.

2) What is your best advice for someone after finishing their first marathon?

I am not the right person to answer this question! I registered for what I thought was going to be my first marathon in June of 1993. In October of 1992, I registered for what was primarily a relay marathon, but it did have roughly 50 solo participants. My plan was to run 20 miles and drop, and a friend would take me to the finish and then back to my car. At mile 20 he decided I looked too good and made me run the whole thing.

So, I was registered for my second marathon before I even finished my first. I guess that's the advice, because after your first marathon you will hurt so much you may not ever want to do another. If you're already registered for the next one, then you won't just stop after one.

3) How many times have you completed a marathon in all 50 States?

4-time certified finisher. 47 states into round 5, but no real finish plan in place for the last 3 states that I still need.

4) Why did you decide to become the "certifier" for the 50 States Marathon Club?

Paula Boone simply asked me.

5) Can you explain the basic difference between a "certified" and "non-certified" 50 State Marathon finish?

Non-certified members have supplied just a list of a marathon in each state. If a member wants to certify the finish, they would additionally need to supply a copy of the results from each marathon on their list of 50.

(Note: At the time this chapter was completed Tom Perri was a seven-time 50 State Marathon certified finisher, Hank Lopez was a first time 50 State Marathon certified finisher, and Beth Davenport was a four-time 50 State Marathon certified finisher.)

Marcela Todd Davie, from Miami, Florida, on what makes her special with her pacing and running.

1) What made you decide to register for your first race?

My first race was the Corporate Run 5K in the year 2000. I work in a Corporate Fitness and Wellness Facility, and was asked by the Team Captain to help organize the Motorola Corporate Run Team, so I did. I also signed up for the 5K myself. I got hooked and the rest is history! That guy (his name is Vince Garcia and he forever changed my life) not only introduced me to running (along with a few others at the time) but he also made me realize how sharing the sport with others can be such a life changing experience for so many. I have since become a pacer, (love helping other reach their goals!) But I also have a Marathon and Half Marathon Training Program in South Florida called Friends in Training, Presented by Baptist Health. We have 4 different locations in Broward County, and we love changing lives one step at a time!

2) How many times have you paced and/or completed the Miami Marathon?

I have completed the Miami Marathon/Half Marathon every single year since it started. Soon will be my 22nd! And have paced about 20 of them!

3) How has the Miami Marathon changed from when we paced the 5:30 Pace Group together (Sunday, January 28th, 2008 finishing in 5:28:49) for the first time?

The race has grown a lot! To the point of selling out in the last couple of years! But the fabulous memories remain and forever will! Lots of smiles!

4) When pacing the Miami Marathon, you fluently speak at least two languages, can you please explain?

Yes, that is true. I am originally from Colombia, South America. The Miami Marathon has a great number of international participants with Colombia being #1 with largest number of international runners. One of the reasons is because we go to Colombia expos and tell runners about the fabulous experience Miami offers. Once here, I can communicate with both Spanish and English speakers.

5) How does that help make your pacing special by being at least bi-lingual?

It gives me a greater opportunity to connect with the runners and make them feel "welcome" and part of the team!

As we run together as a group, I love engaging my runners speaking their language. Some people share some great stories! Some people love connecting and they keep coming back to run with me year after year. Being bilingual is really a great opportunity to connect with more runners!

6) You're approaching your 80th marathon, what marathon will be your 80th if all goes as planned?

YES!! I'm super excited about this!! Shamrock Marathon in Virginia Beach, Virginia, will be marathon number 79, and Paris Marathon will be my 80th marathon! Wooo hooo!!!

Gary Dixon, Liverpool, United Kingdom, on running Comrades and completing 300 marathons plus marathons.

1) What marathon and what year did you do for your first marathon?

My first marathon was on November 7th, 1999, in New York City.

I wasn't a runner and took up the challenge of completing my first (and only) on the back of a drunken bet on New Year's Eve.

My preparation consisted of three half marathons a couple of months before and I was physically sick at the end of each.

My lack of preparation was summed up by the shoes I wore and the fact that I ran it in a thick cotton rugby jersey. In short, I was clueless!

So, when I got to halfway - I had no idea how I was going to double up and do the same again. However, the amazing crowds that support runners through the 5 boroughs dragged me round until I emerged in Central Park still in one piece. Somehow - I managed to finish in a time of 3:56:32 but I swore - never again.

My efforts were recognized by companies I had sponsor my chosen charity (Whizz Kidz) and I managed to raise over £10,000 - so my pain was very much worthwhile.

My running days stopped dead in their tracks and I never ran again until early 2002 when I was offered a charity place to run the London Marathon in April.

2) What marathon have you completed the most and why that marathon?

I have run the London Marathon 18 times and been lucky enough to be an official pacer on 8 occasions - with number 9 being due in April of 2024.

All marathon majors are very special but as a proud Brit - taking part in the London Marathon fills me with immense pride.

London is very similar to NYC in many ways - in particular the volume of support throughout the route. If the weather is good then the crowds are simply immense and make it a real party atmosphere.

In addition to my pacing the marathon I have also completed London in fancy dress on several occasions. My most memorable outfits included Batman; Mr. Incredible; Captain Y Fronts and an England Cricket player including batting pads; gloves and bat!

There are many iconic landmarks that you pass along the way in London but I think that finishing on the mall whilst passing Buckingham Palace with 200 meters to go - is without doubt the best finishing line in the world.

3) With all your many running accomplishments, which one are you most especially proud of?

In 2021 I took on the Challenge of running 10 marathons in 10 days.

To put this in to context - I had never run 2 marathons in 2 days so was going in at the deep end. Add to this the fact that the Windermere Marathon course is very hilly/undulating including one hill aptly named 'ice cream mountain' - I really was extending myself!

Somehow - my body held together and apart from losing both big toenails (mainly due to the downhill stretches on the course) - completed my challenge and managed to average 4:31 over the 10 days!

4) What was your biggest obstacle to completing your 300th marathon and what marathon was your 300th marathon?

I completed my 300th marathon on October 8th, 2023. I opted for it to be in Chester, UK, as this is close to where my family live and it meant that I could run over the finish line with my two young grandsons (Albert 3 and George 2) . In addition, my youngest grandson (Jaxon 3 months) was at the finish line waiting for grandad to hold him.

Having decided that this was going to be the date and venue for my 300th the big challenge was it meant that I had to run 45 marathons in a 12-month period to get there. Luckily my body held up and everything went as planned.

Another reason why I chose Chester was the fact that they had given me my 1st pacing opportunity on October 2013. Wind forward 10 years and I have now paced 76 marathons - something which brings me great joy to look back on.

Pacing is totally voluntary and is a real privilege to be trusted by so many runners to help them with their race goals and targets. People who have run with me remember me more for my pacing style as I always run with a bluetooth speaker and try and make it a party atmosphere all the way round.

5) What about your pacing and running Comrades and any suggestions to people out there that want to do Comrades?

The iconic Comrades marathon in South Africa is without doubt the most incredible road race in the world.

Why they call it a marathon - I will never know. The 'up run' is typically 87.2km and the 'down run' is now 90.2km. You can see from the course profile that it is extremely hilly and very testing.

The race is gun to gun and has a strict 12 hour cut off so if you are 1 meter from the finish line when the gun goes at 5:30pm - despite the distance you have covered it is a DNF (Did Not Finish) ! All that distance; all that time; all those hills and no medal and no finish time. Heartbreaking.

I ran Comrades in 2013 (10:48 up run) and 2014 (10:45 down run) so was never in fear of the dreaded DNF.

Wind forward to 2018 when I was invited as the only non-South African to pace Comrades. Crazily I said yes particularly as being a 'bus driver' that comes with the ultimate responsibility. They gave me the 11-hour 30 minutes bus to pace. Luckily everything went to plan and the bus arrived in the Moses Mabhida Stadium 11 hours 27 minutes later. Never again would I want to put myself under that pressure particularly as you pace solo at Comrades!

One of the things that Comrades does is to reward first time runners who take the challenge the following year to go back. If they do and succeed you are rewarded with a 'back-to-back medal'. By September 2018 a number of runners who had been on my bus in June were asking me to return to Comrades in 2019 to support them achieve their back-to-back goal.

Needless to say, I went and again brought the bus home safely and on time.

I framed my medals and my flag so there is definitely no going back. Nothing could surpass the memories I have already made - so why try?

6) So better to do Comrades on down or up year and your thoughts?

Anyone interested in doing Comrades needs to go on You Tube / Google and watch the videos of the start and the finish. It will make the hairs tingle just watching either!

As its gun to gun - so any time you lose to get to over the actual start line you do not get back. So, in my case - each year it took just about 10 minutes to cross the actual starting line.

When you look at the course profile most people would assume that downhill is easier. Personally, I would say exactly the opposite. On the down run there is so much impact on the quads / calf's it is very easy to get carried away and injure yourself. Uphill there are some parts of the course you have no option but to walk. I found that these walking periods gave your legs time to recover.

Both years I paced I even called walking periods on some of the downhills #bodymanagement.

Any runner that enters Comrades will not be disappointed.

The challenge is incredible; the crowds and the 48 aid stations are simply wonderful; the medals are small but the sense of achievement and pride are immense.

7) Any final comments on your running journey?

Running in many different countries has presented me with so many memories; I have made so many friends and hopefully I stay fit and healthy for many years to come so 300 was only the start of another journey.

Matt Ebersole, Carmel, Indiana, on his running and Personal Best Training (PBT) philosophy.

1) What is your Personal Best Training (PBT) philosophy?

Maximizing the time and effort a person wants to give to running. Balancing preparedness for short term goals with long term development that opens the possibilities for the runner. Meeting the runner where they are now and helping them get to where they want their running to take them.

2) What prompted you to become a runner?

The first runner I knew was my grandfather and he would take my brother and me to the park when we were very young and would run laps around the playground while we played. A few years later I discovered it felt really good to stay in motion and it gave me a rewarding feeling when the run was over. I ran my first race, a 15K, in 1980 and it has been a part of my life since.

3) What race distance is your personal favorite to run?

5 miles/8K is my favorite. There is something about that half hour (used to be less, now it's more!) of hard running that is a great balance of intensity and endurance.

4) How long have you been involved with the Monumental Marathon?

I became the elite athlete and pace team coordinator in 2013.

5) What is one tip you would give to a first-time marathoner?

Prepare the best you can while enjoying the process and without wearing yourself out before race day.

6) What has been one of your best success stories since you started PBT?

Thankfully, there are many candidates for success stories. The obvious great performances of my runners come to mind, but the real successes are far less obvious. Helping people achieve things in running that open the possibilities in their mind for other areas of life. Keeping people in the sport when they need to shift their reasons why they are running or helping them fit it into a very busy life. Of course, as I write this, Jesse Davis just qualified for his 3rd Olympic Trials Marathon with a PR at age 41. After missing the trials in 2020 he was convinced he was done trying to run fast marathons. Fortunately, while training for a range of distances as a new Masters runner, he realized there were still some great performances left. Witnessing his running and personal journey over the 17 years we have worked together is a very special reward for me.

Kristen Fjerstad, Saint Paul, MN, on running her first marathon and possibly going for a second marathon.

1) What was your motivating factor to take up running?

I worked my way through a variety of exercise and training plans, trying to find something I enjoyed enough to stick with. I have always used exercise as a way to decompress after a long day. Running was something I could do on my own (without a gym membership or equipment) . And it allowed me to be able to enjoy the outdoors, be in the sun, and escape the day while listening to music.

2) What made you decide to run a marathon?

Well, my crazy uncle/godfather ("Pacer Tom" - AKA Tom Perri) had run like 300 of them at that point, so I figured I should probably give it a shot! I'm kidding! I was approached by someone who asked if I'd run with her. I didn't really have any interest at first, but when she said it was in Amsterdam, that definitely made it more intriguing. I had also been recently diagnosed with rheumatoid arthritis, so I agreed to the marathon to prove to myself I could do it.

3) What marathon did you complete and why?

TCS Amsterdam Marathon, October 2015. I knew someone living in London at the time and she asked me to run it with her. I agreed and turned it into a 2-week trip to explore Europe.

4) Any thoughts on running a marathon again and what marathon might you want to run?

I have thought about running another one, but it would have to be something pretty fun. I'd need to do another destination run, because I need that extra incentive of a trip to make it worthwhile for me. I have discussed running the Disney World marathon with a friend, but haven't made any real plans.

5) Your mother (AKA Kathy Mutch my older sister) texted me that day totally worried about you as she was tracking you, can you please explain?

If I do run another one, I will make sure that no one tells my mother how to track runners and their progress online. I do not need her thinking I died again when she fails to refresh her screen. I'm sure you remember that story - mom was following me during my marathon and my tracker stopped updating. She started crying because she thought I was hurt or something had happened. Turned out, she just needed to refresh her screen. By the time she figured that out, I had finished the marathon.

6) You studied in Japan during college and you did get to see Mt Fuji, please explain?

I studied abroad in Tokyo during the fall semester of 2003 at Bunkyo Gakuin Univerisity based in Todaimae, Tokyo. There were about 15 or 18 of us in the study abroad program and two or three were pretty emphatic about climbing Mt Fuji. I didn't know much about climbing a mountain, but figured I likely wouldn't get another chance. Ultimately 13 of us decided to make the climb. We started in late afternoon and climbed through the night and made it to the summit before sunrise. I wish I could describe how beautiful that sunrise was. It's not an extremely tall mountain, but we were above the clouds. Seeing that sun start to pop up over that layer of clouds was such an incredible thing. I have pictures, but they don't do it justice. I remember being very cold (I had socks on my hands and many layers on) , but I was completely at peace. I stood there thinking how cool it was I was able to do that. It is still to this day one of my very favorite memories.

7) What is one tip you would give to a runner running their first marathon?

I couldn't believe how much the training impacted me, mentally. I was physically exhausted and I expected that. But the mental exhaustion was completely unexpected. I'm not someone who cries easily and I remember crying at a commercial. It was the worst kind of commercial too, because I can describe in detail what happened, but I couldn't tell you what the advertisement was for. They showed a man running around a track, training for a marathon. JJ Watt was in it, holding a sign that said "your dream is 26.2 miles away" or something like that. I absolutely bawled when I saw it. Then, later, I was describing my emotional breakdown to someone else, and started crying again. I never would have expected the training to impact me so significantly.

8) When can a person donate blood after a cancer diagnosis?

This is a complicated question to answer, as this is dependent on the type of cancer and treatment, etc., For example, some types of cancers will defer someone indefinitely. Others, if the cancer is treated and healed with no recurrence, might be acceptable after a varied period of time. Also, this information does change, so the current criteria could be different next month or year. Sorry, it's really a difficult question to answer due to all the variables.

Jose Maria H Gabriel, from Chicago, Illinois, on his marathon journey to 100 marathons and beyond.

1) What has been by far your favorite marathon experience to date and why?

TCS NYC. I love the course and even the bridges. Going through the five boroughs and its neighborhoods is quite a tour of the city! The crowd support is phenomenal not like any other races I've ran.

2) Which marathon was your 100th marathon and why did you choose that particular marathon?

My 100th marathon was planned to be in Chicago which is my local race in 2019. It was the same year when I also completed my 50 States in Missoula, Montana and it was also the year I finished my World Marathon Majors Sixth Star at Boston Marathon. All three milestones in 2019! What a year!

3) How long do you plan to keep running marathons for?

I'll keep on running as long as my knees allow me to. I'm cutting down on the big races for now and I'll concentrate on smaller races with more generous time limits and do more half marathons.

4) Do you remember how we met?

Of course I do! You were crossing the finish line of the Beer Run in Missoula in 2019 and I thought I recognized you (you were wearing a 50 States Marathon Club hat) . I invited you to meet my fellow Marathon Maniacs friends and of course everyone knew you. It was so funny and embarrassing for me. Haha!

5) Any marathon you suggest for someone running their first marathon?

This is a tough one. Either Chicago or New York City. But the most important thing for a first timer to remember is, enjoy the race. Soak everything in. It's the best running tour you'll ever have done! All 26.2 miles of it!

Kirt Goetzke, from Plymouth, Minnesota, Gordon, on his illustrious running career.

1) At what age and year did you run your first race?

My first race was in September of 1985 at the JJ Hills 2 mile.

2) What race distance have you raced the most often and why that distance?

Definitely a 5K. I mean I can't seem to get away from the need to recover fast enough to go out and do it again especially nowadays that I'm getting older. The 5k distance definitely lets me recover quicker.

3) As of this question (today which is Sunday, October 22nd, 2023) I have 2,363 career races for probably third most races by a Minnesota runner, and the late Rick Recker ended his running career with 2,845 races who is probably currently in second place, and you are undoubtedly in first place with how many?

My total as of this morning on Sunday, October 22nd, 2023, is 2,957 races.

4) The last marathon and year that you ran a sub three hour marathon?

My last sub three hour marathon was on Sunday, October 5th, 2014, the Twin Cities Marathon were I finished in 2:55:59. It should be noted that for the previous two or three years there was nothing under three hours that was just the one where everything kind of came back together a little bit. This was my best come back marathon from my disastrous Twin Cities Marathon on Sunday, October 2nd, 2011, where I finished in 4:35:16.

5) How has your running changed since you turned 60 years old?

I could start focusing on running for comfort and not focusing on the speed aspect. I can look back at my old race results and see the speed when I would run like run a 5k in under a 20 instead of feeling comfortable at 23 1/2 for a 5k.

6) Your best advice for an older person that is just starting to run races?

Best advice is to just a look at your age graded performance at races to see how you are doing and don't be too hard on yourself.

Julian Gordon, from Lake Bluff, IL, on his amazing and legendary pacing and running career.

1) Where did you start your running career?

I just started running Sunday mornings to get out of the house so the rest of the family could get extra sleep. I lived in Basel, Switzerland then. I started running trails beginning at my home. Over a period of years, I slowly extended the distance, running up and down hills and valleys, because that was all there was. I started running point-to-point and rendezvousing with family for breakfast. By that time, I was running about 50 K without thinking it was a big deal.

2) When did you move to Chicago, Illinois?

In 1984 we moved to the Chicago area and I discovered the Lake Forest Lake Bluff running club and started running with other humans. I found that other people run more than once a week and run races. I joined in and was doing all distances: 5K, 10 K, Half marathon. Again, no big deal, my body was used to any distance.

3) What year did you run your first marathon?

Then in 1986 my son announced that he was going to do the Chicago Marathon. I decided this would be an opportunity to make up for my neglect of the father-son relationship. He got shinsplints and never did it, and I went on to complete it. My son was a great tri-athlete, but never went on to do a full marathon. While it never resulted in improvement of the father-and-son thing, it did bring me closer to my brother in London, with whom I otherwise did not have much in common. That was 1991 when I did my first Chicago Marathon. And it hurt so badly that I swore never to try to do anything like that again.

4) How many times have you completed the Chicago marathon?

In 1992 I was overcome by curiosity and thought I would try just one more (Lake County Races, in the Spring) , and perhaps I just needed to train a bit better. Then a did Chicago again. Each go, my times were getting better and better. I eventually did 22 Chicago Marathons.

5) Can you talk about your breakfast with Sir Richard Branson before the London Marathon?

Jeffrey, my brother had always been big into sports, unlike me. I ran a couple of UK marathons with him in 1993 and 1994. He had run all London Marathons up to that time, 2011, and I became a special guest as a family member in the Virgin London Marathon. I had run the London Marathon with him in 2001, without him in 2015. So happened the Sir Richard Branson Champagne breakfast in 2011.

6) How old were you at the last Chicago marathon that you successfully paced and what pace time did you have?

My best time ever was in Chicago in 2001, 3:47. That was also the first year I ran as a pace team leader. I paced in Chicago every year after that, until my body quit in 2018, at 81 years old.

7) What is your best running related accomplishment?

I only just realized that, besides inspiring other runners as a pace team leader for many years, I was also an inspiration to the other pace team leaders.

Jeff Hill, from Chattanooga, TN, on creating the 50sub4 Marathon Club and

running journey.

1) What was the first race you registered for and why did you register for it?

The first marathon I registered for was the 1989 Charlotte Observer Marathon. I was fresh out of college, and did not know anyone who had actually ran a marathon and thought it sounded like a good challenge. I finished in 4:11 in what was a very painful learning experience. The marathon distance was a humbling experience.

2) What marathon have you completed the most and why that marathon?

I completed the Houston Marathon 10x in order to gain "Legacy" status with that race. I lived in Houston at the time and it was logistically very straightforward.

I have run Boston 9 times and qualified (but not by enough) for 2024. Boston is just a special race and I'm hoping to finish this more than 10 times.

3) Of all your many running accomplishments, which one accomplishment surprised you that you accomplished it?

Comrades Marathon in South Africa on the day before my 50th birthday. As you know, Comrades is almost double the marathon distance and I had never run anything close to that distance prior. I had many ups and downs in the race and had tears in my eyes when I finished.

4) What five states do you think are the toughest to complete a sub-4-hour marathon in?

Alaska - logistically challenging just to get there.
Colorado - altitude issues.
New Mexico - altitude and few races to choose from.
North Dakota - few options to choose from and variable weather conditions.
Wyoming - no easy courses.

5) What was your deciding factor to create the 50sub4 Marathon Club?

It was out of curiosity to see if anyone else in the running community shared the same goal as I did. To me, running a "quality" marathon (which I arbitrarily defined as a sub-4-hour marathon) was just as important as covering the distance.

The 50sub4 challenge is one of the hardest challenges in the athletic world in my opinion. It requires consistency, financial resources, good luck and logistical planning.

6) If someone is looking to join the 50sub4 Marathon Club what is the easiest way to join?

Go to our website - www.50sub4.com and complete the online application. Very simple and free!

7) Any next big running goal you are working on?

I'd like to get my 7th WMM (World Marathon Major) star in Sydney in 2025 and also complete a marathon in all the Canadian provinces.

Mel Jolosky, 81 years old, from Maple Grove, Minnesota, on his running his one and only marathon.

1) What was your motivating factor to take up running?

Looking back, the reason that I took up running is two-fold.
1. Physical health
2. Companionship in running with others and we have been lifelong friends.

2) What made you decide to run a marathon?

For me it would be a challenge and also a great feeling of accomplishment.

3) What year and what marathon did you complete?

I ran in my one and only marathon in October, 1992, just shy of my 50th birthday. I had been running for a number of years and a couple of my running buddies were going to run The Twin Cities Marathon in 1992. I gave it some thought and decided to participate with them. The three of us trained together and come race day I stayed with them for about 5 miles and told them to go ahead, since they were faster runners than me. I completed the race with my family at the finish and felt great.

4) How did you discover you had prostate cancer?

In mid-2008, my doctor suggested that going forward, we should test my PSA every 6 months instead of 12 months, since it had started to inch up. The next PSA test showed an increase higher than normal. At this point, my PSA was still quite low but my doctor suggested a biopsy. The results came back positive. I had prostate cancer.

5) How are you managing your prostate cancer?

The prostate was removed 4/15/2009 and have not had any problems since. I feel very fortunate that my doctor was proactive in testing for prostate cancer. Since I had back surgery in 1997, my running was limited, so when I was diagnosed with prostate cancer my running was not affected. I have continued to work out 5-6 days per week switching between aerobic exercise and strength training.

6) What would be your advice to someone that might not be sure if they want to run a marathon or not to encourage them to register for a marathon?

If someone is thinking about running a marathon, my suggestion is to talk to a few people that have run one. This will give them a good perspective as to the huge commitment it is. They need to be aware of hours spent training, watching their diet. and family and friends supporting them. Also, training for a marathon is much easier when running with others that run the same pace or close to the pace you are currently running.

Lisa Keller, from Chicago, Illinois, regarding finishing the 50 State marathon journey and the quest for a 50sub4 State marathon finish.

1) You have a nickname that you go by when running, so please explain how you got that nickname?

My running nickname is Crayola. I love to run in lots of colors, especially at races. At the Des Moines Marathon expo in 2015, I was chatting with another Maniac (Tina Hauser) who had also run the Chicago Marathon the week before & when I showed her what I was wearing, she said I was "Crayola." The name stuck!

2) What was your favorite marathon out of the 50 marathons that you submitted for your 50 State Marathon certified finish?

It's always hard to pinpoint a favorite marathon, but my Boston to Big Sur experience in 2017 sticks out. It was my first Boston Marathon, but I lost my cat suddenly 5 days earlier & was swamped at work so I wasn't sure how it would go. I somehow drew strength from seeing animal charity singlets & finished with my 2nd fastest marathon time to date. Then 13 days later, I ran the beautiful & hilly Big Sur Marathon, taking 300+ pictures while almost getting another BQ. (I even beat a professional athlete, Tiki Barber.)

3) Which of the Six Major Marathons was your favorite experience?

Like my favorite "state" marathon, I don't really have a favorite WMM (World Major Marathon) . But the 2010 Chicago Marathon was my first marathon and that was the start of getting me "hooked.". Since it's my local race, I've since run it 7.5 more times (I took a planned DNF in 2023 due to my goal race being 6 days later) and am excited to run it again in the future.

4) How close are you to a 50sub4 finish?

I have 3 states left for a 50sub4 finish. Unfortunately, they are "hard" states with only a few marathons in each state, so it's tricky to plan - NM, NJ & NH.

5) Your best advice for someone trying to run a Sub 4-hour marathon in all 50 States?

My advice is to not give yourself a time limit for completing the quest, as life & world events can derail even the best plans. And have secondary goals you can celebrate if sub-4 gets delayed as in 2023, I celebrated visiting my 50th state in NH (even though it wasn't a sub-4) , my 49th state marathon at the 49th running of the mayors Marathon in the 49th state of Alaska, and my "regular" 50 state finish at the Sundance to Spearfish Marathon (along with a milestone birthday) .

6) Your toughest state so far to run a sub-4-hour marathon in?

I have had to repeat a few states. But the most challenging may have been Mississippi. My first Mississippi marathon was my first double & before I knew about the sub-4 club, so time did not matter. Then I was registered for one in December 2020 but DNT (did not travel) due to having lost my running mojo.

I ran that race the following year, but could not tolerate the course's Powerade & ended up walking a lot (but made lemonade out of the Powerade by helping a first-time marathoner finish!) . I finally got my sub-4 (barely) in 2023, but my flight the day before got cancelled so I was scrambling last minute to figure out how to get there at a reasonable time (thanks United for flying when Southwest could not handle "weather") .

Geneva Lamm, from Little Rock, AR, who is the Race Director for the Little Rock Marathon.

1) How and why did Little Rock create a marathon?

I started the marathon to help subsidize operations of Little Rock Parks & Recreation. Most city parks departments are underfunded. That was 2002. We had our first race in 2003.

2) Any significant roadblock that was overcome to create the marathon?

The only roadblock was the running community thinking we couldn't put on a marathon successfully.

3) Why the importance of diversity and fun for your marathon?

There are plenty of races out there that are serious. We wanted to be different. At the time, walkers were looked down on and not considered marathoners. I didn't think that was right, so I set out to change the discussion. I think I did. Lol. The race reflects my outlook on life. Love everyone. Love what you do. Love to give back!

4) One word to describe the Little Rock marathon weekend experience:

FUN

(Note: Tom Perri has completed the Little Rock Marathon 14 times, starting in 2004 (the second year of the marathon) to simply get the state of Arkansas for his first time 50 State Marathon certified finish. Since then, he has paced the Little Rock Marathon 13 times.)

Dean McGovern, from Missoula, Montana, regarding pacing and running and especially the Missoula marathon.

1) What was your motivating factor to take up running?

The search for peace motivated me to start running. When I run, my problems and the problems of the world melt away and I am free. The strong sense of community has kept me running.

2) What made you decide back then to become the Pace Coordinator for the Missoula Marathon?

Community, plain and simple. When our community decided to create a Marathon in 2007, I knew I wanted to be part of this great event. Building community is important. Pacing is making your running matter to others, helping them reach their goals and succeed.

3) How did the untimely and incredibly sad death of the past Race Director affect you and possibly change your life?

Tony was a wonderful community member, outstanding leader, and a good friend. His death was a loss. Even in death, he continues to bring people together. To me, that's a sign of a life well-lived.

4) Why the infamous cowboy hat when you pace?

I hope it's not infamous. People tend to like it. I get lots of good comments about it from runners and spectators. It started by simply trying to keep the sun out of my eyes. However, it caught on and runners told me, "I just kept looking for the cowboy hat while I was running. If I can keep the cowboy hat in sight, I'll be OK." The hat became a beacon of hope and a marker of progress for folks, so I just keep wearing it.

5) I remember being at a Pacer meeting on a Saturday at Noon, and then unexpectedly taking you to the hospital, do you remember why?

In 2019, the day before the race, I took a friend's kids out mountain biking. They were visiting and really hadn't biked like that before. We were puttering around when I realized I needed to get back to town for the Pacer Meeting. I hustled back and was riding on the bike path, when a young couple, with a big bulky tandem bike was coming at me up a hill. They kept drifting over into my lane. I kept moving over further to accommodate their weaving. But, alas, we could not avoid each other and crashed head on. I flipped over the front of my bike and landed on my head and shoulder. Eventually, I hobbled into our meeting, but dazed and confused. Margie, a physician, insisted I get to the ER. You were kind enough to take me there. All the testing checked out, nothing broken, just sore. I paced the marathon the next day.

6) "I come from Minnesota to the Missoula, Montana, for the huckleberry dessert and the Beer Run, 5k, and marathon I do because they are offered" Any idea why I say that?

To graciously receive what is offered is a great human skill. It needs to be practiced. You do it well.

7) Any advice for someone that is not sure or possibly a little afraid of running their first marathon?

Fear is quite normal. It is also quite limiting. It takes courage to try something new. Courage is not the absence of fear, it's acting in spite of it. So, my advice to first time marathoners is to summon the courage by focusing on the wonderful process of distance running and the great satisfaction of finishing.

(Note: Missoula Marathon will always hold a special place in my heart as I completed my 2,000th career race at the Missoula Marathon on 7/9/2017.)

(Bonus trivia: If you have ever watched the YouTube video - The Missoula Marathon Experience - then you have seen Dean and myself. Just look for the pace coordinator/pacer/runner with the Cowboy hat and a runner sitting at a picnic table talking about his "280th marathon today.")

Todd Oliver, from Carmel, IN, and the Race Director of Fair on the Square Marathon and accomplished runner.

What made you decide to run your first marathon?

The running club I ran with had many encouraging runners and first timers. Knowing I would not be alone, I decided to give it a try after multiple half marathons.

Why did you become a Race director?

My career is in sports marketing; working 15+ years in auto racing along with stops at a venue on the ATP tennis tour and Sports Medicine. I was approached to produce an event when I was president of the local running club and thought, 'yes, we can do this.'

Why the Sub 4 50 State Marathon goal?

That goal came much later into my running. I met some folks in the Marathon Maniac club and they were talking about the 50 sub 4 club. All of my marathons were under 4 hours so why not join the club in case I wanted to continue to run more states.

What challenges you are seeing for the newer runners?

The challenges for newer runners are still the same for every runner. Carving out the time to make running a lifestyle versus something you should do. Once you cross that boundary where running is a must, you will realize the benefits of physical activity and be proud of the lifestyle.

Can you please share a roadblock that you personally overcame to accomplish your goal?

There are many roadblocks in life; personally, professionally, financially, etc. Professionally as a Race Director, every event we produce experiences a roadblock in some fashion. Examples include road construction, lost medals, and business owners not happy. Many times, you cannot solve the issue so getting past the roadblock means to make the situation as best as it can be while keeping your customers in mind.

What did you ultimately learn from this experience?

That first glance, it may appear there is no solution. Don't give up but continue to work through and in every occasion, you will come up with a solution.

Sue Olsen, from Burnsville, Minnesota, on her record setting ultra running journey over the years.

1) Which race did you first register for and finish?

My first Ultramarathon was the 1990 Edmund Fitzgerald 100km race. I had run the Edmund Fitzgerald as part of a relay race in 1989, and realized that people ran further than the marathon, so I decided to try it in 1990. At the starting line, I found out that this was a World Cup race, and there were runners from around the world there. I was wondering what I had gotten into! I finished the race in under 9 hours (my goal) and stated that I was never going to run that far again. I had placed 3rd of the United States women, which qualified me to be on the first U.S. International team going to Italy in February. When I found this out, I decided that I would run 100KM again, this time in Italy!

2) When you began running what percentage of the runners on average would you say were female that were registered or even finished the race?

When I first started running Ultramarathons in 1989, there would be very few women. I would estimate about 15% were women.

3) Tell us about your unique running story with Grandma's Marathon and the FANS run in 1995?

When I became pregnant, I wanted to continue to run and stay in shape. My doctor was in support of this. She said the most important thing was to stay hydrated. I was lucky, and did not have any issues with my pregnancy. I had an ultrasound done before I ran Grandma's Marathon, and was given the OK to run. I completed it in 4 hours and 53 seconds. This was an easy pace for me at that time.

2 weeks later, I got the OK to run FANS, but was told to sit out during the hottest part of the day. I did what the doctor told me, and also slept some during the night hours. I ran 62 miles, and then had my son the next day. I named him John Miles.

4) Of all your many running accomplishments, which one are you most especially proud of?

The running accomplishment I am most proud of was setting a North American/US Record in the 48-hour race. It was held in Surgeres, France. I ran 216 miles.

5) With women now running a 2:11:53 World Record in the marathon at the Berlin Marathon in 2023, do you anticipate a sub 2:10 marathon by a female anytime soon?

I believe that with all the new training knowledge and technology, women will run a sub 2:10 marathon in the near future.

6) What is your best running tip specifically for a woman that wants to try an ultra race for the first time?

The advice I would give to women who want to try running ultras is to plan, train for the distance, and practice your drinking and eating during your training runs to figure out what works for you.

Eddie (AKA Fast Eddie) Rousseau, from Minneapolis, Minnesota, on his running and sobriety.

1) When did you realize you had a problem with alcohol?

I knew since my teens that I drank and got drunk but I was in denial till age 44 and my 6th DWI when I finally accepted it.

2) How long have you been sobering for?

40 Years on September 28th, 2023.

3) Were you running when you were drinking or only after you became sober?

Started running in 1978 in Iran so I could get home from drinking before martial law curfew allowing me an extra round of beer.

In USA, 2 DWIs in 1979, treatment and serious running. But relapse in 1981 to 1983 though still running PRs, and TCMs. Running PRs peaked at age 45, in sobriety, but 24 Hour, 100 Mile PR at age 54 and 6- day PR at age 63.

4) Why do you do the FANS 24 Hour run every year? Have you have done all the FANS 24 Hour runs?

FANS 24 Hour, my first 24 at age 50 for Inner City Kids college fund. I have run them all, 30+ years, now at 3000 miles total, some 800 miles ahead of next male. Definitely slowing down. Best FANS. 116 miles at age 51. Now happy with 70+.

5) What is your proudest overall win or Age Group award in your running career?

Oh my! All are treasures in their own way. The people I meet and the friends I make, like you from 5Ks to 6-day events are all like family to me. But my first 24 Hour Nationals at age 54, where surprisingly I won gold and set 3 USA age group records, 12 hours, 100 miles and 24 Hours 121 miles, stands out.

Daniel Ruckert & Jesse Ruckert, from Saint Cloud, MN, about running and the Mainly Marathons.

1) One word description to tell us about the Mainly Marathon experience?

Supportive.

2) How and why did you decide to buy the Mainly Marathons?

Jesse and I first came across Mainly Marathons during the 2023 Day of the Dead Series. Jesse and I were in the process of completing marathons in all 50 States together, and Jesse suggested knocking out three states in a single trip. Taking time off work and spending a whole weekend for a single race or even two races, if we were able to navigate the traveling logistics, was starting to take a toll on our vacation time and finances. Even though, the sounds of an out-and-back lap structure seemed mind-numbing and boring, we decided to jump into the world of Mainly Marathons. Little did we know, that first toe-dip was just what we needed before diving in head first! Fast-forward a handful of years and a couple dozen Mainly races, Jesse and I were contacted by Clint and Hanne Burleson (the original owners and creators of Mainly) about potentially buying the company from them. After discussing it together and figuring out all the necessary legal and financial pieces, Jesse and I decided to leave our office careers and join the caravan of roaming crazies...later to be known as loons!

*A quick aside and important note, Jesse's wife, Katie, and our mom, Brenda, were a big factor in Hanne and Clint reaching out to us, as Katie and our mom had volunteered with Hanne at nearly all our Mainly adventures. I think their time at the aid station planted some seeds that we would be suitable stewards of the Mainly ship.

3) Any significant roadblocks that you have overcome like the challenges of COVID, etc.?

Due to our streamlined overhead, we were able to overcome the financial hardships of COVID. We had to cancel nearly all of our 2020 events; although, we were still able to host our longest continuous series, our 20in20. The 20in20 had us hosting 20 races in 20 days, all of which took place in the St. Cloud, MN area. We originally planned the 20in20 to encompass our Heartland Series, Summer Camp, and Prairie Series which would been 20 days of races in 13 states. We also held our first virtual series with our "We Run this Country, Virtually Together!" This virtual series encouraged participants to rack up mileage by virtually completing races (5k, 10k, half-marathon, marathon, or 50k) in all 50 States. Participants earned medallions for each state completed, and for every five medallions they would earn a medal that held the five medallions.

After states started allowing outdoor events, we found that each state had its own set of restrictions and safety measures that needed to be met. The protocol for safety measures varied widely with some including masks before the race started, masks throughout the race, no uncovered containers, temperature checks, and many others. These protocols would change and frequently adjust, which created some difficulties for us. With that being said, we were happy to be back with our running family and providing opportunities for people to strive towards their amazing accomplishments!

4) You basically have the "no runner left behind theory." Why is that so important to your marathon philosophy?

Mainly has some of the most accomplished and toughest runners in the world. Many of them are not as fast as they once were, they still have a list of goals that they are working towards and our "no runner left behind" policy gives them the opportunity to keep knocking out their goals. Mainly Marathons' ethos is to be inclusive to all, and part of us following through on that culture is to keep and promote the "No runner left behind" policy.

5) What have you two personally seen with runners and their battle with cancer that keep on trying to run and accomplish their goals?

We already know that we have some of the toughest runners that have overcome a lot of obstacles and many have been told that their goals are impossible, yet we see them exceed expectations repeatedly. I wish that I could say that this always holds true. Sadly, we've also seen the toughest runners coming to grips that their enduring spirit cannot overcome the health issues, including cancer. There is one Loony Legend, which is like the Mainly Hall of Fame, that was tough as nails and had the grit of a dedicated cowboy. When her cancer spread, all the grit in the world could not power her through the miles that she was used to. Her spirit lives on and still motivates people to accomplish hard things.

6) Your favorite motivational song or songs for runners?

"Alive" by Empire of the Sun is one of my favorites.

Jan Colarusso Seeley from Champaign, IL, the Race Director of the Illinois Marathon

1) How has your life been impacted by cancer?

In January 2011, my husband, Joe, was diagnosed with acute myeloid leukemia. For 21 months, which included two lengthy hospitalizations at the University of Chicago and two stem cell transplants, Joe battled the disease before passing away at the age of 52 on October 13, 2012. We were college sweethearts, married 26 wonderful years, and the parents of two sons, Jake and Paul. Joe was my soulmate and my biggest fan. I miss Joe every day and nothing will ever change that.

2) Can you explain about "Joe's Pacers" for the marathon?

The Christie Clinic Illinois Race Weekend has had a pace team for marathoners and half marathoners since Year 1 in 2009. After Joe got sick, our pace team coordinator Jim Crist asked our family if the pace team could be renamed Joe's Pacers. The first year of Joe Pacer's, Joe was still with us. After Joe died, the program continued running in Joe's memory on race weekend. As Jim Crist explains, "Joe was always one who wanted the best for other people. He was always helping people and that's our mission with MarathonPacing.com"

3) You used to be involved with the magazine Marathon & Beyond so can you explain how you were involved?

I was with Marathon & Beyond from its inception in 1997 until its end in 2015. I became the publisher of the magazine in August 1998, when editor Rich Benyo and I purchased the magazine from Human Kinetics Publisher, the original owner. The bimonthly magazine focused on marathons and ultramarathons and we had subscribers all over the globe. We published 114 issues of the magazine before ceasing publication at the end of 2015.

4) What was the late Mark Knutson's impact on the Illinois marathon?

Mark is best known as the director of the Fargo Marathon, but he holds a special place in our hearts because he was also the founder of our Christie Clinic Illinois Race Weekend back in 2009. It's been over a decade since Mark was involved with our event, but we will remember him as a visionary who helped us create a life-changing race weekend here in Champaign-Urbana. He impacted our lives and our community indelibly.

5) How has running marathons changed since you became a Race Director?

Over the past 16 years, we've seen the rise of MEGA marathons, with marathons like the Bank of America Chicago Marathon, London Marathon, and the New York City Marathon hosting fields of almost 50,000 runners. We've also seen the creation of scores of new marathons across the Globe, giving marathoner wannabes race options everywhere. More women are also running marathons than 20 years ago.

(Note: Tom Perri was a Pacer and Legacy runner for this marathon for 10 years and ran his 400th marathon at the Illinois Marathon. Unfortunately, Tom needed to pace the London Marathon in 2019 so he ended his Legacy status to work on finishing the Major Marathons.)

Adam Smith, Glen Ellyn, Illinois, on his first-time marathon experience at the Chicago Marathon on Sunday, October 8th, 2023.

1) What prompted you to run the Chicago marathon?

I started running on June 18th, 2023. I had tried some high-intensity interval training (HIIT) on the treadmill at the gym the week prior, which I shared about with my friend Mike who is an experienced runner. I told him about how I had cranked the treadmill up to level 10, and how the intensity was taking a toll on my ankles. Mike invited me to run with him and the Glen Ellyn Runners (GER) the next day. Once I realized that GER trains as a group for the Chicago Marathon every year, I thought I'd better try to get in!

2) What about your running shoes and how you picked them for the marathon?

After my first 'long run' of the Marathon training season with GER on 6/18/2023 (6 miles, the farthest I had ever run) , I thought I had better inquire about and invest in a quality pair of running shoes. Mike had suggested I go to Naperville Running Company (NRC) in Wheaton, where GER members get 10% off. Monica with NRC was very helpful, had me step on their FootBalance scanner, and picked out a few pairs of shoes for me to try on: the New Balance Fresh Foam X 880, Asics Gel Nimbus 25, and Hoka Clifton 9. As the training season progressed, I bought all three, starting with the Fresh Foam X 880, and ultimately choosing the Clifton 9 for the marathon.

3) What was your biggest surprise while running the marathon?

My biggest surprise while running the marathon was the support from the people. Everyone, including you whom I ran alongside with up until just before Mile 20, to the strangers standing/sitting and cheering us on the entire way, as it brought tears to my eyes as I ran and made me feel so loved and appreciated and grateful.

4) How did running with a pacer help you?

Running with a pacer helped me to enjoy my first marathon experience to the fullest, running at a conservative pace. An all-too-common mistake in the marathon is to start out too quickly and fade at the end. You helped me conserve my energy for the latter stages of the race.

5) Would you advise a first-time marathoner to run with a pacer?

Yes, absolutely!

Gwen Thomas, from Fargo, North Dakota, on her love of dogs and pacing and running.

1) What marathon and year was your first marathon?

Fargo Marathon, 2008.

2) You best tip for a first-time marathoner?

Don't worry about running a certain time. Take the whole day in. Enjoy the course. Pick up energy from other runners. Use a pacer and finally, have fun.

3) *Why the name of "Lost Dog Pacers" for your pacer group name?*

This came out of a conversation with Brock Jenkins. Our group was originally loosely called Twin Cities Pacers. We felt this didn't truly fit the team as not of all the pacers live in the Twin Cities. Also, as our team expanded and added more races, we found that Twin Cities just didn't work. We started spit balling and trying to come up with a name that was memorable. We tried something about being on time or getting you there in your goal time. Then we tried something playing on "not all who wander are lost.". Several of us have dogs or love dogs so "Lost Dog Pacers" was born.

4) *Why are dogs so important to you?*

Someone once said, that a dog is the only creature on Earth that loves you more than themselves. I firmly believe this to be true. For as long as I can remember, I have been involved in dog rescue and will continue to be as long as I am able.

5) *I hear lots about your beloved dog "Scout"," why is Scout so special to you?*

We currently have two rescue dogs, Scuttle and Scout. Scuttle was a foster failure, and Scout was born while he was at the rescue. They are both great dogs and have run with me on and off throughout their lives. This summer, Scout was diagnosed with Immune-mediated Thrombocytopenia (ITP) , which means his body was destroying his palettes leaving his body incapable of clotting blood. We caught it early and rushed him to the emergency animal hospital. While there, it was touch and go for several days. He was ultimately released from the hospital on approximately five or six different medication that he had to take several times a day. While he is not completely out of the woods his health does seem to be getting better.

Unfortunately, there is no known cause for his case of ITP and he will likely need at least one medication the rest of his life. As he recover's he is getting all the love and belly scratches that he can handle.

Kathy "Rat" Waldron, from Green Bay, Wisconsin, a legendary Boston

310

Marathon finisher.

1) Why did you want to run Boston Marathon that first time?

I dreamed of running the Boston Marathon since I was 5 years old when I heard the results broadcast on the radio. I asked my Pa if he thought I could run that marathon one day, and he gave me an emphatic "Yes, you can"! I only knew it was a really long run, but kept those encouraging words close to my heart until I finally ran my first marathon in 1991 and my first Boston Marathon in 1992. God Bless my parents, siblings and kids for their encouragement and support!

2) How many attempts at running a marathon to get your Boston Qualifying time?

My first attempt at a marathon and qualifying for Boston resulted in a DNF! Back then I thought more miles were better and had to drop out at mile 20 with an overuse injury. So, I tried again in 1991 at Fox Cities Marathon in Appleton, WI where I qualified for Boston, running 3:10:24.

3) What year did you run Boston as an Elite athlete and what was your finish time that year?

In 1995 I was super excited to learn that I was assigned an elite runner number (F-86) . I really didn't feel deserving, but what a special feeling that was! My qualifying time for Boston 1995 was 2:56:05, which I ran at the Lakefront Marathon in Milwaukee, Wisconsin, in October of 1994. But my finishing time in Boston was slower that year, 3:17:05. But no matter, I feel Blessed to run Boston!

4) How many Boston Marathons have you completed and how do you rank among number of Boston

Marathons completed among women?

I am thankful to say I have completed 32 Boston Marathons. Patty Hung from Boston has the women's record for most Boston Marathons, at 37 as of 2023. She is amazing! When I first made the Boston Marathon Quarter Century Club in 2016, there were 6 other women on the active list and that number is growing every year.

5) Please explain what is the Boston Marathon Quarter Century Club that you are a member of?

The Boston Marathon Quarter Century Club is a group of runners who have qualified for and completed at least 25 consecutive Boston Marathons. I am so grateful to be part of this club, and I could not have done it without the support of my parents, siblings and kids.

Jun Ulama, from Lakeville, Minnesota, on trying to reach 200 marathons/ultras goal and beyond.

1) What was your first registered race and the year you completed the race?

My first ever registered race was a 10K in Minneapolis, Minnesota at the Race for Kids 5K/10K in June 2013. I started my marathon journey on September 13, 2014 with no goal then but just to finish and the race was at the Madison Garden Marathon, a really small marathon in Madison, Wisconsin.

2) What was your highest weight you have been and your lowest weight?

My highest weight I have ever been was at 308 pounds when all I did was to play golf, go to the all-you-can-eat buffet restaurants after golfing and drink my favorite beer! I started to lose weight in 2012 and was at my lowest at 175 pounds in 2017 when I trained for my first Ironman and at the same time running a bunch of marathons.

3) How many full Ironman events have you completed and your best completion time?

I have completed 8 full Ironman events since September 2017 (and 6 half-Ironman races at the same time) . My best completion time was 14:44:45 at the Ironman Indiana in October of 2021.

4) What has been your biggest obstacle to completing your 200 marathons?

I started running marathons with pre-existing knee issues and that has been my biggest obstacle. I decided to have a full knee replacement on my left knee in March of 2022 when the pain became so unbearable. But because of the extreme motivation I get from you - who is unquestionably a legendary pacer and a passionate runner - my recent surgery did not hinder me from doing what I love to do.

5) Do you recall how you and I met?

I met you at my first Grandma's Marathon in June of 2015 in Duluth, MN. That was also my 3rd lifetime marathon, and I was so awed (and really shocked!) when you said you were already in the hundreds of marathons then!

(Note: Jun UIama did reach his 200th marathon at the Manchester City Marathon on Sunday, November 12, 2023. Congratulations Jun on your accomplishment!)

Ryan Westin, from Little Rock, Arkansas, on his running and pacing journey.

1) What year was your first half marathon and why did you choose that particular half marathon?

My first half marathon was the Tom Walker Milhopper half marathon in Gainesville, Florida, in 1993. It was right after my freshman year of high school cross country and wanted to run a marathon but my mom said longest, I could run was a half.

I know I did the race again the following year as the race sent all finishers got a mug with your name and finish time on it and I use it now to scoop chili into my bowl.

2) Why did you decide to become a Pacer?

I was very fortunate to run my 50th state In Vermont at the young age of 32 on July 8, 2012. After I completed all my goals, my goal since that day has been to help others reach theirs. Whether it is pacing a marathon, guiding a vision impaired runner or helping a friend with their goal in a race.

3) What race did you first Pace at and how did it go?

In 2013, I was ready to hit the ground running and start pacing. I got the opportunity to
pace 3:35 at the Little Rock Marathon which is the local race in my town.
I was very new to pacing and always chose not to run in a pace group due to the crowd and
never had much trouble keeping pace or run for a specific time.
A half mile into the Little Rock Marathon disaster struck. I tore my calf muscle. I walked for a few hundred yards and thought I could still walk the rest

of the way but chose not to as I didn't want to increase level of injury.

4) Your best Pacer experience with a runner at a race when and where?

I have a new favorite pacing experience but I'll choose to keep that experience between that runner and myself as it was very personal for them.

The best pacing experience is hearing the stories of the runner who overcame so many obstacles and were resilient.

One of these stories that comes to mind is a story that just gets you feeling great from Go! St Louis!

A female runner fell back to our pace group around mile 23. She decided after battling Hodgkin's Lymphoma and turning 26 years old that she'd run her first marathon in 6:00 hours!

You could see and feel how significant a moment it was for her, her fiancé, parents, grandparents etc., as they were at the finish line to celebrate with no dry eyes around.

5) What is your best advice for someone wanting to be a pacer for their first marathon?

I would highly recommend that they pace with an experienced co-pacer. Take it seriously. Others are counting on you and relying on you to lead them to their goal they've dedicated the past 16-20 weeks.

Make it fun! Keep runners distracted. Tell some short fun stories, make some jokes, be vocal and engaging. The more fun the runners are having the more likely they're be less stressed and not even realize they're running 26.2 miles.

I tell my pace groups each time that this will all be a memory before you know it so Let's make it a great one. Make it a great one! Every pace group is different and if something goes wrong, do not panic. If you fall behind on pace, slowly get it back.

Read the body language of those you're pacing. The more you pace the more you'll notice when runners will need you more. Talking less, breathing changes, etc., as these are the runners who need that extra encouragement, extra attention and motivating.

Pictures

Pacing with Stage 4 Cancer

Berlin Marathon 2023

Little Rock Marathon 2020

Fargo Marathon 2022

Med City Marathon 2021

Hatfield & McCoy Marathon 2022

Eugene Marathon 2023

Chicago Marathon 2022

Des Moines Marathon 2019

Mesa Marathon 2022

Mad Marathon 2023

Louisiana Marathon 2024

Grandma's Marathon 2022

Sue Olsen & Tom Perri, Twin Cites Marathon 2014

Steve Yee & Tom Perri, The First Light Marathon 2015

Steve Boone & Pacer Tom, Mississippi Blues Marathon 2015

Jeff Galloway & Tom Perri, Moose's Tooth One Mile Run 2016

Craig Swanson, Tom Perri, Robert Britain, Mike Swanson
Torchlight 5k 2018

"Fast Eddie" Rousseau, Tom Perri, Henry Rueden, Frank Bartocci
Paavo Nurmi Marathon 2018

Vincent Ma & Pacer Tom, Pocatello Marathon 2018

Benji Durden, Tom Perri, Amie Benson, Amie Durden
Kalakaua Merrie Mile 2022

Dick Beardsley & Pacer Tom, Grandma's Marathon weekend 2021

Jim Simpson & Tom Perri, New England Series Day #4 2022

Kirt Goetzke, Steve DeBoer, Steve Plasencia, Tom Perri
Langford 4 Mile Race 2023

Bob Kennedy & Pacer Tom, Manchester City Marathon 2023

Sid Howard, Pacer Tom, Gail Waesche Kislevitz
NYC Marathon Expo 2018

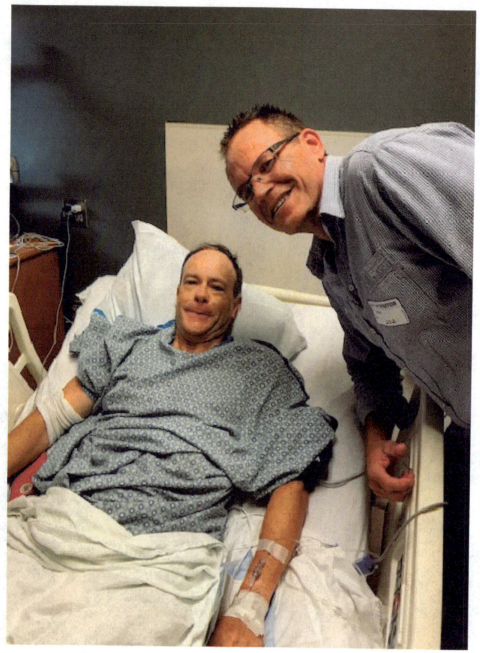

Steve Cirks & Tom Perri, St John's Hospital 2019

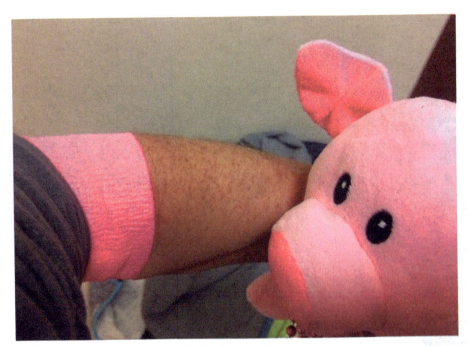

PSA test 2019

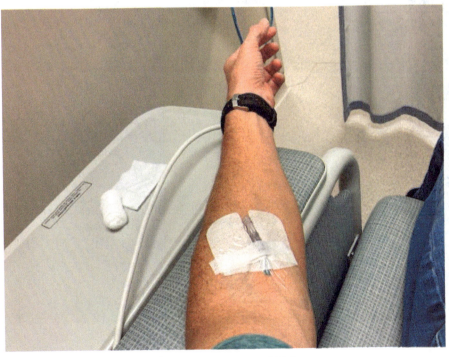

Scan preparation 2021

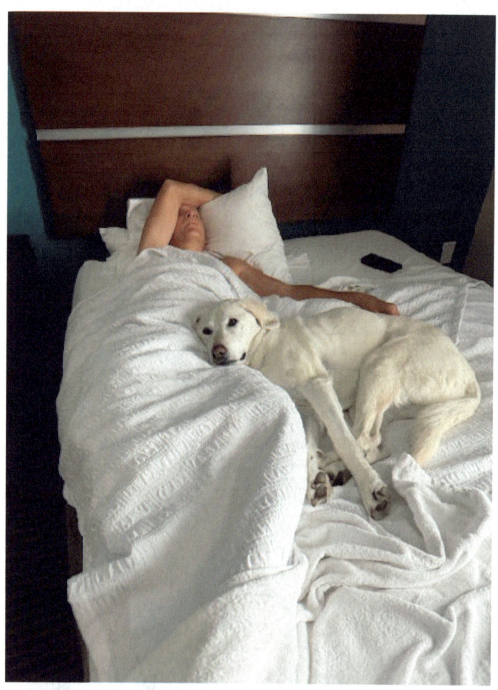

Maggie & Tom Perri, October 2023

Otto & Tom Perri, February 2023

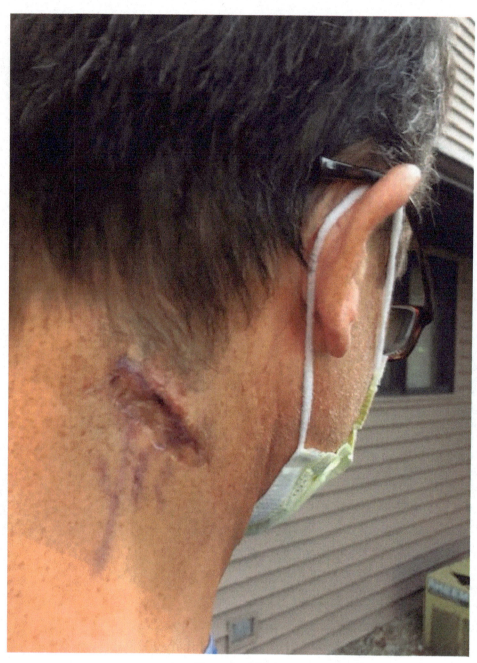

Surgery 2021

341

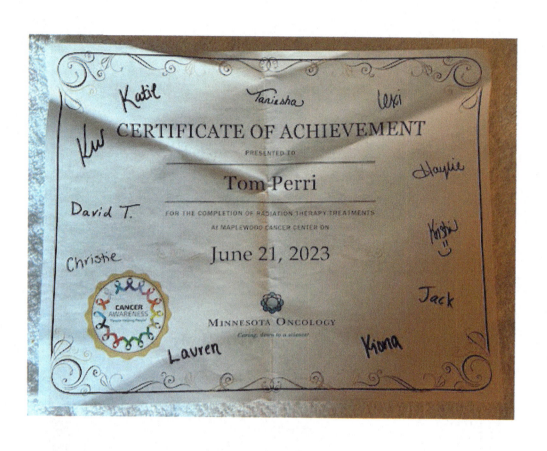

Katie Taniesha lexi

CERTIFICATE OF ACHIEVEMENT

PRESENTED TO

Tom Perri

FOR THE COMPLETION OF RADIATION THERAPY TREATMENTS

AT MAPLEWOOD CANCER CENTER ON

June 21, 2023

David T.

Haylie

Kristin

Christie

Jack

CANCER
AWARENESS

MINNESOTA ONCOLOGY

Caring, down to a science

Lauren Kiona

Pacing Experiences

For my first ever pacing event in 2022, I was paired with Pacer Tom at the Jack and Jill Marathon in Washington State. Tom provided me with much joy and wisdom for the five hours that we paced together. He put me in the correct mindset and made me feel at ease both as a runner and as a pacer. The few hours I spent with Pacer Tom provided me with invaluable experience about how to be a better runner. Tom's generosity and professionalism in running is inspirational and serves as a model for how I want to run and pace every race, and has definitely motivated me to pace nearly a dozen races this year, making me a much better runner in the process.

Simon Li
Plano, Texas

I am a rookie pacer who wanted to pace an ambitious time. The pace group owner who is a very kind soul herself decided that the best person I could learn to pace from was "Pacer Tom" Perri. I had heard of this legend before but never had a chance to meet him. On race day he comes with his race gear on and a trash bag over it to retain some heat. Even in Florida, there was a little chill in the air in January of 2022. He walks up to me and says: so, you will be teaching me how to pace, yeah? This is my first marathon. I completely missed what he said under his breath -"for today". Through the course which was 2 loops, I learned some bit of his battle with cancer, his journey with trying to defeat cancer, and then accepting that he may have to live with it. What I learned even more was the way he lives. He lives as if he will never give up or give in to anything which he doesn't want to. He is such a seasoned pacer that he did not have to worry about the time or pace throughout the race, so he had time to do other things - pick up every beer ticket that fell off from racers' bibs, so much so that other racers would pick it up and hand it to him. Talk to every woman along the course from a 7-year-old to a 65-year-old. We all were charmed by him. He also got a first-time marathoner to finish strong and finish happy. In those 5 hours, I learned so much about life, passion for a sport, enthusiasm to live, and commitment to give back.

Tom: Thank you for being a mentor of life and for life!! "

Harsha Raman
Irving, Texas

One year prior to my first marathon, I laced up my running shoes in a last-ditch effort to find something, anything, to help me gain victory over a personal struggle that waged war against me for over 20 years. I found life in running and the completion of my first-ever marathon was meant to be a celebration, and that it was. Having Tom as a pacer reconfirmed the renewed vitality of my life the entire 26.2 miles. I don't think he will ever understand how meaningful his presence was to me and how grateful I am to have shared that experience with him. It was absolutely perfect, thank you, Tom!

I swear I cry and will continue to cry every time I think of the experience. You were heaven sent and it would not have been what it was without you!

Jodi Williams
Largo, Florida
Clearwater Running Festival

Testimonies

I have been running and hosting races for over 40 years and never had the insight into the spirit of a runner that Tom Perri has shared in *Running: My Salvation from Stage 4 Cancer.* Inspirational. Insightful. Spiritual. Joyful. Stories from the heart.

Dori Ingalls
Race Director
Mad Marathon, Mad Half & Relays

Tom's influence, impact, and indomitable spirit can't be contained to a couple of hundred pages, but this book is a heck of a start!

Attitude is everything. His story, and others within this book, speak to the power of gratitude and positivity in the face of adversity. It's not about running. It's not about cancer. It's about living regardless of what life throws at us and the lives we touch along the way.

DC Lucchesi
Co-host, The Running Around Charlotte Podcast

This book has something for everyone. Whether you're a runner looking for a tip or motivation, or just enjoy learning about the human spirit, you'll find compelling stories throughout. Tom Perri is a true inspiration!

Paul Miller
Pace Team Coordinator
Bank of America Chicago Marathon

I met Tom Perri in 2005, and he first paced for the IMT Des Moines Marathon in 2007. Even though that was long before his cancer diagnosis, I found his running accomplishments and desire to help other runners achieve their marathon goals admirable. The fact that he has continued pacing while battling Stage 4 prostate cancer is inspiring. I am honored to call Tom Perri my friend and I hope that you will find his book as inspirational as the man himself.

Tara J. Thomas

Tom Perri……….. An inspiration to me!

I met Tom Perri many years ago when he was working as a youth worker for a nonprofit in the northwest suburbs of Minneapolis and I was employed as an administrator in a suburban school district in the same area. When Tom asked me if I would care to add some of my thoughts to his book, I was excited to do so because I possess an enormous amount of gratitude for Tom Perri, his friendship and his story!

When we first met, we worked together to develop a Youth Yellow Pages to distribute to junior high students. This small pocket-sized publication we developed was written to give students a list of community resources to help them access counseling services, recreational activities, emergency phone numbers, etc. I remember one of the areas of the book that Tom contributed a great deal to was the section on Suicide Prevention. Through this project we became friends.

We have stayed connected by way of the health club we both work out at regularly. As a result, I have been able to keep up with Tom's dedicated marathon running life style and the endless records he has not stopped piling up! Tom's enthusiasm and love for running showcases his joy of living. His passion for running and those that are part of his running community (of which there are many) give him one of his major purposes in life!

Through my ongoing contact with Tom, I noticed that, as he encountered his surgeries and hormone therapy, he refused to let these difficult treatments pull him down - constantly gathering the intestinal fortitude to somehow keep running through all of his trials and tribulations! Because I personally went through hormone therapy, I could not believe what he was doing was even possible.

I went to Fargo in May of 2022 to watch him run his 600th marathon and at the moment of Tom's step over the finish line I was overwhelmed by what he had accomplished, knowing what he had been through and is still going through, to treat his cancer. (As of this writing I believe he has finished 666 marathons!) Through his ongoing example Tom has positively helped change my life. In addition to motivating me to work harder to meet the difficult challenges we all face, I also stepped up my game and am pushing myself to work out with more vigor and time commitment. If Tom can do the nearly impossible I can surely do much better! There is no doubt that Tom has helped make me a better person!

Like I said....TOM IS AN INSPIRATION TO ME!

Lee Skavanger
Maple Grove, MN

"Closing Time" (Semisonic)

It is finally time for me to stop writing. Note that I didn't say "permanently" so you will likely be hearing from me in the future.

I wish I could thank everyone personally who has touched my life in any way. Simply saying "thank you" seems insufficient.

The running community has been such a big part of my life for nearly fifty years. It truly has been an amazing experience, and this never became more apparent than when I started the Twin Cities Marathon in 1993 and then finished the marathon. When I finished the Twin Cities Marathon that day my life was forever changed. Every marathon I finished after that Twin Cities Marathon was just "icing on the cake" as my mom might have said.

As more people than just myself told you in this book, running and doing a race *will* change you forever.

But as previously noted: *Warning: this can become addictive.*

I want to be the first person to say to you: I told you so!

Goodbye for now!

Stay happy & healthy & safe.

"Pacer Tom" Perri

My mantra: I celebrate everyday with gratitude for my family, friends and faith and for this precious time I've been given to walk on this amazing planet!

Father Michael Alello

Epilogue

I started my journey in life on July 30th, 2019, with Stage 4 cancer. It was on the morning of Sunday, January 14th, 2024, at Catholic mass at St Joseph Cathedral in Baton Rouge, Louisiana, that I started that day with being blessed by Father Michael Alello. A few hours later that day with Father Michael's blessing I was able achieve my goal of a marathon/ultra in all 50 states with my Stage 4 diagnosis at the Louisiana Marathon carrying a pacer stick that simply stated "Run with Tom" in 5:47:25. What made it extra special that day was that Ivan Nguyen finished his first marathon that day with me in 5:49. Congratulations Ivan!

Thank you, Louisiana Marathon, for this incredible experience and lifetime memory.

Also, on Thursday, January 18th, 2024, at the first day of the Aloha four-day series marathon in Kapaa, Hawaii, I was first male winning the marathon in 5:14:34. I finally reached my goal of an age group award, first male, or overall winner in all 50 states.

Also, because I like doing things twice, I won the overall marathon on day four of the Aloha series running 5:23:50 in Kapaa, Hawaii, on Sunday, January 21st, 2024.

Ready, set, go, and off to my next race and run.

The American Red Cross

At least 1 million people every year are diagnosed with cancer for the first time and many of them will need blood. Just one pint can save up to three lives. If everyone who reads this book donates at least one pint the impact would be phenomenal. My current plan is to raise money for the American Red Cross and run the Boston Marathon with them in 2025 for the third time.

The website for GivenGain donation for myself, which will benefit The American Red Cross of Massachusetts, will potentially be active in September of 2024.

See the following websites at that time.

https://www.givengain.com/#

https://www.redcross.org/local/massachusetts.html

Made in the USA
Columbia, SC
17 February 2025